A GEORGIA LAWYER

S. Price Gilbert

A Georgia Lawyer

HIS OBSERVATIONS AND PUBLIC SERVICE

by

Stirling Price Gilbert

Former Justice of the Supreme Court
of Georgia and for forty-four years a
Judicial Officer.

THE UNIVERSITY OF GEORGIA PRESS
Athens

Paperback edition, 2010
© 1946 by the University of Georgia Press
Athens, Georgia 30602
www.ugapress.org
All rights reserved
Printed digitally in the United States of America

The Library of Congress has cataloged the
hardcover edition of this book as follows:
Library of Congress Cataloging-in-Publication Data
LCCN Permalink: http://lccn.loc.gov/46022584

Gilbert, Stirling Price, 1862–[from old catalog]
   A Georgia lawyer,
      xiii, 257 p., 1 l. front., plates, ports. 23 cm.
   1. Judges—Georgia—Correspondence,
   reminiscences, etc. [from old catalog] I. Title.
KF373.G55 A33
46-22584

Paperback ISBN-13: 978-0-8203-3537-7
ISBN-10: 0-8203-3537-1

TO
THE GEORGIA BENCH
AND BAR

Foreword

Shortly before his death, Chancellor S. V. Sanford told me that Judge Stirling Price Gilbert had written a book and that he wanted me to read the manuscript with a view to its possible publication by the University of Georgia Press.

As I wrote Judge Gilbert some weeks later, I am grateful to my good friend and mentor, Dr. Sanford, for the privilege of seeing this script and of placing it in channels whereby it emerges as a book with the imprimatur of the oldest chartered of the state universities. The word *privilege* is used advisedly. Some manuscripts and books which I must read are in the nature of a chore. But not Judge Gilbert's. It was indeed a pleasure — as I am sure it will be for all those who read this memoir in book form — to become better acquainted with the Judge's long, useful, and distinguished career.

A Georgia Lawyer possesses strong reader-interest and enduring values in several directions: (1) as superior autobiography; (2) as original Georgia history; (3) as wise legal commentary; (4) as colorful descriptive writing; (5) as good entertainment; and (6) as inspiration, especially for young persons, in terms of personal achievement and good citizenship.

All of which adds up to the fact that *A Georgia Lawyer* is Georgiana in the best sense of the word. It is both the memoir of a man who has meant much to his state, and a commentary on many matters of pertinent interest to all Georgians, especially lawyers and those in public life in any way. For alumni of the University of Georgia, the book has special significance in that Judge Gilbert —

not a graduate of the University — has during the years been one of the institution's best friends. He made possible a beautiful new infirmary on the Athens campus, is a Regent of the University System, and in other ways has shown that he is very much concerned with the proper development of higher education in this state.

JOHN E. DREWRY, *Dean*,
Henry W. Grady School of Journalism,
University of Georgia.

Preface

There is a tradition in my family, supported by information said to be among state records in Hartford, Connecticut, that five Gilbert brothers came from Devonshire, England, in the year 1640 and settled in Connecticut and Massachusetts. Among them were Jesse and Thomas Gilbert. The Gilberts, numerous today throughout the New England states, spread south through New York, Pennsylvania, Virginia, the Carolinas, Georgia, and other states. One branch left Virginia and went westward to the Pacific. My great-grandfather, Jesse, resided first in Virginia and later moved to North Carolina where my grandfather, Thomas Gilbert, one of fourteen children, was born. My grandfather is my authority for the statement that our Gilbert family descended from one of the brothers mentioned above, perhaps from either Jesse or Thomas.

My father's mother was Margaret Carswell, a member of one of the numerous and well-known families scattered all over Georgia. The Carswells came from Scotland via County Antrim in North Ireland. Our Scotch ancestor is credited with having been too outspoken and otherwise obnoxious to the ruling Scotch royalty; that doubtless explains his presence in Ireland, where he married, and the presence of the Carswell family in America.

My father, Jasper Newton Gilbert, was born on a farm in Hancock County, Georgia, on December 27, 1830. Of him more in Chapter I.

The author wishes to thank sincerely all the many who have materially assisted in the preparation of this work: Former Governor John M. Slaton, Atlanta; Judge David

S. Atkinson, Savannah; Mr. Harold J. Friedman, Brunswick; Mrs. Margaret D. Cate, Sea Island; Miss Ella May Thornton, State Librarian, Atlanta; Mr. W. Clyde Woodall, Columbus; Mr. James J. Gilbert, Columbus; Mr. William W. Brewton, College Park; Mrs. Talbot Smith, Darien; Judge William S. Tyson, Darien; and for helpful criticism and aid in arrangement of material Mrs. Dorothy M. Crosland, Librarian, Georgia School of Technology, Atlanta; Prof. John E. Drewry, Dean, School of Journalism, University of Georgia, Athens; and Prof. S. Walter Martin, Department of History, University of Georgia, Athens. I am grateful to the following authors and publishers who have permitted me to use material from their publications: American Historical Society, *The Story of Georgia*, by Walter G. Cooper; Little, Brown and Company, *Constitutional Limitations*, Vol. I, by Thomas M. Cooley; Charles Scribner's Sons, *Reminiscences of General John B. Gordon;* Wirt Armistead Cate, *Lucius Q. C. Lamar;* and Thomas J. Norton, *Losing Liberty Judicially.* My thanks to Mr. Fred C. Wickham of Columbus, Georgia, for furnishing a photograph of the Steamboat *W. C. Bradley* and to Mr. Lamar Dodd, Head of the Art Department, University of Georgia, for painting the "Country Doctor on Horseback."

S. PRICE GILBERT.

Contents

		Page
	Foreword	vii
	Preface	ix
I.	My Father—The Country Doctor	1
II.	A Georgia Country Boy	13
III.	Vanderbilt and Yale	24
IV.	Gordon and Lee	43
V.	Member of the General Assembly	58
VI.	Riding the Judicial Circuit	72
VII.	Old Columbus Days	96
VIII.	Appointed Supreme Court Justice	114
IX.	The Supreme Court of Georgia	125
X.	The U. S. Constitution and the Supreme Court	147
XI.	Retirement	167
XII.	Georgia's Coastal Paradise	180
XIII.	Wars	201
XIV.	Travels	221
XV.	Georgia History and Men Who Made It	241
XVI.	Higher Education in Georgia	249

Illustrations

	Facing Page
S. Price Gilbert (*Frontispiece*)	
The Country Doctor on Horseback	2
Steamboat on the Chattahoochee	100
Mrs. S. Price Gilbert	104
Price Gilbert, Jr.	105
Francis Howard Gilbert	105
Lanier Oak	178
Oglethorpe Oak	194
Old Governors' Mansion at Milledgeville	250
Chapel, University of Georgia	252
Library, Georgia School of Technology	253
Gilbert Memorial Infirmary	256

Of Thinking

Reflection is a flower of the mind,
    giving out wholesome fragrance,
But reverie the same flower,
    when rank and running to seed.
Better to read little with thought,
    than much with levity and quickness;
For mind is not as merchandise,
    which decreaseth in using,
But liken to the passions of man,
    which rejoice and expand in exertion;
Yet live not wholly on thine own ideas,
    lest they lead thee astray;
For in spirit, as in substance,
    thou art a social creature;
And if thou leanest on thyself;
    thou rejectest the guidance of thy betters,

. . . .

Yet listen often, ere thou think much;
    and look around thee ere thou judgest,
Memory, the daughter of Attention, is the teeming
    mother of Wisdom,
And safer is he that storeth knowledge than he that
    would make it for himself.

                      Tupper's *Proverbial Philosophy*

CHAPTER I

My Father--The Country Doctor

MY father was a country doctor. He was country-born and reared. He fitted precisely into the picture; he knew the country and loved it. When he arrived at maturity he launched out for himself to cultivate the soil, to live the only life he knew, that of a farmer on Georgia soil.

The following incident changed his whole life. His small farm was rolling, very rolling, terrain. He had barely begun to farm. It was springtime; he had prepared his land for planting; the ground was soft and therefore heavy rains could be destructive. He was awakened one night by a heavy downpour of rain, colloquially known as a "trash mover." For seemingly hours he listened and visioned all of his carefully prepared land turned into gullies, the few seeds that he had sown washed away with much of the top soil into the swampy waste places below. When morning came, conditions proved that his fears were fully justified. He sold his farm and all of its accompanying personal property and with the proceeds he entered the medical college at Augusta, graduating in 1855, at the age of twenty-five, and at once began to practice at Union, a cross-roads settlement in Stewart County, Georgia. His practice grew rapidly, and he was constantly traveling, chiefly on horseback.

I can see him now on horseback, riding across plowed fields or along a trail through the woods en route to some remote farm house. His office and his drug store he carried with him in his saddlebags. Often he was stopped on the way by some Negro working in the fields who would tell the doctor his troubles and then hold out his hand expecting a magic cure. Out of the saddlebag would come a large bottle of powdered quinine or calomel, and the powder would be poured into the upstretched hand. With one gulp the bitter powder would be swallowed without benefit of water, and with no sign of distaste. Smacking his lips, the field hand would bow his thanks while the doctor poured an additional portion for future use and wrapped it in a piece of scrap paper. As the Negro returned to his work, the doctor would ride on neither asking nor expecting pay, but with the satisfaction which is so great a part of the reward of all men of the medical profession.

In the saddlebag days the country doctor was a unique character. He was as beloved by his neighbors as he was important in his community. Many writers have pictured the country doctor in his heroic and unselfish devotion to duty. One of Honore de Balzac's best known novels, *The Country Doctor*, portrays the main character, Dr. Benassis, as the beloved country doctor of Grenoble — a truly great doctor, full of human sympathy, who treats the rich and poor for all ailments, advises the peasants about farming, and brings happiness where sorrow and misery had been. Another novel, *Beside the Bonnie Briar Bush*, by Ian McClaren, presents, in Dr. McClure, a noble country doctor of Scotland. Henry M. Flagler, creator of modern Florida, once said to me that this novel of McClaren's was his favorite of all novels because of "Doctor McClure." More exciting than any fiction is the true story of Dr. Ephraim McDowell which James Thomas Flexner has told in *Doctors on Horseback*. Dr. McDowell, who lived between the years 1771-1830, practiced medicine in Danville, Kentucky, and the sur-

Doctor Gilbert on His Favorite Saddlehorse, Fannie

rounding mountain country. One day in 1809 he rode through ice and snow to see a mountain woman who was dying of tumor. Her faith in him gave him courage to take her on horseback sixty miles to Danville and there perform one of the most important operations in the history of surgery, the first successful removal of a tumor from the abdomen. Neighbors, friends, and even his own nephew, a doctor himself, denounced him. Even his life was openly threatened by a mob when it was learned that the doctor intended to perform an operation that required opening of the abdomen. Such an operation had never been undertaken, and it was considered nothing short of murder. Of course there was no anaesthesia. It was thirty-four years later that Doctor Crawford W. Long discovered and used ether in Jefferson, Georgia. Ephraim McDowell is an outstanding example of the courage and self-reliance that marked the best of the country doctors in the early years of our country.

The present chapter concerns the country doctor as he was known in our own Georgia during and immediately after the War Between the States. The latter period, which was worse than war, has been portrayed by Claude G. Bowers in his book, *The Tragic Era*. The story of that tragic era, however, has not been fully told, and perhaps never will be. Margaret Mitchell in *Gone with the Wind* has a wonderful story of conditions in and around Atlanta, but all could not be told even in that great book. It is of the country doctor under the conditions and handicaps of those years that I write here.

The country doctor, as a rule, had a hard life, especially during the period from 1855 to 1875. For several years just preceding the war, slavery agitation seriously disrupted agricultural pursuits, making things difficult for all who made their living from the soil. Doctors, lawyers, preachers, and teachers shared the same hardships. These difficulties were greatly increased with the opening of hostilities. The Confederate Army took most of the white men, leaving behind only those who were physically unfit. Farming went from bad to worse, with only women to look after most of the farms, for the slaves left behind were not as universally hardworking as they have been pictured. This does not mean that all the Negroes became trifling or undependable. Some could be depended upon, and in some instances Negroes even managed farms successfully. There were Negro women who were sheet anchors of protection and angels of mercy to the sick and heart-broken white women of our farms. As for those Negro women, all right-minded people have agreed that our debt of gratitude is one that can never be fully paid or sufficiently extolled in song or story.

Four years of war had left the South exhausted of nearly every means of existence. Much of the flower of Southern manhood had been killed or maimed for life. Slaves who had supplied practically all demands for common labor before the war had been emancipated, and then made citizens with all rights of voting and holding office. Those cruel and oppressive measures of the United States called "Reconstruction" came in the midst of near chaos when war passions had not subsided and when nearly every family was in dire distress, mentally and physically.

These measures were often administered in a vindictive manner by incompetent and dishonest adventurers. This situation brought into existence the Ku Klux Klan which operated much like the "underground" in World War II. Though this organization drifted into excesses, disorder, and lawlessness, as all such orders usually do, it is credited with doing much to restore order and protection to persons and property. The Ku Klux of that day resembled the Vigilantes who operated in the formative days of our Western states and territories. The methods of both were often primitive, but many of the results were good. However, the present-day Ku Klux Klan is a spurious imitation of the Klan of Reconstruction era. It is wholly bad; its influence is contrary to good order, peace and dignity of the state. It can lead to no good end and should be suppressed.

Secession and war soon exhausted all United States money in the South, and the States which attempted to secede began issuing State money, while the Confederate Government also issued its money. State and Confederate bonds were issued; but as the ill-starred fortunes of war more and more destroyed public confidence in the ability of the Confederate Government to win the war and independence, money and bonds lost value in buying power and market price. Upon the collapse of the Confederacy, which many Southerners confidently expected all the time, all such money and bonds became worthless. Imagine, now, about one-third of the people of the United States finding themselves without food, clothing, and shelter, or money with which to procure these necessities. Such was the actual situation. When it was said above that the Southern States "attempted" to secede, the term was used advisedly; for in the case of *Texas* v. *White*, 174 U. S. 700, the United States Supreme Court decided flatly that all secession legislative enactments by Southern States were null and void and that the States were never out of the Union.

I was too young to realize the suffering during the war, and I recall only that of the Reconstruction. Because my education was obtained in three separate states—

Alabama, Tennessee, and Connecticut — I have never felt the sectionalism so commonly felt by others. I had never heard expressions of sectionalism or of hatred of the North in my family. Consequently, when, in 1887, I was invited to deliver the Confederate Memorial Address at Columbus, I used the following words without any thought of inappropriateness of the sentiments.

"No prouder heritage could be left to our common country than the valor of the blue and gray. And in the light of this day of good feeling and national pride, the names of both Lee and Grant belong to America. The knightly heroism of Lee finds its counterpart in the tenacious bravery of Grant; the Christian resignation of the one in the noble magnanimity of the other. Their tombs are priceless gems in the diadem of America's future greatness."

My father lived through the hard years of the war and Reconstruction, supplementing the earnings from his practice by farming. He had grown up on a farm and he knew farm life. Most professional men in the South in his day knew farm life, since many of them ran farms in addition to prosecuting their professions. My father's farm produced enough to help support himself, his family, his farm laborers, and his farm stock. Of course, such luxuries as coffee and sugar were rare, and even flour was not often in evidence. Various substitutes were used. Sugar cane, from which syrup was made, was grown on the farm. This syrup was used in sweetening the imitation coffee. Extra boiling produced a brown sugar from the syrup also, and this was used. Among the coffee substitutes tried, none was quite so satisfactory as parched corn, or, as we said, roasted corn. Perhaps the cereal "coffee" now used in some health resorts is a legitimate descendant of the concoctions used as coffee substitutes

My Father—The Country Doctor 7

during the days of Reconstruction. Clothes were made over and over again by my mother. Could a person now see an entire neighborhood or state dressed as did those we knew, the sight would bring bursts of laughter or tears of sympathy, according to temperament or point of view. Confederate money and bonds were worthless, and in Stewart County there was hardly any United States money. The country doctor accepted pay from his patients in chickens, pigs, or in any kind of produce, however small in value. He had no bookkeeper and never mailed statements of account to his patients. What was the use? Postage stamps and stationery were expensive, and it was doubted that they would produce what they cost. Such bills were not expected to be paid until the fall of the year when cotton had been sold. When that time arrived, most of the country doctor's debtor friends would call and settle of their own accord. Long after my father had moved from Stewart County to Columbus, old patients would travel twenty-five miles to his new location to have him prescribe for their ailments, often bringing with them a chicken, a turkey, or, if they had nothing else, a "mess of greens" — turnips, cabbage, or collards.

It was always as the country doctor that he wished to be thought of and remembered. He was certainly typical of his class. The country doctor was consulted, regardless of the trouble, whether it related to health, the farm, or politics. Maybe it was toothache. If so, he acted as first aid until the sufferer could reach a dentist in the faraway village or city. He was arbitrator in many family and neighborhood disputes. He traveled the country on horseback or by horse and buggy. My father had two excellent horses for the saddle — Fannie and Prince. The former was coal black, beautifully formed, docile and trustworthy. As a very small boy I could handle her with ease. Prince was fine and durable but not so trustworthy. He had one brown eye and one which looked like glass but was sound. It gave him a queer look. When my father returned from his round of calls, it was his custom to tie his horse to the hitching post. Immediately the stable boy would take charge. The horse was rubbed, watered, fed, and stabled to rest until the next round. There were always calls for my father upon his return home. Any pending emergency call would be answered by using the other horse which had been resting. Later, as conditions grew better and a small family was to be considered, the buggy came to be used when suitable to the road which had to be traversed; but necessarily the rate of travel was slower, for on horseback the doctor could cut distances by using paths, private plantation roads, or by going through forests, or even riding through streams through which the horse sometimes had to swim. Such routes, however, were often better than the roads we then knew, even in the best of weather. In bad weather the buggy could hardly ever be used. As a little fellow, I often went with my father when he used the buggy, and he sometimes took me up in front of him in the saddle when he was riding around in our immediate neighborhood on horseback.

My mother was very young when she went with my father to a country home, isolated, far from neighbors. It was too far, in fact, for a call to be heard had she been in danger. As my father's practice grew, he had to be away from home day and night. After I was old enough to understand, my mother often related to me how much she was alone. Of course, at that time the telephone had not been invented.

My father's farm was operated by a former Negro

My Father—The Country Doctor

slave, John Redding, who was as faithful in freedom as he had been in slavery. John Redding and a pack of foxhounds were the protection of our home. No stranger dared enter our yard without challenge. He would be given ample warning by the baying of the hounds. A stranger had to stand outside the gate until the dogs were ordered to be quiet — else he entered at his peril. How well do I remember those fox-hounds! It was they who told of my father's approach, even when he was half a mile away. The clatter of his horse's hoofs on the hard clay road was their signal. Out of the front porch, through the yard, over the fence at a leap, and away — they were gone to meet their master. Leaping and baying all around his horse, they escorted him home. Those were days of isolation, but they were days of home.

After twenty years of such strenuous labors during all hours of the day and night, my father began to feel the effects of such a hard life, for it was not on the agenda of the country doctor to turn down a call, regardless of the hour or the weather. The country doctor had to be a leader in the various problems of the system under which he lived, as did the preacher and teacher.

The maintenance of schools and churches was as important to the country people of my youth as it is today. The preacher usually supplied several churches. He was a circuit rider, just as were the physician and the lawyer. Usually being a man with a family, the preacher lived in a rented house supplied by the combined churches of which he was pastor. Sometimes there were as many as six in a charge on a circuit. At least this was true of the church to which we belonged, the Methodist.

An interesting custom at that time which was never disregarded was the manner in which the people were seated at churches. Of course, I speak primarily of our country church. There may have been a different custom elsewhere, although we certainly were a representative community in so far as Georgia was concerned in those days. Under this custom, the men and women did not sit together in church. Husbands and wives sat in different sections of seats, or rather, on opposite sides of the church. There were two front doors side by side and precisely alike. Husbands and wives, couples engaged, young men and women, and boys and girls entered by separate doors — the males all going in at one, the females at the other, regardless of ages. The only exception to this was the rare occasion when very young children were taken to church. Couples who arrived together would stand around outside, weather permitting, discussing the various topics of social interest, until time for the service. Then they would separate and enter. After services and when cordial adieus had been spoken, they returned to their homes or to those of neighbors for dinner. Of course, hotels were virtually unknown in our community because of the sparseness of the population.

The schools were small, one-room, wooden structures with wooden shutters. The only way to heat the room was by a wood fire. Often the school house was itself one of the churches of the community. The patrons financed the school, since there was no general state-wide or county-wide system of public finance for education. The teachers received small salaries as compared with those of today, but they usually received as much as the patrons were able to pay, and besides, their living expenses were extremely small. It was not surprising that we usually had a new teacher each year. Each school had but one teacher who generally taught only the most elementary courses. After four or five months he would resign and cause a delay in educational instruction. During my attendance the teacher lived in our home parts of three years. Naturally, the country doctor took his turn in boarding the teacher.

Something like three-quarters of a century have elapsed since the days when my father was a country doctor in Stewart County. A great volume of water has passed under the bridges and over the dams since those days. Our world, even that part of the world with which this story is concerned, has experienced a marvelous change. Discoveries and inventions coupled with enterprise and energy have well nigh made a new world. Modern hospitals and new drugs to combat disease have lengthened the lives of men and played their part in the progress of this world. Notwithstanding all such changes, the "country doctor," though doubtless much reduced in numbers, has not been pushed off into utter extinction, nor has he been lost to memory, nor has his page of honor in the history of our early days been forgotten. Certainly one genuine example still survives — a splendid citizen and a generous contributor to the welfare and happiness of his neighbors and his country. I have known him well for half a century and am proud to claim his friendship. He is Doctor Neal Kitchens, Warm Springs, Georgia, all-round physician, home-builder, grower of good things to eat, philosopher, insatiable student of public affairs, unsurpassed admirer of Franklin D. Roosevelt, and a fisherman who has never known surrender — fish or no fish.

There were other country doctors in Stewart County during the "Tragic Era," and as a group they were a stabilizing influence at all times. Their influence lent encouragement, patience, and hope to a broken and crushed people. The picture of conditions in Stewart County and in most of the Southern States during the dark days of the so-called "Reconstruction" was one of chaos and suffering. Under such circumstances the people of Georgia and all the Southern States literally worked out their existence from wreckage. Southern women furnished the inspiration, but let us credit the country doctor for his part in the darkest days this land ever knew. It has been my wish to leave some tribute to my father as a representative of the country doctor during these dark days and to my mother who was his helpmate, because their lives and labors have been a beacon unto my path all the days of my life.

CHAPTER II

A Georgia Country Boy

MY mother was Sarah Louise Redding. She was born in Zebulon, Pike County, Georgia, on June 16, 1841. She was only eighteen years old when she married my father in Stewart County on October 18, 1859. She died in Columbus, Georgia, on April 13, 1920, having almost reached the age of seventy-nine. My only sister, Margaret, always called Maggie, was born in 1860 and died in 1937.

I was born on January 31, 1862, in a sparsely settled section near the Chattahoochee River in Stewart County. Our home, a farm, was isolated as were most farms in that day. There was no railroad in the county. I walked to and from school, as all pupils did. There was an all-day session, regardless of the weather. School terms were too brief to permit a day's absence.

At that time the section where we lived was infested with malaria. Nearly everyone suffered from chills and fever. In my case, it seemed that I was never free from that affliction. New methods of combating malaria have since improved conditions. The infection stunted my growth and reduced my strength, clinging to me, more or less, for many years.

The earliest recollection that I have of my home takes me back to the age of about three. The time was just after the end of the War Between the States. The slaves on my father's farm were now free. Our cook and her son, Anderson, who was the yard boy and who had "looked after" me, were leaving. They were free, and freedom meant leaving the farm and going to the "Big

Town." I had a strong attachment, almost love, for Anderson. He had been my bodyguard and my playmate. My heart was filled with sorrow, and I cried because he was leaving me. I went to the road with him and his mother. I can remember standing with feet apart, in the middle of the road, with tears streaming down my face, waving goodbye to my two friends. Every hundred yards or so, they would turn around and wave. This kept up until they were out of sight. I was a desolate little boy. I didn't see Anderson again until he was grown.

In rural Georgia where I lived, boys under seven or eight years of age wore boots in winter. These boots had rather heavy soles and brass toes; that is, there was a narrow strip of brass across the toe of the boot to prevent wear. Boys played marbles much of the time and hence were hard on knees and toes. In summer we preferred "hoofing it" with bare feet. This was especially a delight when we followed the plow, because of the feel of the freshly turned earth to the feet. I was too frail to undertake real plowing, but I enjoyed following the plow and dropping the seed into the open furrow. My father made me a small plowstock and attached to it a light plow point. My pony would be hitched to this, and for short periods it was my delight to plow in my "patch" near the house. Our residence was always called "the house." It was never spoken of as "residence" because we did not like the more pretentious term.

Like all country boys of my time I was interested in dogs, chickens, pigs, goats, steers, and colts — about in that order. Every boy then loved the dog, and certainly I did. All these domestic animals came in for their share of boyish affection, but the dog never fell from the place of supreme attachment. This brings to mind a very pretty legend about the friendship of Man and his Dog.

A Georgia Country Boy 15

When God created the heavens and the earth and the animate and inanimate things and observed their habits, their lives, their likes, and dislikes, He decided that Man should be separated from the lower animals. So He ordered that Man should go one way and all lower animals should go another. He created a great and wide gulf to separate them. The lower animals moved away — all save one, the Dog. The Dog turned and, looking across and beyond the gulf, he saw Man, who had turned to look at the Dog. The Dog, quick as thought, sprang to follow his friend. He made a mighty leap for the far side of the gulf, but could reach the landing-edge with only his two forefeet, his body hanging precariously. Then his friend, Man, grasped him by the forelegs and drew him to safety and caresses. Man and Dog have ever after been the truest of loyal friends.

My dog was my most loyal friend and companion. He was a bench-legged, rather long-bodied mongrel, but in courage and intelligence and indeed in loyalty, he was an aristocrat among animals. So I named him "Lion." I spent many happy hours in the fields and forests with my dog and my gun. I had a single barrelled, muzzle-loading shot gun. Modern breech-loading guns were not then in existence — at least, not in my neighborhood. My powder was carried in a horn hung from my shoulder by a cord tied to both ends of the horn. Although we traversed the surrounding neighborhood, we did no great damage to the wild life.

After I had become a Justice of the Supreme Court of Georgia, a case involving the dog fell to me for writing the decision. Immediately the memory of my dog Lion filled my mind. In fact, my heart was touched, for no man ever loses his regard for a loyal playmate, whether human or beast. There came over me a desire to seize the opportunity to place on the enduring pages of the decisions of our Supreme Court a tribute to the dog, which would also be in some sense a memorial to Lion. I wrote such a decision, and it appears in volume 169 at page 746 *et sequitur* of the *Georgia Reports*. The opinion opens with these words: "From the dawn of primal history the Dog has loomed large in the art and literature of the world, including judicial literature. So it doubtless will be until the 'crack of doom'." The opinion comprises about five pages. It was a poignant regret to me that the greatest dog-lover among my associates on the Bench, Justice Atkinson, was disqualified from participating in this decision because he was related to one counsel in the case.

Reverting for a moment to the "goat era" of my boyhood, I must mention my one possession that was the envy of all my boy friends in the neighborhood. My father purchased a pair of fine, large goats for me — Bill and Jack. Then he made a set of harness to fit them and a wagon for them to pull. With this outfit I was occasionally sent to a grist mill some two miles away, carrying a sack of shelled corn which I would have ground into meal. On rare occasions, my "turn-out" was my means of transportation to and from church. It so diverted the attention of the other boys from worship, however, that I had to discontinue this practice.

The present generation cannot appreciate the vast improvement in transportation in Georgia within the lifetime of some of us now living. The same has been more or less true all over America. At the close of the War Between the States, in 1865, there were few railroads in Georgia and no paved roads. City and town streets were very little better than the best of country roads. Automobiles and trucks and busses were unknown. Passenger travel was by horseback or muleback, sometimes on backs of oxen, or, when roads permitted, in carriages, buggies, and gigs. (A gig was a light, two-wheeled, one-horse vehicle.) These vehicles were generally useful only in dry summer weather. That explains why there was very little social intercourse between farm families in winter.

My father resided twenty-five miles from Columbus and fourteen miles from Lumpkin, the county seat of Stewart. Columbus was the larger market; so our cotton was carried there by wagon for marketing. On the return trip the wagons usually brought supplies for the farm. The road to Columbus ran along the general course of the Chattahoochee River and not far distant from it. Several creeks emptied into the river and had to be crossed near their mouths, the most difficult parts to cross. Generally the old covered bridges afforded a passage, but they were often in need of repair because of long usage and the damage from swollen streams. Some streams were small, shallow, and unbridged.

When I was a boy, a journey to Columbus was a great event and always involved the element of adventure. For several days before the "start," as it was called, there was excitement on the farm and much talk about who would go, how many bales of cotton would be carried, and how many mules would be used. Usually the wagon would be loaded high with as many bales as it was safe to carry. Six mules would furnish the "motor power," with the driver on the back of one of the two mules nearest the wagon, the four mules ahead in pairs. The "lead" mule was one of the first two and had to be both strong and spirited. There was never any question of who would drive — it was always John Redding.

My father would make the trip to Columbus in a buggy, unless the roads were too wet and muddy. In that case he resorted to his saddle horse. If the buggy was used he took me along, and that was a wonderful experience. I do not remember my mother ever undertaking that hazardous and always uncomfortable trip. On the appointed day, the wagon having been loaded the day before, the farm was astir long before daybreak. The driver and his assistant were busy having their breakfast and feeding the animals that were to bear the heavy burden of the journey. Then at break of day the mules were hitched to the wagon with old John Redding seated on the back of his mule. There would be the crack of the whip, a cry from him of "Git up, mules!" and away the team would go, knowing as well as the men that the road was long and the trip would be hard. Still, they were off with spirit.

The team would be given an hour's start before my father would take his leave. This gave him time for a more leisurely breakfast. Then off we would go, planning to overtake the wagon before nightfall. There were places along the road, well-known to travelers, which were suitable for camping. These places were always interesting to me, for I longed to "camp out" with the wagons, but that permission never came. As the short winter afternoon wore on, we would watch for the wagon until finally we came up with it at camp. My father would halt only long enough to examine the mules and question the driver; then our buggy would be off again, headed for the home of my Grandfather Gilbert, a place which today is a portion of the great Fort Benning to which I refer elsewhere. We crossed a very clear stream just before reaching my grandfather's place. I always looked forward to crossing this crystal-clear stream that ran over a solid bed of bright-colored pebbles. I know of no other stream like it. We next climbed a rather long hill, by which time the day's journey had brought us such fatigue that a mile seemed like two. Just before reaching "Grandpa's" my father would tell me that the first thing I would see would be my grandmother sweeping the porch. He was nearly always right, for she was constantly busy keeping her place immaculately clean.

In those days dinner was eaten at noon; so our first meal there was always supper. After a perfect night's rest on a good bed, followed by a hearty breakfast, we felt like new. We awaited the arrival of the wagon, anxious to learn its condition. Then we drove the last lap of eleven miles to Columbus. This was over a better road and would be uneventful. There was one stretch of about a mile where the fences on both sides of the road were covered with Cherokee rose vines. I saw it several times when the roses were in full bloom, and I can never forget its unsurpassed beauty — just two lines of wild loveliness. Since those days I have loved the Cherokee rose and have several in my flower garden at Sea Island. This rose is now Georgia's state flower, and a finer choice could not have been made.

On arrival in Columbus, we met the wagon at the warehouse of Burrus & Williams, cotton dealers. This would be headquarters, where we met and where all our purchases were sent for loading on our wagon. On one of these trips, when I was six or seven years old, I wore pants my mother had made out of an old pair of my father's, turned inside out. It was only about four years after the war, when clothing was scarce and when wives and mothers made all the clothing their children wore. Wearing these trousers, I arrived at the warehouse and found several boys waiting to play with me while my father attended to his business. We leaped from cotton bale to cotton bale and were having a "big time" when suddenly we discovered that something had happened to my pants at a very embarrassing portion thereof. There I was, far from home, by father down town somewhere, and I with no change of trousers. For a boy, such a predicament is the height of embarrassment. However, one of my playmates, Thomas Salisbury, used his head. He lived just across the street, and while some of us were wondering what to do, he ran home and quickly returned with a message that his mother would mend my pants. Of course, I went with Thomas to his room, divested myself of my pants and waited while his mother mended them. That experience ended my jumping from one bale of cotton to another. However, it did not end my friendship with Thomas Salisbury, for since those days our friendship has been strong and true.

At fifteen I finished the grammar school in Columbus, that is, so the school authorities said. Looking backward, I am convinced that they were mistaken, for there was much in a first-rate grammar school that I had skipped. These omissions affected adversely all of my subsequent education. My father had moved from a really rural section where educational advantages were almost primitive. I had attended parts of three elementary school terms, and then entered school at Columbus in the next to the highest class, "sliding through" that class and then the highest class in two school years. Because I had suffered from malaria and was not strong, the going was difficult. I wanted to quit school and go to work as did a large percentage of my comrades. My father thought otherwise, but he was too smart to force me to attend school against my will. He owned a drug store, and he readily agreed to give me a job and ten dollars per month. My duties were to rise very early, open the drug store, sweep out the store and sidewalk, then go to breakfast.

A Georgia Country Boy

After breakfast my work was chiefly in the cellar under the store, washing bottles into which medicine would be poured. After that they were to be corked and labelled.

Soon my mind was on my boy friends who spent the long, hot, summer afternoons playing baseball, while my duties would call me to that cellar where there were bottles and more bottles to be washed, corked, and labelled. My mind suddenly changed. I told my father that I wanted to go back to school. He said I could join a number of comrades who were going to Park High School, Tuskegee, Alabama, the next month, September, 1877.

At the Tuskegee school, it was my good fortune to fall under the guidance of a really great educator, the late James F. Park. I shall never forget him. His influence remained with me even after I entered college, for which I now began to prepare myself.

Some years after our family removed from Stewart County to Columbus, and after I had become a Georgia Circuit Judge, an amusing incident occurred with a Negro to whom our farm in Stewart had been sold. The Negro, Joe Muns, had bought the farm on credit; had worked the farm and earned the funds with which to complete his contract, and had his deed of conveyance. Naturally, in such a transaction continuing about nine years, Joe had grown to depend upon me (my father having passed away) to finance him on all occasions.

One morning Joe appeared, peeping through the partially opened door, and said, "Good-morning, Boss." I was sitting at my desk in the Judges' Chambers.

"Come in, Joe," I said. "What do you want now? You have your land, all free of debt. Surely you don't want to borrow!"

"Yes Sir, Boss, I sho' does, fer I'm in one terrbul fix."

"What in the world has happened?" I inquired.

"Well, Boss, it's lack dis: I's been conjured. My folks is all sick; my chickens is all dead; my cows done gone dry and dey won't eat nothing; my hogs is all dead; and lastly an' most pertickeler, my mule, she tuck sick and died; I jist ain't got no mule to plow."

"Well," I said, "that does sound pretty bad, but how do you know you're conjured, and what do you propose to do about it?"

"Boss, Judge, I knows what to do, an' it ain't but one thing can stop all dis trouble and dat's why I come to you as I is always done. De conjure man, he put a piece er red cloth on my do-step, and dat is de way de conjure-man tell you what he is done. He say 'lessen I leave three hundred silver dollars on dem steps, so he can cum and git hit in de night time when I is shet de do' and sleepin' in de bed, dat de conjure goin' git wuss. An, Boss, I wants to git dat money fum you so I can pay de conjure man and my folks and my things won't be sick no mo'."

"Why must all of the money be in silver dollars?" I asked.

Joe replied, "I dunno, but hit jest have to be dat away."

By this time I had become certain that Joe's fertile mind had spun a complicated scheme which he was sure would achieve his purpose. So I said, "Joe, there is only one thing of which I'm very certain about your story, and that is that you are a crazy man, and a contract with a crazy man is not binding. So you can't get a cent from me to pay the conjure-man."

Joe looked as if I had pronounced a death sentence, and slowly departed as if in great suffering. I had about fixed my attention on a pile of court papers on my desk, when a newspaper reporter, a friend of mine, came in and asked if there were any news. I told him the above story, and he printed it in the Columbus morning paper. Two weeks passed and the incident had been completely forgotten when Joe appeared again at my office, the whites of his eyes shining with a new light.

"Come in, Joe," I said. "What is it now?"

"Lord, Boss, you done ruint me. What I gwine do now? I went out to Lumpkin to see if I can git de money fum de bank. When I goes to de bank winder, de bank man was sittin' dere readin' de Columbus paper, and he say 'Is dat Joe Muns?' I say 'Yas sir, dis is Joe, and wants to git you to loan me three hundred dollars, please sir.' I starts to tell him my troubles, and he say, 'Wait a minit, Joe. I'se been reading in de Columbus paper about you and Judge Gilbert,' and he say de bank is 'zackly lack Judge Gilbert, hit don' lend no money to crazy folks, and dat's how I sho' am ruint."

And then he added: "Judge, Boss, I's sorry I tole you dat lie about de conjure-man. I now gwine tell you de truf'. I tole you all dat to git de money to buy me a new mule — won't none of de things true what I tole you."

Joe's credit was no better than before he first told the conjure-man story.

CHAPTER III

Vanderbilt and Yale

THE selection of Vanderbilt University as my choice among colleges grew out of the influence of my roommate at Park High School in Tuskegee. This friend was Paul LeGrand of Montgomery, Alabama, who was going to Vanderbilt and urged me to accompany him. I decided to do so since I had no predilection for any other university.

Vanderbilt University in Nashville, Tennessee, was established in 1873 and was named for Cornelius Vanderbilt who desired "to help heal the wounds of war and to aid the Southern people in reviving their fortunes." It was only six years old when I matriculated on a warm September day in 1879. The campus was large, and the buildings were new. The home of the president and the homes of many members of the faculty were on the campus. The President of the Board of Trustees was none other than the celebrated Bishop Holland N. McTyeire, a noted scholar, a great religious leader, and a bishop in the Southern Methodist Church. Twelve years later his *History of Methodism* was to serve so well in the instruction of members of the Northern as well as the Southern branch of the Methodist Church. Bishop McTyeire and his faculty laid the foundation stones of a great Southern university. Beginning with the first commencement, Vanderbilt has graduated an unusually large number of governors, senators, congressmen, one speaker of the United States House of Representatives, Supreme Court Justices, both Federal and State, one "roving" ambassador, a president of the American Red Cross, bishops, and many noted educators.

How one's life is altered, even molded, by the friends one makes, especially at college! I was to make friends who were to influence me the remainder of my years. At Vanderbilt I became associated with many young men who afterwards became great in the world's estimation, who became illustrious and successful business and professional men. First of all, there is Justice James C. McReynolds, that staunch oak of the Constitution, who was to sit on the bench of the Supreme Court of the United States for so many years, who was to warn his country against departing from the Constitution as our fathers declared it to be, and who, before this service, was Attorney General of the United States.

Thinking back to the first time I saw James C. McReynolds, I remember the campus of Vanderbilt. There were many benches on the lawns of the campus for the convenience of students who might wish to sit and ponder over their problems or wait for the next class. One day shortly after I arrived, I was occupying one of these outdoor seats and gazing over the scholastic panorama which to me seemed quite grand, albeit I must confess to a touch of homesickness, when I was approached by a most distinguished looking student. He was tall, fully six feet or more, slender, and very erect. In a most friendly manner he sat down beside me and introduced himself as James C. McReynolds of Elkton, Kentucky. I later learned that he had been born in that town on February 3, 1862. He was exactly three days younger than I, but I must admit that on that particular day he evinced a greater degree of self-confidence than I did, my thoughts being far away on my mother and home. This new acquaintance was to become my roommate and constant companion. It seemed as though from the moment we met our lives became interlocked. Nearly two decades later, when I was married to Mary Howard of Columbus, Georgia, on December 12, 1895, none other than McReynolds was my "best man."

James C. McReynolds' career, from the day he entered college, was so unusual that I must touch upon it more in detail. His legal fame was to spread far beyond the boundaries of Tennessee where he began the practice of law. This future member of the Supreme Court of the United States, whose blistering dissents were to challenge wreckers of the Constitution, was early looked upon by both faculty and student body as the outstanding leader of the school. He led his class in grades nearly all the time, and he was so earnest a devotee to duty, so faithful to method and discipline, that he was a tower of strength at the University and was looked upon somewhat austerely as an "example." Notwithstanding the fact that he finished the four year academic course in three years, receiving highest honors from both students and faculty, he was able to participate in extra-curricular activities and was editor-in-chief of the student publication, *The Vanderbilt Observer*. It was then the custom for the faculty to name the graduate who had won the highest grade during the entire course, from matriculation to graduation, as winner of the first honor and of the gold Founder's Medal. The graduating class also selected its most representative member, regardless of scholastic grades. The students named for these honors were to deliver addresses at Commencement exercises. McReynolds was the man chosen by both faculty and class. He declined the faculty honor, but accepted the class honor. How did he achieve this enviable record? The answer is simple — by self-discipline — though to have followed in his steps might not have been so easy. He planned his tasks and refused to deviate one iota from his schedule. His hours for study, sleep, and recreation were fixed in advance, and he never changed them to please friend or foe. He was of a friendly nature, but this did not prevent his rigid compliance with that methodical life which did accomplish so much. His rules were unbreakable no matter what temptations came his way. This characteristic was to follow throughout life. It later caused him to be called austere, but it kept him from bending to mob psychology when he had to construe the Constitution.

McReynolds was a candidate for Congress in 1896 on the Palmer and Buckner ticket with full knowledge that defeat was certain. He was in politics to serve the public good — not to get an office. As prosecutor of the tobacco and other trusts by government employment under Theodore Roosevelt, as Attorney General of the United States by appointment of Woodrow Wilson, and as Associate Justice of the Supreme Court of the United States by appointment also of President Wilson, Mr. McReynolds was the same unswerving devotee to duty, the same loyal Knight of the Constitution *as written*. He refused to agree to change it to suit any "changed conditions" or any government policies or so-called emergencies. He stood adamant against the theory of amending the Constitution by construction to suit "changed conditions," temporary emergencies, or administrative policies. In this he was in harmony with the great Constitution authorities.[1]

Possibly the next most remarkable student, after McReynolds, entering Vanderbilt in 1879 was Duncan Upshaw Fletcher, afterwards a distinguished member of the United States Senate from Florida. He was born in Sumter County, Georgia, but at the time he went to Van-

---
[1] See chapter X.

derbilt he lived at Forsyth, Georgia, in Monroe County. He was an outstanding student in every respect. There was not a more popular boy on the campus. His winning personality made him liked equally well by faculty and students. He held the affection of all. He was the top-ranking orator of the college, as was evidenced by his triumphs on anniversary and Commencement occasions. After winning his academic degree, Fletcher entered the Law Department, and there again, notwithstanding certain misfortunes that would have overwhelmed most men, he excelled. He was engaged to be married to a lovely young woman of Barnesville, Georgia, and in order to speed his marriage day he was taking two years of law in one. One attack of illness after another overtook him, and as a final blow, his fiancee was stricken with a fatal illness. He left the university for his home, intending to abandon his ambition to become a lawyer — his hopes of happiness and a coveted professional career having thus been cut short.

Then, with no common purpose, no concerted plan of action, the students loaded the mails with letters to Duncan. These letters were filled with condolences and entreated him to return. Finally, he yielded and returned to his classes at Vanderbilt. Both students and faculty knew it would be impossible for him to make up for the lost time. He returned with it clearly understood that he would not try for or expect a diploma. Ultimately he moved to Jacksonville, Florida, where he began to practice law and where he entered politics. That city remained his home, and Florida became his home state. Fletcher's career ended in perfect accord with what had been the general tenor of his whole life. He died after a long period of service in the United States Senate, beloved in Washington as he was in the State of Florida.

Among my other classmates and friends were Malcolm R. Patterson of Memphis, next to Duncan Fletcher the best orator at Vanderbilt, who became a Congressman and Governor of Tennessee; George H. Armistead, later the brilliant editor of the Nashville *Banner;* William H. Jackson, who was in later years appointed by United States Attorney General McReynolds as United States District Judge for the Panama Canal Zone; Claude Waller of Kentucky, who graduated with first honor the year after I received my diploma and who became General Counsel for the Nashville, Chattanooga, and St. Louis Railroad; Robert F. Jackson, who became a leading lawyer in Nashville and for whom I was a groomsman when he married; William H. Ellerbe, who at the age of twenty-eight became Comptroller General of South Carolina and was later Governor of that state; Hunter Meriwether, first honor graduate in 1883; and Morris Brandon, who became a leading lawyer in Georgia.

I began a life-long friendship with Morris Brandon, whose home in Dover, Tennessee, was just across the state boundary line from the home of J. C. McReynolds in Elkton, Kentucky. These two college friends had been students together in grammar school. So intimate did Brandon and I become that we agreed to practice law together when we finished college, and this understanding was arrived at even before either of us entered the Law Department. Our agreement was to practice in Atlanta, the sequel to which will be found in a subsequent chapter.

While at Vanderbilt, I joined the Phi Delta Theta Fraternity. Classmates who were fraternity brothers became more intimate friends. During the years 1886-89, I served as national treasurer of this organization. Years later when I was blessed with two sons, they followed my choice and joined Phi Delta Theta; Price, Junior, the Georgia Delta Chapter at Georgia Tech; and Francis, the Georgia Alpha Chapter at the University of Georgia.

After four years at Vanderbilt University, I was awarded the degree of Bachelor of Science and a certificate from the Law Department entitling me to be admitted to the bar to practice law. I was so admitted in June, 1883, in Nashville, Davidson County, Tennessee. It was my intention not to enter the practice until I had studied further.

After thorough investigation of law schools, I decided to attend Yale University, New Haven, Connecticut, whose law school was unsurpassed anywhere in the land, in my opinion. My good friend, Morris Brandon, joined me in that conclusion. In the fall of 1883, I proceeded to New Haven, with Brandon coming shortly thereafter. Soon after I entered Yale I suffered a severe blow — I was stricken with typhoid fever. My physician, becoming alarmed and convinced that I could not recover, telegraphed my father to come at once. After consultations with the attending doctor, my father decided to take me home, regardless of my condition, since my one consuming desire was to see my mother. There were no through sleeping cars from Connecticut to Georgia; so I was placed on a mattress and loaded on the train. We had to change trains several times before we finally arrived in Columbus. Nursed by my mother, I soon had a sudden turn for the better, and in due time I recovered. I was still determined to go through the Yale Law School; so I went back in the fall of 1884 and graduated in law in 1885.

Morris Brandon had remained at Yale. He received his law degree in 1884 and returned to Dover, Tennessee, where he entered the practice of law with his father for a year.

Vanderbilt and Yale

My roommate at Yale during the year 1884-85 was Charles K. Holliday, of Topeka, Kansas. He was educated in academic work at Heidelburg, Germany, but came to Yale for law. We became very close friends. His father had preempted the land where the city of Topeka stands while Kansas was a territory. After Kansas became a state, Topeka was made the capital, and that made Colonel Holliday, the father, very wealthy. He built the Atcheson, Topeka, and Sante Fe Railroad, which no one at the time thought he had a ghost of a chance to build. The railroad contributed to his wealth. Colonel and Mrs. Holliday came to Yale to see their son graduate in June, 1885. Both of his parents urged me to go to Topeka to begin the practice of law. They told me that Charles had stated to them that unless I did so he would not enter the law practice. They were keenly anxious for him to be a lawyer. They offered me unusual inducements — far more than I could possibly have been worth to them or to Charles. I told them that I, too, was an only son and must return to my home in Georgia. I did accompany them back to Kansas for a visit, after graduating. The Colonel gave us a vacation at Manitou Springs, near Colorado Springs, Colorado. Mrs. Holliday, a sweet and lovely woman, went with us. Her charm resulted in numerous social affairs at which Charles and I met many lovely girls. She introduced us as "her boys," and we had the time of our lives. We had just finished school and had not yet learned how hard it was to make a living at law.

Hardly had I returned to Georgia and entered upon the task of finding a law office for Brandon and myself when I received a letter from Charles Holliday urging me to return to Topeka. The inducement was that a beautiful young kinswoman would be a guest at his home for several weeks, and he wished us to meet. I declined for sundry reasons. Shortly afterwards they were married. His decision not to practice law being unalterable, his father bought him a daily newspaper (called the Topeka *Capital*, as I recall). It was Republican in politics. Kansas was then, as it is now, a Republican state. Colonel Holliday was a leading Republican, but Charles, who had become so intimate with many Southern boys at Yale, became an ardent Democrat and follower of President Cleveland. Shortly after Cleveland began his second term, he appointed Charles as one of the World's Fair Commissioners. Each state had two commissioners, one a Democrat and one a Republican. Charles was the Democratic appointee for Kansas. The Fair opened in 1893, one year late, since it was launched to commemorate the four hundredth anniversary of the discovery of America by Columbus. I attended the Fair and saw Charles for the first time since our parting in 1885. We met only once again — during the 1922 annual convention of the American Bar Association at San Francisco. Charles had become a citizen of Sacramento, California, and a very fine and useful one. He has gone to his last rest, as have so many of my old friends of those old days.

During a cruise of the Caribbean some four or five years ago, Mrs. Gilbert and I visited most of the West Indian Islands and Caracas, Venezuela. The memory of Charles Holliday was brought back to me. In his young days he was quite outspoken in his opinions and prejudices. In the second administration of President Cleveland, an interview in the New York *Herald* related the return of Charles and his bride from Caracas, where he had spent a brief period as minister. The period was so brief, in fact, that the reporter inquired the reason for his resignation and return. He replied to the effect that he could not remain in any country where it was believed that a bath would mean certain death. Of course he was joking, and his real reason for returning was not given.

Mrs. Gilbert and I found the West Indian Islands attractive and the people friendly. Some of the islands were obnoxiously infested with hordes of persistent beggars. Kingston, Jamaica, was one of the worst with respect to beggars. Curacao, the Dutch island, and Havana, Cuba, were outstanding in cleanliness. Caracas, in some respects a very modern city, is in the interior of Venezuela and is approached from the harbor, LaGuaira, over a splendidly engineered, concrete-paved highway. The President's Palace was open to tourists, and though not pretentious, it was quite attractive. We voyaged on the Dutch steamer, *Rotterdam*, sailing from and returning to New Orleans.

Joseph R. Parrott of Maine was a member of my law class at Yale and also a member of the varsity crew. We also had a member of the varsity football team named McCrory. These two kept our class keyed up on athletics. Parrott asked for advice as to a Southern location for himself just before we graduated. He liked Southern boys and saw no future for himself in Maine. I suggested Jacksonville, Florida, and gave him a letter to my Vanderbilt friend, Duncan Fletcher. Parrott took the suggestion, established himself in Jacksonville, was successful, and became General Counsel and First Vice-President of the Florida East Coast Railroad and of the Flagler tourist hotels, as well as chairman of the Board of Trustees that administered the estate of Henry M. Flagler upon the latter's death.

As would naturally be supposed, a university graduating as many men as did Yale built up a large reputation for successful and prominent alumni. The student body was so large no student could know a large percentage of those in attendance. The university was made up of many schools and colleges. There was the usual classical college, awarding such degrees as A.B., A.M., etc.; then there was the Sheffield Scientific School, or "Sheff," as it was called, awarding scientific degrees; the theological college, the law school, etc.

In the large student body, containing many who were justly entitled to admiration and who afterwards were leaders in many lines of American life, Amos Alonzo Stagg was outstanding. He attained prominence at once, and justified it throughout his Yale career. It has been a long time since I graduated at Yale (1885), and some of the details about Stagg have become confused. As I recall, I wrote about Stagg having earned a part of his first year at Yale by rooming over the stables of a wealthy New Haven citizen. Feeling not quite certain as to these facts, I wrote to him for verification. He promptly replied most cordially, saying, "I am sorry not to be able to corroborate the 'stable boy' story. Probably there is a bit of confusion." Then he explained that in 1884 he spent five months at a "prep" school preparing for his entrance "exams." "I earned my board and a good room in the barn where the cow was kept . . . by milking it, cutting wood, and doing other chores." (I'm sure these chores were all faithfully and well done.) He passed the "exams" and entered Yale Theological School. I regret that the plan of this work does not permit much more space to be devoted to this fine man. His story should be an inspiration to thousands of youths. An entire book, *Touchdown!*, about Stagg has been written by Wesley Winans Stout. In it we learn that Stagg entered Yale to become a preacher and came out a football coach. He is noted as a football player and athletic director. He was, as he insists, a baseball pitcher — always an amateur, but a brilliant one. He is still coaching football — now at College of the Pacific, Stockton, California. He has graciously permitted me to use the above stated facts.

Differing from those of most colleges and universities, fraternities and societies at Yale were class organizations in my day, as they may still be. "Skull and Bones," or "Bones" as it was called, was a senior society, limited to a membership of fifteen who had been upgraded from the junior class and were distinguished in some activity: athletics or scholarship. "Bones" was the oldest of the senior societies. In my day at Yale there were also two others — "Scroll and Keys" and "Wolf's Head." The first choice, the ambition of every junior, was to be called to membership in "Bones." So far as I ever heard, only one man ever rejected membership after being "tapped" for this society, and his reason seems never to have been learned. The invitation to become a member was conveyed to the fortunate selectee by his being "tapped" on the shoulder. The word went forth each Commencement that on a certain day the memberships for "Bones" for the ensuing year would be selected. A crowd gathered; all dormitory windows would be open and filled with gazers watching the ceremony. "Bones" members would go out on the campus one at a time where the crowd of students had assembled, and fifteen selected persons would be tapped on the shoulder. Then "Keys" selected its new set of members in the same way. When a selectee was tapped on the shoulder, he would follow the man who tapped him to some private room for instructions as to his induction. "Wolf's Head" did not pursue this plan.

An old custom at Yale, never deviated from in my time, was fence sitting. Around the front side of the campus and in front of the dormitories was a fence with two or three round stringers running through a row of posts, the stringers being about the size of a man's leg. A student could conveniently sit on the top rung or stringer while resting his feet on a lower one. The different classes had their exclusive panels. The seniors had the extreme right, looking toward the "green," as the lawn was called, and away from the dormitories. That placed your look outward and toward the "petticoats" who passed. The juniors were on the left of the seniors, then the sophomores, then the freshmen. However, it was always told me at Yale (I was only in the Law School there) that freshmen were never allowed to sit on the fence until they had defeated the Harvard freshmen in baseball. If Yale was the victor, the "Fresh" would form a line at the athletic field, headed by a brass band, would march back to the campus, and, on reaching their part of the fence and having saluted the seniors with the Yale yell, would break ranks and make a wild rush, some falling over the fence and climbing back. They would sit there until called to other duties.

Yale prowess in football was more noted when I was there than it is today. Yale usually had the outstanding football team in the country at that time. In recent years many colleges have received fame and prominence because of their football teams. Yale has many times gone down in defeat. I shall never forget the scene on Sanford Field, Athens, 1929, when Georgia defeated Yale. It was the occasion of the dedication of the field. The day was beautiful, and the crowd of Georgia alumni and supporters was keyed for victory. The Georgia "Bulldogs" christened the field by winning from the Yale "Bulldogs." Georgia has also defeated Yale at New Haven.

During my student days, Yale played Princeton at the

Polo Grounds in New York. A huge gathering of gaily dressed girls and chaperones and "sporty dressed" men saw the entire game played in several inches of snow. It began and ended in snow. There were fifteen of us who engaged a tally-ho coach, decorated in Yale blue and equipped with bugles to let the world know that we were present. We boarded our tally-ho at the old Hoffman House at Madison Square and travelled to the Polo Grounds. All of us, well wrapped to guard against the icy weather, were seated on top, blowing the bugles incessantly. We drove as near the side lines as possible and noisily witnessed the game — and Yale's defeat. Then we made a very subdued return.

For a single event, the annual boat race with Harvard was the most colorful. It was run at New London on the Thames. For a month or more before the race the crew, with its substitutes, was sent to Gale's Ferry, a few miles upstream from New London, to practice over the actual course where the race would be run. The course was four miles, ending at New London. The boats — long, light, and narrow — were called "shells." For the varsity race, eight oarsmen and a coxswain — the latter to guide the boat — sat single file. At Gale's Ferry there were comfortable living quarters where the crew remained strictly on the job of practice rowing; of course, also carrying on class studies. One or more professors went along to assist in keeping up studies and for general steadying purposes.

Special trains packed with enthusiasts were run, as today, from Cambridge and New Haven. At New London the crowds transferred to flat cars on which were seats running lengthwise. The tiers were so arranged that spectators in the rear could see over the heads of those in front. These trains of flat cars parallel the river and run at a speed which permits the spectators to observe the race from beginning to end. They are sent to Gale's Ferry before the race and return along with the racing boats.

A short time after arrival of the spectators at Gale's, seemingly hours, the crews are seen silently and smoothly moving out from their separate boat houses to the starting point. Cheers and all sorts of deafening noises rise over the waters of the river and the hills above. Horns are blown to increase the din. The bedlam is indescribable. Excitement reaches a fever pitch. Someone, more intimately acquainted with the personnel of the crew, discovers and publishes that the Yale "stroke oar," the pride of the crew, is ill and cannot row as usual. Sure enough, the Yale boat drops behind, and Harvard forges ahead. The Yale supporters are thunderstruck, dismayed; defeat is almost certain; the tin horns begin to grow silent; then all of the horns are thrown overboard. Yale has lost; Harvard has won the race. Sad looking, the Yale Blue and its following return to New Haven. Harvard, wild with joy, noisy, or raucous, as it seems to the Blues, returns to Cambridge to chalk up a victory.

When I saw this race as a student, one Yale student, a sporting youth, bet his all on the race — money sent him for his return home after Commencement. Yale's loss caused the youth great grief, but *mirabile dictu*, when the stakeholder reported, it was found that this bet had been called off by the Harvard better; and the money, imagined lost, was returned to the Yale youth's pocket.

There were other days, before and since, for Yale, because the string of victories does not run evenly for any college. Harvard and Yale have long been traditional competitors; in fact, each is the other's chief competitor.

When I was at Yale, democracy was the shibboleth.

Yale considered that Harvard was "blue blood." True it was that wealth and family prominence counted for more at Harvard than at Yale. Yale decried this Harvard sentiment as unjust and discreditable. Furthermore, Yale ridiculed it as is quite well illustrated in the following toast proposed by a Yale student at a banquet attended by both Harvard and Yale students:

> Here's to the City of Boston,
> The home of the Bean and the Cod,
> Where the Cabots speak only to the Lowells
> And Lowells speak only to God.
>
> And here's to the Town of New Haven,
> The seat of Learning and Light,
> Where Brown speaks to Jones
> In the very same tones
> He addresses to Hadley and Dwight.

Another traditional custom rigidly adhered to at Yale during my time was that every freshman was expected to buy one or more tickets to the Senior Promenade, but he was not allowed on the dance floor. All freshmen ticket holders were seated in the gallery where they could see the gay dancers and partake of refreshments, and one may be sure that they did full justice to the latter privilege. However, none of these traditions obtained in the professional schools. As I was in the Law School, my knowledge of the custom was derived solely from observation of what went on around me. I was not involved in it myself.

I did enjoy one experience not common there. Charles Holliday and I were members of a "Mess Club," a group which ate together, composed of ten members. The other eight were seniors in the academic department. This association meant more than might at first appear. The friendships formed at a common board attended by a limited group are lasting, and they sink deeply into the consciousness. Every member of that club knew well the sentiments of every other member.

Noah Porter, who was President of Yale when I was there and who signed my law diploma, delivered an address some years before (1881) on Yale, that great democratic institution of learning, in which he said: "It has proposed no royal and easy paths to learning or intellectual power. It has carefully refrained from odious comparisons to the disadvantages of sister institutions... Its windows are open in every direction, towards the rising as truly as towards the setting sun, and it is ever ready to welcome new truth from any quarter, and to try new methods, by whomsoever they are suggested, if they are recommended to our judgment or are enforced by experience. But it believes in the past as well as the future, holding it to be eminently becoming in those who have received the torch of knowledge from those who have gone before them to despise none of the wisdom which the past has inspired or confirmed."

I commend most heartily those sentiments to all units of our University System, as well as to all institutions of learning, high and low, everywhere.

Both Yale and Harvard have always been popular in Georgia. A list of Georgians who studied at those institutions would include many of our foremost men. Within my own knowledge, two of our Associate Justices of the Georgia Supreme Court, Hiram Warner Hill and James Kollock Hines, contemporaries on that court, were students at the Harvard Law School. Judge Hill was a graduate of the Harvard Law School. Judge Hines attended that eminent institution for instruction in law one year. He would have finished the course there had he not decided to enter the practice of law when the course was half covered, because of pressure in his circuit in Georgia, where he was being urged to seek judicial office, an urge with which he complied some three years after leaving Harvard.

Among Georgia Yale graduates have been Joseph E. Brown, our War-Between-the-States Governor; William A. Little; and Beverly D. Evans, who became a Justice of the Georgia Supreme Court and later United States District Judge. Evans was at Yale when I first entered.

I consider myself especially fortunate in having had the opportunity to study law at Yale under Professor Simeon E. Baldwin, who later served Connecticut as Governor and also as Chief Justice, and as President of the American Bar Association. I never knew a man more deeply learned in the law. He was figuratively a law library in himself. I recall also that Frank D. Brandegee, the eminent United States Senator from Connecticut, was at Yale when I was there.

Yale is a great institution with a long and creditable history. It is situated in a wealthy section of our country and consequently draws patronage from a wealthy class, though many who go there are poor. In its long career it has become heavily endowed and has many rich alumni. Georgia universities in the undeveloped South need and deserve all that Georgians can contribute to their welfare. Yale has less need of us.

However, without disparaging Yale or Harvard in the least, I must state emphatically that neither can offer Georgia students anything better than that which they can get in their own state. Of course, going away to college opens up new horizons and gives a comparative study the youth does not get at home. He learns the mental reactions of many other people, strange and new to him.

This broadens him. I cannot see, however, where my stay at Yale changed any opinion I ever had or influenced me more than other general associations have done. My student contacts were about the same as they had been in the South. The press broadens our fund of knowledge by increasing our information. Travel does the same, and in some respects it is the greatest educator of all. Travel in foreign countries has meant much to me. It broadens the sympathies and makes it possible to form clearer judgments. Especially is travel really worthwhile if the traveller keeps a diary instead of merely seeking to digest — in lumps, as it were — all he sees and hears on the spot.

I have often been asked why I went to Vanderbilt and Yale. There was no special reason in either case. My father was very indulgent; I was an only son; and like many other youths, my decisions were made for superficial, rather than sound reasons. In selecting my schools I acted simply upon what I had heard. I must confess, from this latterday view, that I have always regretted that I did not go to the University of Georgia. Inasmuch as my younger son graduated at both Georgia and Yale and so soon thereafter passed away, I have endeavored to take his place in devotion to our University. On the campus at Athens I have built an Infirmary as a memorial to my father and my deceased son. During World War II it was used exclusively by the United States Navy for general war purposes of a medical nature. Now that the war is over the Gilbert Infirmary is again serving the students of the University of Georgia.

CHAPTER IV

Gordon and Lee

IN the spring of 1886 a marble statue of Georgia's great and beloved Senator, Benjamin Harvey Hill, was unveiled in Atlanta at Baker Street, the junction of Peachtree and West Peachtree Streets. It was later moved to the State Capitol where it now stands on the main floor, facing the north entrance. Major J. C. C. Black, a great orator and renowned citizen, had been selected as the speaker of the occasion, and he delivered a masterful address which fully measured up to his reputation.

Jefferson Davis, old and feeble, who was then living at Beauvoir, his home on the Gulf Coast of Mississippi, had yielded to the great urge for his presence. He had placed great reliance upon the advice and counsel of Ben Hill during the most trying days through which he and the South had passed. In an effort to show a token of appreciation of Hill's loyal support, he had come to Atlanta to pay homage to his late friend, volunteering this break in his own self-imposed privacy.

These features and others united to attract a great concourse of people. I was in the crowd and fortunately managed to secure standing room not far from the speaker's stand. No audience was ever more reverent or more surcharged with patriotic ardor and hero worship. I had never before, nor have I ever since, witnessed such an occasion.

The great Georgian, Henry W. Grady, editor of the Atlanta *Constitution*, was master of ceremonies. He had planned the event in all its details to make it a never-to-be-forgotten occasion. The eloquent Grady, at this time the pride of all Georgians, introduced Davis in the following words:

> My countrymen, let us teach the lesson of this old man's life, that defeat hath its glories no less than victory. Let us declare that this outcast from the privileges of this great government is the uncrowned king of our people and that no Southern man, high or humble, asks greater glory than to bear with him, heart to heart, the blame and the burdens of the cause for which he stands unpardoned. In dignity and honor he met the responsibilities of our common cause. With dauntless courage he faced its charges. In obscurity and poverty he has for twenty years borne the reproach of our enemies and the obloquy of defeat . . . . This moment finds its richest reward in the fact that we can light with sunshine the shortening end of a path that has long been dark and dreary. Georgians, countrymen, soldiers and sons of soldiers, and brave women, the light and soul of our civilization, rise and give your hearts voices as we tell Jefferson Davis that he is at home among his people.[1]

As with an electric current, the throng was swept off its feet, and when Davis arose the cheering was deafening. He was overcome with emotion, and his voice could scarcely be heard beyond a few feet.

General John B. Gordon was there, along with thousands of Confederate veterans. It was a day of reunion and of memories. These veterans completely gave themselves to the spirit of the occasion, living over old days of victories and defeats, of joys and sufferings. The day belonged to them, and there was none to dispute the glory which this day was theirs.

During the time Grady was planning the details of the ceremony, he was keeping in mind a situation of another character, one more important to Georgia. It was the year for the nomination and election of another Governor.

---
[1] Walter G. Cooper, *The Story of Georgia*, Vol. III, p. 306.

Major A. O. Bacon, one of the ablest of Georgia lawyers, who had been Speaker of the House of Representatives in the General Assembly of Georgia for several terms, was already an announced candidate. In fact, his nomination was thought by many to be assured. He had many friends and admirers in Georgia. No one questioned his qualifications. In later years he was elected to the United States Senate where he served until his death. He held high rank among leaders there, being for a time president pro tem of the Senate.

But Grady had other plans as to who was to be the next Governor, and the time to act was at hand. On the night following the Ben Hill unveiling, Confederate veterans crowded the lobby of the Kimball House, which was then Atlanta's main hotel. These veterans worshipped the knightly John B. Gordon. He had led them for four years throughout the war; he had been one of them. As a leader he held their complete confidence and affection. He had won promotion from Captain of the "Raccoon Roughs" to Lieutenant General in the Confederate Army, although he was not a West Point man. He had received a wound in the face,[2] but had survived to stand by the side of Robert E. Lee at Appomattox. Now he was their leader in binding up the wounds of defeat and in showing them the way to full citizenship in the nation they had opposed.

Suddenly a voice in the Kimball House lobby rang out: "Gordon! Gordon for Governor!" Those veterans

---

[2] It is said that during a former campaign Gordon and Bob Toombs, who had also been a General in the Confederate army, met at a joint debate and Toombs, who affected a profound disgust with what he called Gordon's posing, strutting, and capitalizing his military record to get votes, confronted Gordon with the reproach that if his wound had been *behind* instead of in front the candidate would not be showing it. "If you had been where I was, that's exactly where you would have gotten it," Gordon is reported to have replied.

and all others in that vast crowd were on fire — a fire of enthusiasm for Gordon that spread quickly throughout the State. The Governorship was settled there that night. At once Grady began to point his editorial championship to the Gordon candidacy. General Gordon "took to the stump." He was splendid in his manhood — tall, slender, soldierly, and as brave as "Richard the Lion-Hearted." He could not fail to inspire all who came in contact with him. In addition to all that, he was an orator of the first rank. His marvelous voice and his every movement majestic, the facial wound to attest his heroic service and to prove he got it *facing* the enemy, and his personal magnetism combined to make him irresistible. As he carried his campaign from county to county where he found Bacon Clubs already numbering more than a majority of the voters, opposition melted away like snow under a hot sun. His old soldiers, many of whom had already joined Bacon Clubs in good faith, could not deny their old leader and quickly changed to his support.

The late Judge James K. Hines, with whom I served on the Georgia Supreme Court, was then practicing law in Sandersville, Georgia. He told me the following story. Hines was chairman of the Bacon Club of his county (Washington), which numbered much more than a majority of the county's voters. When it was announced that General Gordon would speak on a named day in Sandersville, Hines called the Bacon Club into session to consider how they might meet the demands of the occasion. After some discussion it was decided that the Bacon Club was so strong and confident it might well afford to show every courtesy and respect to General Gordon because of his distinguished war record. Moreover, they decided they should do him the courtesy of attending his speaking, since their failure to attend and a slim audience might indicate a direct discourtesy to the hero, resulting in their own discredit. The Bacon Club even offered Hines, its chairman, to the Gordon supporters as the speaker to introduce Gordon. The Gordon committee accepted because of the fact that it did not have available in its own ranks a suitable member.

The day came; a great outpouring from all adjoining counties swelled the Washington County crowd, and it seemed that Bacon supporters vastly outnumbered their opponents. Hines arose, advanced to the front of the platform, and began: "Fellow citizens, it is my pleasure and privilege to introduce General . . . ."

The great audience at once broke out: "Gordon! Gordon! General Gordon!" They let loose the "Rebel Yell," which increased in volume, bringing on a tremendous Gordon ovation. Hines, who at once saw that his remarks were futile, since Gordon needed no introduction, paused, looked around at General Gordon who had arisen to bow his acknowledgment, and took his seat. Gordon stepped to the front and began: "My fellow countrymen," whereupon there was another roar. During his speech he frequently would pause, point to some old soldier who belonged to the Bacon Club, and say, "Bill Brown, they tell me you are against me." Bill would immediately shout back with moist eyes, "It's a lie — you know I wouldn't be against you!" Thus it continued until the Bacon sentiment in the crowd had utterly vanished. Hines and his Bacon Club, which shrank rapidly, saw that "the jig was up." The county went over to Gordon. This situation was repeated in county after county supposed to have been for Bacon, although in these counties the scenes were not quite so dramatic.

I had only a few months before returned to Columbus for the purpose of entering upon the practice of law.

That spring was for me a waiting period which most young lawyers experience. They have to wait for clients. The waiting in my case afforded ample time for every kind of activity which might attract me. Clients apparently did not know that my services were available. I was keeping abreast of public events, especially in Georgia. The Gordon campaign was filling the newspapers. I read of General Gordon's engagement to speak at Cusseta in Chattahoochee County twenty miles south of Columbus, and decided at once to attend and hear him. I had seen him but had never heard him speak. On the day of his speech, I arose very early and, with a rented horse and buggy, I started upon my journey. The weather was hot and the road was deep in sand, but I arrived at Cusseta in time for the speaking. There were about as many ladies in the audience as men. Gordon's speech was superb, even irresistible. Most of the women carried palm leaf fans. While the men shouted, the women wore out their fans by beating them on the backs of benches.

That afternoon General Gordon left Cusseta for Columbus, where he was to speak the next day. A large cavalcade followed him, and I fell in with it. I sought out the Gordon Club, or campaign committee, in Columbus and joined up "for the duration." Most of my time until the end of the campaign was spent around the Gordon headquarters where I performed all and sundry campaign duties my inexperience permitted. It is needless to say General John B. Gordon was overwhelmingly nominated and then duly elected Governor. In 1888 he was re-elected without opposition. In 1890 he was elected United States Senator, though in that race he met with more formidable opposition.

This opposition grew largely out of the fact that at

this time we had no popular election of Senators. They were elected by the Legislature. Hence the Gordon oratory and magnetism were not so available or effective. Moreover, by now the farmers' movement, known as the Farmers' Alliance, had grown until it was the dominating political force in Georgia. It had its own platform of political principles, known as the Ocala (Florida) Platform. It embodied some extreme features which were deemed unsound by most of the leading statesmen of Georgia and of other states. Such men as Charles F. Crisp, who was Speaker of the United States House of Representatives for several terms, and Henry G. Turner, a Congressman from Georgia, opposed it. The Alliance elected a majority of both houses of the Georgia Legislature that year (1890). There were so few lawyers elected that laymen had to be assigned to the Judiciary Committee. When the Alliance "yardstick," as it was called, was applied to him, General Gordon refused to accept it, and the Alliance opposed his election to the Senate. Judge Hines was one of the candidates against Gordon. Patrick Calhoun of Atlanta, a prominent lawyer, accepted the Alliance "yardstick" and was another candidate. Nathaniel J. Hammond, former Congressman, a very able man, was a candidate, opposing the Alliance. Thomas M. Norwood of Savannah was another. There were even others. Of course I, a member of the Georgia House at this time, supported Gordon. After the first ballot, but before the result could be announced by the President of the Senate (it being a joint session of the two houses when the Senate President presided), it became known that no one had a majority. General Gordon lacked *one vote*. Quickly, Representative Norman of Liberty County, who had voted for one of the other candidates, arose and stated that he wished to change his vote to Gordon. Bedlam broke loose on the floor and in the galleries of the House. Gordon was elected United States Senator! He had been Senator once before but had resigned for business reasons, and now he was to return to serve until his death in Atlanta in 1904.

It was the historic career of John B. Gordon with his incomparable personality and the lustre that shone round his head that caused public service to appear attractive to me. I wish to close the chapter by retelling a marvellous story of him which I found recorded in a souvenir booklet distributed at the Gettysburg battlefield some years ago, and which is also referred to in Gordon's own *Reminiscences*, pp. 151-153.

On July 1, 1863, General Gordon and his command arrived at Gettysburg, joining the advance of General Lee's forces. Gordon's command was quickly thrown against the right flank of the Union Army and into the battle which had been raging for some four or five hours. One Confederate general and a portion of his brigade had been captured, and two Confederate generals had been wounded. Gordon's arrival was, indeed, timely. The ranking Federal general on the field had been killed. Every foot of ground was being hotly contested. With a ringing yell, Gordon's men rushed into the bloody and deadly combat – a hand-to-hand struggle. In the midst of this scene where there was, of course, much confusion, a Federal officer, seeking to rally his men, was struck by a minie ball. He fell from his horse. Riding forward on his advanced line, General Gordon saw the stricken officer, apparently dying, with the July sun in his face and with dead and dying soldiers around him. After quickly dismounting and giving him water from his own canteen, Gordon asked the officer's name. He was Major General Francis C. Barlow. It did not appear that he

Gordon and Lee 51

would live many hours. A ball had penetrated his body from the front, passing through and out so near the spinal cord that his arms and legs were paralyzed.

"I am Gordon — General John B. Gordon. Who are you?" the Confederate general asked.

"I am General Barlow of New York," the Federal weakly replied. "Thank you, but you cannot help me. I am dying." Then after a moment the Federal officer continued, "Yes, you can help me. My wife is at the headquarters of General Meade, who is now in command of the Union Army here, or else with General Howard. If you survive the battle, please let her know I died doing my duty."

Gordon said to Barlow that his message would be delivered as surely as he lived. He asked the Federal officer if there was anything else he could do. Barlow replied that he had some letters in his inside coat pocket from his wife and wished Gordon to read one. He seemed to be about to expire. Gordon did as he was asked. "Now, tear them up, General. I don't want them scattered after I die," further requested the Union officer. Gordon complied also with that request; then he had Barlow removed to the rear to a more protected spot. He then mounted and rode away. On the pommel of his saddle, Gordon wrote a note to Mrs. Barlow and dispatched it to General Meade's headquarters by his own staff officer. This officer approached the enemy's lines bearing a white handkerchief on the point of his sword and delivered the note to a Federal officer. In the note Gordon assured Mrs. Barlow safe conduct through the Confederate lines in case she wished to go to her husband.

Because of the desperate battle of the next two days and the retreat of the Confederate Army, Gordon thought no more of the incident except, as he later expressed it, "to number Barlow with the noble dead" of the two armies who had so gloriously fought and faced their fate. Fortunately, however, the ball which wounded General Barlow had not touched a vital organ, and he recovered slowly. Gordon did not know this. In his *Reminiscences*, page 152 *et seq.*, Gordon relates as follows: "The following summer, in battle near Richmond, my kinsman with the same initials, General J. B. Gordon, of North Carolina, was killed. Barlow, who had recovered, saw the announcement of his death .... To me, therefore, Barlow was dead; to Barlow, I was dead. Nearly fifteen years passed before either of us was undeceived.

"During my second term in the United States Senate, the Honorable Clarkson Potter of New York was a member of the House of Representatives. He invited me to dinner in Washington to meet a General Barlow who had served in the Union Army. Potter knew nothing of the Gettysburg incident. I had heard that there was another Barlow in the Union Army and supposed, of course, that it was this Barlow with whom I was to dine. Barlow had a similar reflection as to the Gordon he was to meet. Seated at Clarkson Potter's table, I asked Barlow, 'General, are you related to the Barlow who was killed at Gettysburg?' He replied, 'Why, I am the man, sir. Are you related to the man who killed me?' 'I am the man, sir,' I responded. No words of mine can convey any conception of the emotions awakened by these startling announcements. Nothing short of an actual resurrection from the dead could have amazed either of us more. Thenceforward, until his untimely death in 1896, the friendship between us which was born amidst the thunders of Gettysburg was greatly cherished by both."

It turned out, as he thought, that announcement of the death of his kinsman of North Carolina had caused the misapprehension on the part of General Barlow. Gordon then asked Barlow to relate the story of his recovery. The latter stated that the note Gordon wrote to Mrs. Barlow reached her and, after a perilous trip under fire, she had finally reached his side. She caused him to be conveyed to a surgeon's quarters in a farmhouse nearby where timely treatment turned the tide in his favor.

When the Blue and the Gray met at Gettysburg in 1888, Gordon, then Governor of Georgia, was there. So was Barlow, then a noted New York lawyer. They met upon the very spot where the Georgian had rescued the man from the North!

Here is another interesting story concerning General Gordon. It would seem strange that two generals as important as Gordon and Ewell could have engaged in pleasantries in a battle as heated as that of Gettysburg; yet this took place as the former himself has related as follows:

"Late in the afternoon of this first day's battle, when the firing had greatly decreased along most of the lines, General Ewell and I were riding through the streets of Gettysburg. In a previous battle he had lost one of his legs but prided himself on the efficiency of the wooden one he used in its place. As we rode together, a body of Union soldiers posted behind some buildings and fences on the outskirts of the town suddenly opened a brisk fire. A number of Confederates were killed, and I heard the ominous thud of a minie ball as it struck General Ewell at my side. I quickly asked, 'Are you hurt, sir?' 'No, no,' he replied, 'I am not hurt; but suppose that ball had struck you, we would have had trouble in carrying you off the field, sir. You see how much better fixed I am for a fight than you are. It doesn't hurt a bit to be shot in a wooden leg'."[3]

General Gordon entered the Confederate Army as a captain at the outbreak of the war and was a never-failing strong arm of General Robert E. Lee until the end at Appomattox. Gordon's life and character spread its influence on thousands of young Georgians. In like manner Gordon, younger than Lee, must have been profoundly influenced by Lee. So closely had the two been associated during the four years of war, such influence was inescapable. As Gordon was invaluable to Lee, the association with Lee was, for Gordon, beyond all calculation. Indeed Lee's character and life won and retained the worship, as nearly as a human could, of all Southerners. Later all Americans came to respect, admire, and to claim him as a Great American. As his life becomes known in wider and wider circles, his fame spreads throughout the civilized world.

When the State of Virginia adopted its secession ordinance, Lee was at his home at Arlington, just across the Potomac River from Washington. Virginia selected Lee to command the Virginia troops, and he was later made commander in charge of the Confederate Army. General Winfield Scott was in command of the United States Army and he requested Lee, who was then a Colonel in the United States Army, to confer with him on the situation. Lee had won distinction in Mexico under Scott. A graduate of West Point and later Superintendent of that great army school, he had made the army his life's career. It was part of his life — and his pride. But he was a Virginian, and Virginia, in dire need, had called for her loyal son. One must be a Virginian to know how a native feels about his state. In accepting command

---

[3] John B. Gordon, *Reminiscences of the Civil War*, p. 157.

of the Virginia troops, Lee said to the Governor and the convention at Richmond: "Trusting in Almighty God, an approving conscience, and the aid of my fellow citizens, I devote myself to the services of my native state, in whose behalf alone will I ever again draw my sword."

Lee was a practical man, an experienced and successful army officer, not an immature or an impulsive visionary. He knew the relative resources of the Union and the Confederacy, and we cannot escape the conclusion that Robert E. Lee knew at the outset that the Union Army would win the war. Indeed General Gordon, in his *Reminiscences of the Civil War*, (p. 433), names General Pendleton as authority for a statement about General Lee as follows: ". . . he had never believed that, with the vast power against us, we could win our independence unless we were aided by foreign powers. 'But,' added General Lee, 'such considerations really made no difference to me'." General Pendleton, like General Gordon, was very close to General Lee, and both took part in the surrender with Lee. It was Gordon who led the ragged and hungry remnants of the "Gray" to the designated point where their arms were delivered to the Union Army.

And there had always been crowning civil rewards for conquering war chieftains. General Lee knew that at the end of the war the high office of President of the United States awaited the Commander-in-Chief of the Union Army. He knew the reward of Washington, of Andrew Jackson, and later of Zachary Taylor. Nothing could have been more certain in his mind than that the Presidency would be his reward if he heard General Scott's call instead of that of his beloved state. And was there ever a man who "passed up" a chance like that — even a certainty? That such was not a fantastic prophecy is shown by the fact of General Grant's election to the Presidency.

What did Lee decide? First what did Lee, the Virginian, consider to be his *duty?* We have only to remember that it was Lee who said: "Duty is the sublimest word in the English language." Duty, with him, was the magic word. Where duty called, there Lee set his course. Duty chosen, as Washington declared in the convention which framed the Constitution, the rest is with God. Washington was also a Virginian, and doubtless Lee remembered that Washington was thinking only of duty when he took command against Britain — though, what is of far greater moment, Lee well knew he would be what Ben Hill later said of him, "Washington without his reward." His duty being clear, then so was his decision. Could anything more be needed? Robert E. Lee was indeed and in truth "a Christian soldier" as he has been called countless times. When he walked the floor at Arlington before finally casting the die of decision, who can doubt that prayer went up from his heart to his Maker for guidance? And who, indeed, can doubt that there came before his vision that scene at Gethsemane when the Son of God cried out: "O, my Father! If it be possible, let this cup pass from me; nevertheless, Thy will be done, not mine." Yet Lee has been charged with ingratitude to the United States in making this decision because of the training the Union gave him at West Point. But this charge is specious, for Lee and his State had repaid that debt, if debt it were, in the State's quota for the upkeep of West Point. Moreover, to debate this paltry matter of expense certainly could not have consumed much of Lee's time on this momentous occasion. He weighed against it and all else his *duty* to the state to which he owed, he said, first allegiance.

Gordon and Lee

Forth from its scabbard, pure and bright,
  Flashed the sword of Lee!
. . . .

Out of its scabbard! — Never hand
  Waved sword from stain as free,
Nor purer sword led braver band,
  Nor braver bled for a brighter land,
Nor brighter land had a Cause so grand,
  Nor cause a chief like Lee.

—Abram J. Ryan

CHAPTER V

Member of the General Assembly

SHORTLY after returning home from Yale, Morris Brandon and I projected the plan we had formed at Vanderbilt to establish law offices in Atlanta and start out on the uncertain sea of legal practice. We opened offices, only to learn that the city was literally overrun with new lawyers. We were, at the same time, trying to keep up with the Nine O'clock Cotillion Club. We soon saw we could never pay office rent unless there was a definite improvement in our prospects. We saw none. Morris and I "went into executive session over the matter," the upshot of which was that our firm dissolved in less than a year after it was formed. Morris moved into the offices of Judge Henry B. Tompkins, a successful lawyer, where he soon became junior partner in the firm of Tompkins and Brandon. I shall record at this place that Morris Brandon, before his death some years ago, was recognized as the equal of any member of the Atlanta bar. He became a highly successful practitioner of the law. I returned to my home in Columbus to be nearer the "base of supplies." Even the United States Army can't get too far removed from its base of supplies without disaster or hasty debacle.

It was the winter of 1885-86 that Morris Brandon and I endeavored to launch a law practice in Atlanta. I returned to Columbus in 1886 and opened an office of my own, paying office rent of ten dollars a month by sending a daily news letter to the Macon *Daily Telegraph* until my practice enabled me to pay it from that income.

In 1888 I was elected as one of the two Representa-

Member of the General Assembly

tives from Muscogee County to the General Assembly of Georgia, commonly called the Legislature, for a term of two years. I was re-elected in 1890. The immediate cause of my entering politics at this time was as follows: My law office adjoined that of William A. Little who for several years had been Speaker of the Georgia House of Representatives. He never held any office long before tiring of it. He had decided to retire from the Legislature, and since I had assisted him in every possible way for some time, he decided to inform me of his decision and to suggest that I become a candidate in his stead. One day in the early spring of 1888 he called me into his law office and inquired: "Price, how would you like to be a member of the Georgia Legislature?"

"Why, I have never thought of such a thing," I replied, "and, besides, I hardly think I could get elected."

"Well, I rather think you could," he went on. "Your father is a much beloved physician; some of his patients are his friends of many years, having known him in Stewart County; and many are influential. Besides all that, I do not intend to run again myself, and I will support you, helping you with my own friends."

After a day and night of solemn thought about the matter, I came to the conclusion that I could not lose anything in any event, and I agreed to run. It so happened that at the time I was Captain of a "crack" military company, the Columbus Guards, that had become very popular in Columbus by reason of making a name for itself in competitive drills in various sections of the land. Notably, it had won a large cash prize in such a contest at Houston, Texas. The Columbus Guards had a notable history. When the State of Georgia sent troops to the Mexican War in 1846, a regiment of ten companies met in Columbus in June. It was composed of 898 officers and men. Henry R. Jackson of Savannah was Colonel; Thomas Y. Redd was Lieutenant Colonel; Charles J. Williams was Major; and John Forsyth was Adjutant. The Columbus Guards was the first company, having a personnel of 87 men. This company survived the Mexican War, then went through the War Between the States, fighting notably in the Virginia campaigns and at Chickamauga. After the latter war it was revived, still under the same name. I was Captain of the Guards from 1887 to 1893, having begun my career with them as a private at the Houston event. At the time I became Solicitor General of the Chattahoochee Circuit, I declined a promotion to Major because of my new duties as a public prosecutor. I was already a member of the State Military Advisory Board by appointment of the Governor; and I had delivered in Columbus on Confederate Memorial Day the year before an address which had gained me considerable notice. All of these favorable circumstances, especially the fact I had the support of the members of the Columbus Guards, sufficed to gain for me the nomination which naturally insured my election shortly afterwards. Thus began on my part an era of public service which has continued without a break from 1888, and which will have reached and passed fifty years before my commission as a member of the Board of Regents of the University System of Georgia expires in 1950. The intervening offices I held were Solicitor General, Judge of the Superior Courts, and Justice of the Supreme Court of Georgia, which last office alone accounted for more than twenty years.

 From the first I was disinclined to continue in office in the legislative branch of the government. I wished to study and improve myself in the law, my profession. Political office did not promise the kind of life that I wished and had planned for. The practice of law and service afterwards in the judiciary did promise the calm, studious life that it was my desire to lead. Of course, the latter required much more labor and close attention, because no lawyer can succeed in private practice or judicial office without continuous, unremitting study of the law. New decisions were being constantly announced by the courts of last resort, and success was impossible without close acquaintance with these. On the other hand, it cannot be too much emphasized that my experience as a legislator was of great practical good to me, not only in legal study itself but still more, possibly, in the study of human nature.

As soon as I told my good friend Judge Little that I had adopted his suggestion as to running for the Legislature, he advised me to get out in the country and "electioneer." I hired a horse and buggy and drove out into Muscogee County to see the farmers. There was nothing exciting about the trip, though I had one depressing experience. I met a farmer and told him I was a candidate for the Legislature. I was 26 years old, small in stature, and weighed 120 pounds. Doubting, probably, that I was even of age, he looked at me and said, "Give me old men for counsel."

The State Capitol of Georgia, when I reported to be sworn in in November, 1888, was situated at the southwest corner of Marietta and Forsyth Streets, Atlanta. This building was the old Kimball Opera House which had been secured for a Capitol at the time the capital of the state was moved from Milledgeville to Atlanta in 1868. At this time the Legislature was limited by the Constitution of Georgia to a 40-day session each year, with a further provision that by a two-thirds vote in both houses the Legislature could adjourn to such time as it might wish. There was no limit to such an adjourned term. That was the last session of the General Assembly ever held in this improvised Capitol. It adjourned to meet the next June in the new Capitol, then nearing completion upon an elevated site bounded by Hunter, Washington, Mitchell Streets and Capitol Avenue in Atlanta. The new Capitol, built of Indiana colithic limestone (not of Georgia marble of which there was an abundance) was turned over to the State complete within the original appropriation of one million dollars without a penny of graft. We held the adjourned term of 1889 just after the Capitol was completed and turned over to the State by the Building Commission. Everything was new and looked very beautiful. The legislative halls were handsomely furnished and were very comfortable. That session continued for about five months and accomplished a good deal, much of it being local legislation.

Alexander Stephens Clay of Cobb County was Speaker of the House of Representatives. He was afterwards United States Senator until his death in 1911. Other prominent members in the House were Joseph Rucker Lamar of Richmond, afterwards a Justice of the Supreme Court of Georgia and later, until his death in 1915, Justice of the United States Supreme Court by appointment of President Taft; William Y. Atkinson of Coweta, afterwards Speaker of the House and later Governor; and Clark Howell of Fulton County, editor of the Atlanta *Constitution*, who later became Speaker of the House and later President of the State Senate. Clark Howell was about my age, and I soon became intimate with him, forming a friendship which lasted until his death in 1939. I enjoyed many weekends at his house which was, at that time, situated in West End, Atlanta. When I later came to Atlanta as Justice of the Georgia Supreme Court, Clark

Howell was residing on West Wesley Road, between Peachtree Road and Howell Mill Road. I purchased a tract of woodland across the road opposite his place and built a residence where I still reside during the summer months. Being just across the road from each other, my good friend and I enjoyed many hours together in friendly, neighborly visits.

We built our home in that tract of woodland and there Mrs. Gilbert, as her own landscape gardener, planned, laid out and grew her flower garden. This garden consists of some uncommon plants for this region. She has utilized the beauties of nature by retaining the natural growth of dogwood and wild azaleas of which there are hundreds and hundreds. This garden is, perhaps, her dearest possession and it claims her attention and care beyond that which she ought to endure physically. The garden was well on its way to completion before the construction of the house was begun. She named the residence "Ihagee" for her ancestral home near Columbus, which was built by her grandfather Howard more than a hundred years ago on lands purchased from the Creek Indians. It was named Ihagee from a crystal clear stream that runs nearby, and that Ihagee has continued in the family ownership until the present day. The slaves of Grandfather Howard felled and dressed the lumber, made the brick and built the house, which is still standing. It contains eight large rooms on one floor, with cross halls and four porches or verandahs, making four entrances. The north entrance looks over a pecan grove, which makes a shady walk to the family cemetery where the graves of the Howards and the Calhouns are located. Mrs. Howard was a Calhoun of South Carolina. Although our domicile is Sea Island, we still retain Ihagee, the second, near Atlanta as a summer residence.

Also in the Georgia House were Thomas G. Lawson of Putnam, a man of great intellect and of the highest character, afterwards a Representative in Congress; W. W. Gordon of Savannah, Chatham County, a great civic leader devoted to the public interest, afterwards serving as Brigadier General in the U. S. Army in the Spanish-American War; and William H. Fleming of Richmond County, afterwards Speaker of the Georgia House, member of the U. S. Congress, and a leader at the Augusta Bar.

One of the closest friendships, and the one longest lasting, which I made among these legislative contemporaries, was with H. Warner Hill of Meriwether, who had served one term in the House before I entered it. At the beginning of the session of 1888 in the old Capitol I saw him for the first time and was immediately attracted to him, as he was a man whose very appearance drew one to him. We selected seats side by side in the old Capitol and continued this arrangement after moving into the new Capitol during all the sessions from 1888 to 1892 inclusive. He afterwards became Chairman of the Public Service Commission, at that time called the Railroad Commission, and then a Justice of the Supreme Court of Georgia. There was also in the House John C. Hart of Greene, a magnificent specimen of manhood, of fine brain and big heart. He was afterwards Judge of the Superior Court of his circuit and then Attorney General of the state.

By no means should I omit mention of the picturesque figure from Bartow, Dr. William H. Felton. He had been elected to the U. S. Congress as an Independent, despite the fact Georgia was a "solid" Democratic state. He thus entered the Legislature after his service in Congress. At this time he was old and suffered from palsy. He rarely spoke, but when he did it was an event. He favored me with his friendship, a remembrance of which has lingered with me. His widow, Mrs. Rebecca Latimer Felton, was the first woman United States Senator, being appointed in 1922 by Governor Thomas W. Hardwick to fill a very brief interim in an unexpired term.

In the State Senate, Fleming G. DuBignon of Chatham was President. His untimely death cut short a brilliant career. Also in the Senate when I entered the House was Marcus W. Beck, afterwards Solicitor General, then Judge of the Flint Judicial Circuit, and still later a Justice of the Supreme Court of Georgia.

During that summer session of 1889, R. W. Patterson, a Representative from Bibb County, and I were rooming together at the Kimball House. It was political headquarters of the State, and most of the members of the General Assembly lived there during sessions. Patterson and his colleague from Bibb, W. A. Huff, became estranged because of conflicting views about a measure affecting their home county. This resulted in a challenge under the *Code Duello*, as it was called in the days long past. Naturally, I was partisan to my roommate. Persistent efforts of mutual friends to prevent the duel having failed, the two members from the same county agreed upon a location near Girard, Alabama, just across the Chattahoochee River from Columbus, as the point at which to bring off the encounter. At the last moment the urgent advice of friends did prevail, and the combat was abandoned. This ended what threatened to be a serious action, fraught with great embarrassment to the General Assembly and to the state. The *Code Duello* had been losing favor for some years, and other threats to resort to it, besides the one mentioned, had been abandoned. The practice has now lost favor entirely and has completely gone out of fashion. It is today looked upon only as quixotic.

I served two terms in the General Assembly of Georgia, and saw service in both Capitols. It was during my service in that body that we moved into the new Capitol. During my four years of such service, my chief interest was in two certain measures. One was the charter for an electric street railway in Columbus, which was promptly built and operated. The other was the establishment of the Georgia Normal and Industrial College for young women at Milledgeville, today called the Georgia State College for Women. I was the author of the measure to charter the car line and an active supporter of the educational bill. Both were progressive measures; both have vindicated their importance. The college is today outstanding among institutions of its kind. The street railway was the fourth ever constructed in the United States.

In late years it seems, from newspaper reports, that the members of the Legislature are expected to consult the Governor before selecting the presiding officers, the President of the Senate and the Speaker of the House. This must be a product of modern political organization.

I did not enter the Legislature with visions of future fame or delusions of grandeur. My entry was only that of a young man fresh from law school, offering his services to the public and, at the time, not being overworked by clients. Time hung heavy on my hands — to say nothing of office rent, $10.00 per month. I knew that election to the Legislature would bring my name before the people, especially those of my own county and, incidentally, make known that the practice of law was my profession. Of course, as any right-thinking person must understand, one's service in the Legislature must be that of at least reasonable intelligence, diligent effort to understand all questions upon which he must vote, devotion to the best interest of the state and his constituents, regardless of his own interest or of pressure from without. He must, above all things, resist "pressure groups" who selfishly resort to unscrupulous means of securing legislative action. The interests of "pressure groups" are generally in direct conflict with those of the general public, though I realize that such groups are skillful in making the contrary appear. It has always been my belief that under our system of democratic government public officers must, after making every effort to ascertain truths, facts, and the law, act upon their own individual judgment as to what is wise and proper. The most contemptible course of all is to act solely with a view to gaining votes for re-election.

After serving two terms in the General Assembly, I became a candidate for the office of Solicitor General and was elected by receiving a majority over the combined votes of four opponents, including the incumbent. At about the time and during the time of my service in the Legislature, there was a particularly strong and popular group of young men serving in the offices of Superior Court judges and solicitors general. They had all been elected by the General Assembly (Legislature) by joint ballot as provided by the State Constitution; that is, the Senate and House of Representatives assembled in joint session, just as was done for the election of a United States Senator. These elections always occurred during the opening days of the session for the purpose of disposing of them and the throngs that these elections always attracted. At the opening of each session, there would be about a dozen judges and a dozen solicitors general to be elected, and, as an average, there were two or perhaps three candidates for election to each office. Gathered in Atlanta to campaign for each of these candidates there were usually several friends or relatives. Throughout several days until those elections were all completed, quite a group of candidates and friends of candidates were constantly buttonholing members, soliciting support for this or that candidate. They were usually allowed freedom of the floors of the Senate and House where they continued their solicitations. In the lobbies of the Capitol and in hotels and boarding houses wherever a member could be contacted there were candidates to push their campaigns. Necessarily this consumed all of the time of members both during the actual sessions and afterwards, during all "waking hours." There was little or no time left to members to consider other duties seriously. But there was another side of the question of that mode of election that really very nearly evened the balance of the scales. It was this: That mode of election brought the candidates together for days, in close contact with members of the General Assembly. They saw and heard them informally, heard their arguments, heard what others and fellow members of the General Assembly had to say, and, finally, observed their conduct. These opportunities, as a rule, resulted in good selections. The electors, members of the Legislature, naturally acquired better foundations for making a choice than is afforded the great majorities of voters in a general election by the people. It had its faults. All methods of election have faults. It is not impossible that when a balance is struck one system is about as good as the other. Anyway, a cry of dissatisfaction grew in volume, and along in the latter part of the 1890's the State Constitution was amended to the effect that judges and solicitors general must be elected by a vote of the people of the entire state. But a queer situation then arose. The Democratic Party in Georgia adopted a rule that judges and solicitors of the several judicial circuits should be nominated by a vote of the people in a party primary, each group of counties composing a circuit alone nominating candidates for those offices within the respective circuit. Then as now, the names of all candidates nominated in their respective circuits were placed upon the state ticket voted upon in the general election in November of election year. The result is an unreasonably long ballot to be voted upon and counted, and it is one in which the voter cannot possibly make an intelligent choice. Elections by the people cannot possibly result in good government unless the individual voters are intelligent and *honest*. Under the present system in Georgia the voter must of necessity vote for some, perhaps a majority, of candidates about whom he knows absolutely nothing. In the case of judges and solicitors general, he knows and is concerned only with his own circuit and perfunctorily votes for those who have been nominated in the Democratic Primary. Why not, then, require a state ticket to include in each circuit only the candidates for office in that circuit, together with the names of candidates for state offices?

Reverting to the constitutional change in the method of electing judges and solicitors general, which took effect after my second election by the General Assembly, I observed that in the great majority of cases the same men who had been elected by the Legislature, if they were candidates, were re-elected by a vote of the people. That was true in my case.

I cannot too strongly insist that the existence of a government such as ours, a government of the people, is basically dependent upon the intelligence, integrity, and patriotism of its voters. It is inescapable that no such government can endure where a controlling number of voters is ignorant of the underlying principle of the government. Especially in these modern times our government is complicated and intricate. Even the very wisest of our leaders can not know all the answers. True, we have the best country in the world, and that may seem to some as disproof of the opinion above expressed. I do not think so. Thanks to the natural wealth of our land, the diversities of climate, the genius and industry of our people, leaders in industry and our statesmanship, we have been piloted to the pinnacle of world greatness despite the handicaps with which we have contended.

For some beneficent purpose the will of an omniscient Providence must have sent to Jamestown, Plymouth Rock, and later to the Golden Isles of Georgia such leaders as the ancestors of George Washington, Benjamin Franklin, and Thomas Jefferson. These leaders, and others like them, carved out a new world against difficulties that they could not have preconceived. They planned and set in motion a form of government and caused it to be adopted over the opposition of selfish and ignorant minorities. Their successors, guided by the lamp of experience, have carried on, not with the aid of all the people, but despite the handicaps of ignorance and organized groups. Perhaps the world has never known such strongly entrenched pressure groups as now infest the Federal Government in Washington and many state governments and large cities. Often one honestly believes he hears the voice of patriotism and wisdom when, in fact, what he hears is that of some one or more "Pressure Group." Oh! for some modern Hercules to turn on the river of outraged public opinion at flood stage to cleanse these "Augean Stables."

Benjamin Franklin, the greatest of American philosophers, in signing the newly written constitution of 1789, said: ". . . there is no form of government but what may be a blessing to the people if well administered, and I believe further that this is likely to be well administered for a course of years, and can only end in despotism as other forms have done before it, when the people have become so corrupted as to need despotic government, being incapable of any other. I doubt, too, whether any other convention can make a better constitution."

I have digressed distinctly. So be it.

My legislative career did not end without one achievement of which I have always been proud and which has meant much to me — the formation of lasting friendships among many honorable men. These friendships have even influenced the lives of many of the descendants of my colleagues. I often meet young men whose fathers knew me in the General Assembly and who would say to me: "I have often heard my father speak of you, always with great affection." It is thus no wonder that I have loved my state and all its people.

CHAPTER VI

Riding the Judicial Circuit

ALTHOUGH the legislative department of the government was interesting and a valuable school to a young lawyer, there were features that did not suit me or my purposes. The game of politics was not attractive to me. After two terms in the State Legislature, I abandoned the field in favor of the judiciary. If it had not been objectionable, it was a field in which I possessed no talents. Moreover, it did not promise anything upon which to build a life's work and livelihood. The logical and apparently inviting step was to become a candidate for the office of Solicitor General (State prosecuting officer for a judicial circuit), an office filled by joint ballots of the State Legislature. I was concluding my second term of two years in that body, and I knew personally a large number of members re-elected to the next Legislature. So I bade farewell to the legislative field of public service.

In November of 1892 I was elected by the General Assembly of Georgia as Solicitor General of the Chattahoochee Judicial Circuit for a term of four years. I was re-elected in 1896, 1900, and 1904. My first experience in "riding the judicial circuit" began in January, 1893. The circuit was composed of my home county of Muscogee (I resided in Columbus, the county seat), and the counties of Talbot, Taylor, Marion, Chattahoochee, and Harris.

The average county seat in rural Georgia is a town of about 1,000 population. The business portion is generally built around a square, streets entering from each corner and sometimes halfway between corners. The courthouse, housing all county offices, is in the middle, and generally has a low wall on all sides, leaving on each of the four sides a broad street. The courthouse is a general meeting place for the community, especially political meetings. Even long before women could vote they attended such meetings, or went there to hear speeches by noted orators. It would be a great mistake to underrate the intelligence and information of such people, the people of the small Georgia town. They are keen judges of men — more so than the average city dweller. The courthouse is also the exchange for news as well as for jokes.

In country districts (called "deestricts" by many), the general meeting place was, as of old, the "cross-road" general merchandise store. Such stores usually had a front porch, where could be found traders and others with time to idle away, swapping news and jokes. It was formerly customary in the country districts of counties served by me for some person of special prowess to be looked up to as the "best man," reference, of course, being to physical courage. A story is told of one such hero named Joiner. (He was probably called "Jiner.") On one occasion as the said Joiner rode up to a general store, where his fame was respected, he was greeted with loud acclaim and told that a new man named Story, reputed to be of great might, had moved into the district.

"Where does he live?" asked Joiner. "I will have to lick him."

The boys on the store porch pointed down the road and said, "About a mile."

"All right; I'm going after him," answered Joiner. About a mile down the road he met a fine-looking stranger. Joiner stopped his horse and, noticing that the stranger also halted, asked, "Be your name Story?" The stranger said it was.

"Light and hitch," commanded Joiner. Story wanted to know why. "Because you have got to fight," Joiner explained.

"Fight who?" queried Story.

"Me, of course."

"Well, Mr. Jiner, I never saw you before in my life and have nothing against you," said Story, getting down from his horse as he saw Joiner doing.

"Makes no difference whether you ever seed me before or not — you got to fight," Joiner answered, as the two clinched. It must be said in the interest of justice that Story vindicated his honor, giving Joiner a good licking, to the latter's surprise.

Finally Joiner, between blows, said, "Well, Mr. Story, if you won't succumb, I will."

They both got up, dusted their clothes, and rode back to the store. Joiner told the interested group that he was willing to relinquish his superior place to the newcomer, and then he ordered drinks for all around. The crowd laughed the matter off; they considered this the orthodox manner by which friends are made.

The first county in which Superior Court (called Circuit Court in many states) was held after I became the prosecuting attorney was Talbot, the county seat of which was Talbotton. It was for a special term in January, 1893, the regular term being in March and September. The courthouse, which had been used for many years, had been razed, and a new one was in course of construction. Court was held in temporary quarters consisting of the second stories of two frame buildings used as stores. On the first floor of one of these was a grocery store; on the first floor of the other was a drug store which, at last account, was "still doing business at the same old stand" under the management of the son of the physician and druggist operating it at the time of which I write.

This physician and druggist was the beloved Dr. Edward L. Bardwell who figured in the most famous homicide case that ever came before the courts of that county. One peaceful Sunday evening, a young man, the operations of whose mind can never be positively known, walked into the home of a beautiful and popular young woman. He found her sitting in the "parlor" conversing with another young man, afterwards a prominent lawyer of Talbotton. The intruder carried a shotgun and, quickly, with one shot, killed the young woman who was the object of his affection but who was reputed to have rejected his proposal of marriage. The offender ran to his office in the Talbotton town square, took a heavy dose of poison, cut his throat with a razor, and then ran to a nearby lake and threw himself therein. The alarm soon caused a large body of men to begin a search for the offender. They found him in the lake and drew him out, still alive.

Dr. Bardwell was called and, contrary to the urgent pleas of most of the rescuers, instituted efforts to save the offender's life on the very salutary principle that as a member of the medical profession it was his duty to save life. Strange as it may seem, he did save the young man although he was to bear the marks of his ordeal until his death, not so long afterwards. Dr. Bardwell was criticized on the ground that to postpone the man's death could accomplish no good since he was to be put to death shortly for murder anyway. He was urged not to save the man's life since much suffering on the part of both families directly involved would be obviated by merely allowing him to die. But the good Dr. Bardwell, true to the ethics of his high calling, steadfastly refused; and he was the means of prolonging life in a case where it had virtually ebbed when he arrived on the scene. No one could doubt his sincerity, his loyalty to duty as he saw it; and his popularity increased rather than diminished because of his stand. I am constrained to draw the veil of silence over the aftermath of this crime and the fate of the murderer.

At this special term of court in January, 1893, I came to know the real people of Georgia, the people in general. Nowhere so well as in the country communities can such a superb cross-section of our people be found. I came to know some of the finest characters that ever entered my life. I have continued to enjoy and reciprocate the friendships formed at that time, even to the present day. As many have passed on, their children and grandchildren have stepped in to take their places. Always in old Talbot, as in other counties I served, there was a warm, a cordial welcome, and a good-bye with generous words of commendation for my official endeavors. That meant very much to me, as I am sure it would have meant to any young man just entering upon official life, or even to one grown old in the service.

My predecessor in office, Honorable A. A. Carson, had drawn some indictments in every county in the circuit which were still pending in the courts. In September, 1892, he had convicted a Negro man named Gilbert, charged with assault with intent to murder by reason of his having shot another who, however, was only wounded in the toe. The case was appealed to the Supreme Court and heard in October, 1892, two months or more before I took office. A decision was rendered on January 6, 1893, reversing the court below and granting Gilbert a new trial on the ground that the evidence did not show an intent to kill, but only a wounding in the toe which might have been all that was intended. This decision was written for the Supreme Court by Chief Justice Logan E. Bleckley, one of Georgia's greatest legal lights, who was master of many branches of learning besides the law, being, notably, a poet, mathematician, and story-teller of unrivaled excellence.

By the time the Supreme Court's decision was handed down I was the Solicitor General; and since it was customary to publish with the decisions the names of the Solicitor General and Judge in the court below, my name appeared. The law required the Solicitor General to file in the Supreme Court a brief with respect to every case taken there from his court; so of course there was a brief by Carson on file in the Supreme Court in the Gilbert case. It did not bear my name as I had not participated at all in its preparation and had no connection whatever with the Gilbert case. That my name appeared with the first published report of the Supreme Court's decision was due altogether to it being placed there by the reporter as a mark of recognition that I was Solicitor General at the time the high court's decision was *rendered*, though not at the time the case was *argued* in the high court. This first publication of the appellate decision was by a private company before the official publication thereof in the *Georgia Reports*, published by the State of Georgia. In that advance publication there appeared the following entry:

"Leonidas McLester, by brief, for Plaintiff in Error; S. P. Gilbert, Solicitor General, and A. A. Carson, by brief, *contra*."

McLester, the attorney for the defendant in the court below, became Plaintiff in Error on appeal.

Because of the fact that the able and amiable Chief

Justice used the case as an outlet for his incisive comment on the brief for the state, I became the innocent butt of a rather embarrassing, if amusing, situation which continued in the legal minds of Georgians for decades. In fact, the matter figured in one humorous paper after another at annual meetings of the Georgia Bar Association. Judge Bleckley wrote: "Both briefs furnished us in the case at bar are sufficiently striking to deserve mention. That of Mr. McLester is intensely classical. It opens thus: 'When the mother of Achilles plunged him in the Stygian waters, his body became invulnerable except the heel by which she held him; and afterwards when he and Polyxena, the daughter of the King of Troy, who were lovers, met in the Temple of Apollo to solemnize their marriage, Paris, the brother of Hector, lurking behind the image of Apollo, slew Achilles by shooting him in the heel with an arrow.'

"The brief of the Solicitor General is less poetic, but equally irrelevant. It cites seven cases from the *Georgia Reports*, not one of which has any bearing on the question, for in each of the cited cases the attempt to kill was successful. When a homicide actually occurs from the voluntary use of a deadly weapon, an intention to kill is very much more certain than it is when the man assaulted is not killed but only shot in the toe."

Of course, Chief Justice Bleckley's use of the language, "the brief of the Solicitor General," coupled with the entry ahead of it, "S. P. Gilbert, Solicitor General," would cause all the lawyers in the state to think I was the author of the brief filed in the Supreme Court in behalf of the state.

The comment on the brief of Mr. McLester was not only justified but must have been precisely what he desired and expected. The quoted passage constituted the entire brief. However, the great Chief Justice did not need any argument or citation of authority; the law on the question was settled and well known. Moreover, the court reversed the judgment of the trial court, thus sending the case back for a new trial. What more could Mr. McLester have done, even with the most complete and unanswerable brief on the law involved? Also he had derived the satisfaction of having evidenced on the pages of the Supreme Court *Reports* his familiarity with the Greek classic — the killing of Achilles, in the presence of his bride, Polyxena, by Paris.

The opinion of the Chief Justice was sound; the grant of a new trial was just; *but* the keen thrust of the truth-loving jurist inadvertently struck an innocent bystander. The bystander was young in years, and younger still as a Solicitor General. My term of office had begun five days before the decision of the court was rendered, and it probably was written even before my term of office began. I was embarrassed at the thought of entering the important duties of the Solicitor General with that introduction from the highest court in Georgia. What would my friends and the lawyers of Georgia think? Surely they would all read it, and as surely they did. Had I been older and more experienced in such matters, doubtless the incident would have been regarded as of little or no consequence.

It was simply too much; so I repaired speedily to the chambers of the venerable Chief Justice in Atlanta. I found him in a highly propitiatory frame of mind, as indeed he was usually found by those who approached him upon subjects opening up his vast and discursive mind. As I entered his room, he said, "Good morning, Price. How are you?"

I replied, "Judge Bleckley, you have ruined me!"

"How is that?" he responded; and I forthwith detailed all the above facts.

At first he insisted that there was no error in the statement of the case, because when it was printed I was actually Solicitor General. When I insisted that I had never seen the briefs and had not known, prior to his decision, that there was such a case pending at all and that any reader of the advance report would naturally assume that I was the author of the State's brief, he called for the briefs. Finding that the brief for the State did not show my signature but that of my predecessor, Chief Justice Bleckley turned and wrote a memorandum as follows: "The brief for the State was prepared by the predecessor of Mr. Gilbert in the office of Solicitor General." He immediately instructed that this entry appear in the report of the case in the *Georgia Reports*.[1]

As the reader may well conclude, this did me very little good, if any, for seemingly it merely attracted attention. The Court's opinion did supply an ever-recurring need. Generally, the program for the annual meetings of the Georgia Bar Association includes one or two papers of a humorous character. Material found between the covers of the Supreme Court *Reports* is eagerly seized upon and put to use. This case supplied a number of papers read to these gatherings and lightened the proceedings, many of which are devoted to serious discussions and frequently to learned dissertations. Usually, someone has to be "the goat," and that was my turn to serve. I cannot see where the incident did me any permanent professional injury. Of one thing I wish to make absolutely certain. It is that the incident related above never at any time marred my trust and attachment to Chief Justice Bleckley. His purity of purpose, his im-

---

[1] See *Gilbert* v. *The State*, 90 Ga. 691 *et seq.*

partiality as a jurist, and his keen sense of justice were never left in doubt.

Around a judicial circuit lawyers and court officials, very much like youths at school together, make warm and lasting friends. I became very fond of the clerks and sheriffs in the various counties, as well as of the judge and court reporter. A friendship developed between George Currell Palmer and me, beginning when both of us were members of the Columbus Guards and continuing unabated until his death. His first court office was that of official court reporter. His duty was to report stenographically and transcribe on typewriter the records of all major criminal cases and civil cases when called upon. Like many others in those days, George had begun work at the age of sixteen to assist his parents. When William B. Butt was elected Judge of the Chattahoochee Circuit, he appointed Palmer court reporter. Palmer had a very quick mind and made an excellent official, and in the course of his duties he became interested in the law. He took up the study of law and carried it forward at all available times — in court hours listening to the judge's rulings, the lawyers' speeches, the examination of witnesses, and all proceedings. He was soon competent to pass the bar examination successfully.

Now being a duly licensed lawyer, Palmer began to accept employment and to try cases in court, the less important at first. His remarkable memory enabled him to recall the strongest speeches he had heard while studying law. During that time I was Solicitor General, at many of the county seats George and I usually shared a room, the hotels being limited in rooming capacity. It was thus we came to know each other so intimately. He was an excellent man, an ornament to the legal profession, who held the law and the courts as the very palladium of the people. When I became judge, George Palmer succeeded me as Solicitor General. He filled that office eight years as faithfully as he had that of court reporter. Later he was appointed by the Governor to fill an unexpired term of C. Frank McLaughlin, deceased, as Judge of the Chattahoochee Circuit; and was thereafter duly elected to fill a full term. Unfortunately, he did not live to finish the full term. The State lost an upright and efficient judicial officer, and I lost a beloved and irreplaceable friend. During sickness and health, good and evil fortune, his loyalty was unshakable; no obstacle was too great or could in any way deter him from rendering every aid and comfort to me. He passed away on September 24, 1942.

It was not my purpose to remain long in the office of Solicitor General; no longer, in fact, than an opportunity was offered to obtain the office of Judge of the Superior Court — the promotion next in line. This court, in Georgia, is the chief trial court and has general jurisdiction in all civil and criminal cases. In some states it is called "Circuit Court," which is appropriate; but in New York State it is called "Supreme Court," which apparently is a misnomer as it is not the supreme court of New York. While I served as Solicitor General for nearly sixteen years, I had the opportunity of gaining valuable lessons of law and the rules of court by practical observation, although I began to grow tired of the office. I did have the happy good fortune of knowing and valuing the sterling qualities of the people of the circuit. That experience was interesting and educational. Above all, one could not serve long on a country judicial circuit without being tremendously impressed with the importance of the judiciary and the opportunity it afforded to promote the "good order, peace, and dignity" of the community.

In return, such efforts bring their own reward — the

friendship, cooperation, and even affection of the peace-loving and law-abiding citizens. The six counties linked together to form the Chattahoochee Judicial Circuit and the citizens, having neighborly and family connections, all have individualistic characteristics. From my first experience with the Chattahoochee Circuit, long before I became judge, the public respect always paid to the judge impressed me. It was respect for the office of Superior Court Judge, irrespective of the person holding the office. In the local hotel the judge always was assigned the best room; he sat at the head of the table; it was his official right, so understood. If a new judge took office, he immediately took over these privileges, although his predecessor was also present unofficially. The judge, unless circumstances prevented, was always warned of a meal about to be served so that he could be served first. In one county there was the same old, efficient, and popular Negro porter, waiter, and general utility man who always came to my room before opening the door to the breakfast room. His announcement was always in the same words: "Mr. Judge, breakfast is now gwine on; them as gits thar fust, most in ginrally gits the best." When I first knew him, Wesley (abbreviated to "Wes"), in answer to my friendly inquiry as to how many children he had, answered, "Fourteen, thank God." Each year when I asked the same question, the number would be increased; so his reply would be, "Fifteen, thank God," and so on until my last year when he said, as I now remember, but not under oath, "Thirty-six, thank God," or was it thirty-eight? He confessed to having had three wives — not all at one time, however.

It was in 1908 that I was elected Judge of the Superior Courts of the Chattahoochee Judicial Circuit. I was re-elected in 1912. It so happened that my first court as judge was also held in Talbot County. I had been nominated for the judgeship in the state primary held early in September, 1908. My predecessor, Judge J. H. Martin, with whom I enjoyed cordial relations all during our contest for the judgeship, resigned at once, whereupon Governor Hoke Smith called me on the telephone and tendered me the appointment as judge to fill the unexpired term of my predecessor, extending from September 8 to December 31, 1908. Of course, the regular full term to which I was elected in 1908 was to begin January 1, 1909. The regular fall term, 1908, of Talbot Superior Court was due to convene within a few days after Governor Smith tendered me the interim appointment. Of course, I was still Solicitor General, and I might have been excused for wishing to spend the brief period to prepare myself before going on the bench for the term to which I had been elected. However, I had already asked the people of the circuit for the office of judge, and they had accorded it to me; so it seemed proper for me not to permit a vacancy to arise or make necessary the appointment of someone else for the interim. I accepted, was sworn in at once, and was on hand to preside at the opening of the fall term of Talbot Superior Court. As a token of esteem, my Talbot friends had purchased a most comfortable chair and installed it upon the bench. A card was attached expressing their good wishes for my new tour of duty. What a lovable people! As I have said, throughout my entire twenty-four years of legal service in that circuit, the friendship of those fine folks never wavered. It is a precious recollection to me, and I am glad to record it here.

What is said about Talbot County and the people of its county seat, Talbotton, applies to the people of the other counties of the circuit, though possibly I experienced more expressions of the above kind there than elsewhere. The old town, Talbotton, is far more renowned than many in Georgia realize. Governor George W. Towns had resided there, and so had Chief Justice Hiram Warner. The Talbotton Railroad, famous for its great extent of seven whole miles, brought the town fame. It ran from Talbotton to Paschal, a junction point with the Central of Georgia Railroad, and was even classed as an interstate railway due to the fact that it received from the Central (and still does, I assume) goods originating in shipment from without the State of Georgia. What this celebrated seven-mile line lacked in length it made up in another unusual aspect. Its president, engineer, conductor, and single station agent apparently were all one man at that time — Tucker Persons, everybody's friend. He was keenly interested in state politics and usually was quite vocal about it. In one race he was strongly supporting William Y. Atkinson for Governor. At that time the counties did not hold elections the same day. Wherever possible, the Atkinson forces caused the "safe" Atkinson counties to hold their primaries early. Every time "Tuck" arrived at Paschal and learned that Atkinson had carried a county, he would quickly begin his return trip to Talbotton and would pull his bell cord and blow his whistle every foot of the seven miles. The people in every direction for miles would know that Atkinson had carried another county. Atkinson became Governor, and old "Tuck" was happy.

Marion County was named for Francis Marion, the Revolutionary hero, the "Swamp Fox" of South Carolina. Its people imbibed something from the fame of the man whose name they retained. They were, and are, an independent, courageous people. They always loved good jokes and have supplied many anecdotes to the legal lore of Georgia. The county was the home of Mark H. Blandford. He once lived at Tazewell, the first county seat of Marion. For many years it had been a diminishing settlement of prominent families. When Blandford was running for Justice of the Supreme Court, opposed by Judge Bassinger of Savannah, the latter made the plea that Savannah had never had a member of the Supreme Court. Blandford countered with the remark: "Neither has Tazewell." Blandford won.

Once while I was holding court in Buena Vista, the county seat of Marion, a young man was convicted of carrying whiskey on his person to a church, a penal offense that was very unpopular in rural sections. As was usual, the young man's lawyer rose and made a rather impassioned plea for clemency. He insisted that the convicted young man was very poor, that he lived with his mother who worked with him on the farm, and that there was nobody to help her with the housework, cooking, washing, etc., although she was between 70 and 80 years old. I told the young man to stand up and then asked him if it were true that he, a vigorous young fellow, allowed his poor old mother to work on the farm and do all the housework as the lawyer had said. He replied, with heat: "No sir, Judge; there ain't a word of truth in all that." The youth's lawyer was compelled to laugh, along with the entire crowd in the courtroom.

In Marion County there was a lawyer noted for telling stories, even at his own expense. I shall call him Bill Bunkley, not by any means his true name. Buena Vista, where he lived, had a charter provision that licenses to sell liquor could be issued only upon a petition signed by two-thirds of the freeholders of the town. A man whom I shall call Fall made application for a license, and Bunkley was one of those who signed his petition. Bunkley belonged to the Methodist Church. When it became known he had signed a petition for a liquor license, he was hailed before the Quarterly Conference on the question whether or not to turn him out. The conference was held out in the country. It took only a few minutes to convict Bunkley. The meeting then adjourned and everybody started back to town. Bunkley, who was walking, was overtaken by a steward who had voted to turn him out of the church. "Git in, Bill, and I'll take you to town," said the steward. "Brother Fair," complained Bunkley, "I don't see why you folks turned me out — I have done a hundred things worse than that." "Yes, we all knowed that, Bill, but we been waiting ten years to get something on you we could try before a mixed congregation," answered the steward, who thus convinced Bunkley he had better be satisfied.

Another lawyer was tried on the same charge by the same church. He complained, "Brethren, you can't afford to turn me out. We haven't got enough money now to pay what we owe." The Presiding Elder replied, "Yes, we looked all that up before we sent for you. You paid, last year, fifteen cents." Of course this ended the lawyer's membership.

I distinctly recall another story of a huge hoax pulled off by two lawyers, both of whom later became prominent in their profession. One was W. B. Butt, familiarly known as Bill Butt, who was Judge of the Chattahoochee Circuit when I was Solicitor General. The other was Mark Blandford, who became a member of the Supreme Court. It was while I was riding the circuit with Judge Butt that he told me the story. A farmer named Mullis died, leaving his property to his two sons, John and Bill. John, the elder, was executor and had possession of the lands, while Bill resided on another farm. Bill passed his father's farm each time he went to the county seat. There was on this farm an especially fine patch of sugar cane which excited his desires. One day he halted, entered the patch, cut three stalks of cane, and took them with him. Shortly thereafter, John, coming home, sighted Bill's tracks. After turning the matter over in his mind and after questioning several neighbors, he decided that the trespasser was his brother. He went to town to get a warrant for Bill's arrest. He told the J. P. (Justice of the Peace) that his brother had been stealing cane time after time and he meant to prosecute him.

John further told the J. P. that he had heard of a "dead warrant" and wanted one for his brother. The J. P. asked him what a "dead warrant" was, and John replied that it was a warrant by which the serving officer would have to bring in the party "dead or alive." He said the constable would have the power under it to call out the entire male population of the community to find the culprit. Lawyer Blandford had told him so.

The J. P. seemed to be in doubt as to how to draw such a warrant, and John told him that Lawyer Blandford had said that all you had to do was write on the face of the paper: "This is a dead warrant." The J. P. so wrote it out and turned it over to his constable to serve. Soon the news of the matter had spread all over the district, and Bill heard about it. He went to Butt, his lawyer. It so happened that Butt had been told all about the matter by Blandford who suggested to Butt that he have his client hide out and stay in hiding several days or until the search had been abandoned or until the matter died down. He also told Butt to warn Bill that the constable would have to call out the *posse comitatus*,[2] any member of which might shoot him on sight.

Bill stayed out of sight for several days; then one night he slipped into Butt's room and hid there. Butt told Bill he had caused the matter to die down by promising to produce him in court at the time of trial. Bill agreed. On reaching the courtroom that day, they found that the whole community had turned out to see what would be done with a "dead warrant." When the case was called, Lawyers Butt and Blandford arose, and with great seriousness and dignity they requested that the court allow them a few minutes to consult, since the consultation might result in arriving at a peaceful settlement. The J. P., still puzzled himself to know what to do with a "dead warrant," readily assented. The lawyers withdrew but shortly returned. In the same dignified strain they declared that happily they had reached a wise solution of the matter for their clients which would meet all requirements of justice. They said solution was that John and Bill should pay their respective attorneys five dollars as a fee and that Bill should pay John fifteen cents, the prevailing market price for three stalks of sugar cane, while the court costs were to be divided equally between them. The J. P., greatly relieved, approved the settlement as the judgment of the court; the two clients fell in with the agreement as one which would forestall more trouble for each; and the audience suddenly awakened to the realization that probably there was no such thing as a "dead warrant" save in the brains of the scheming lawyers.

Just before his death Judge Butt sent for me to come to

---

[2] Literally, "the power of the county." It consists of the general militia, or entire male population, regardless of whether official or private, of a county who may be ordered by a sheriff or other peace officer to aid in making an arrest or preventing an escape, in disregard of which order any citizen may himself be dealt with by the law.

see him. He said to me: "Price, I am going to die in two or three days, and word of it is going to get over Buena Vista, and some farmer from out in the country will hear of it. On his way back home he will meet another farmer and will say, 'Whoa, mule.' The other farmer will stop, too. The first farmer will say, 'Old Bill Butt's dead.' The other farmer will reply, 'So I hear — git up, mule!' Price, that will be all there will be to it." And Judge Butt, whom I greatly esteemed, laughed so heartily he fairly shook his own death-bed. He died within the time he predicted.

The Chattahoochee Circuit extends from the river for which it was named on the west to the Flint River on the east. (As has been stated elsewhere, these two rivers unite near the Florida line to form the Appalachicola River.) The easternmost county is Taylor — named for Zachary Taylor, hero of the Mexican War and later elected President of the United States. The wide belt of sandy land that runs through the state from the Richmond County region to Chattahoochee County is apparent in much of Taylor County, especially in the northwest portion. Quite a different and more fertile land is seen in the southeastern portion where the thriving little city of Reynolds is the trading center. Notwithstanding the nature of the soil, the sandy section and the county seat, Butler, can boast of a thrifty and well-to-do population and one of the best weekly papers that I have known. The latter fact contributes substantially, no doubt, to the enterprising character of that section.

A few years ago Taylor County constructed a handsome, new courthouse. In the Superior Court room, over the judge's rostrum, laid into the wall, rests a marble slab which it was my honor to contribute. Upon it is cut the following inscription: "The object of all legal investigation is the discovery of truth. The rules of evidence are framed with a view to this prominent end, seeking always for pure sources and the highest evidence." These words comprise the first section of the Law of Evidence as set forth in the *Code of Georgia*.[3] Being within the gaze of all, this inscription serves as a constant reminder to those who participate in trials within that room. Could there be a more exalted sentiment offered to court officials and jurors? When I sat on that bench, it was my constant intent and endeavor to impress the principles here announced upon the minds of jurors when instructing them upon the laws applicable to cases on trial.

These words have long been in the Georgia law. They have been handed down from Code to Code, as revisions of the statute law of the State became necessary in order to accommodate additional acts of the Legislature. The strength of our codified law lies in the fact that we have never permitted new enactments to cause the omission of the fundamental principles of law, which have descended to us from the earliest developments of the science of jurisprudence.

Chattahoochee County is of small population. Its county seat, Cusseta, is its only town. But the county is famous; it is the seat of Fort Benning, largest infantry training center in the world. Every class graduating at West Point goes there immediately for post-graduate training. Just before the armistice of World War I was signed, this military post was begun with a single two-story building. The government had bought 97,000 acres of land in this county. It is interesting to note that this amount of land was about half of the county. The post was named, quite appropriately, Camp Benning, in honor

---
[3] *Code of Georgia* (1933), Title 38, Section 38-101.

of the Confederate Brigadier General Henry L. Benning of Columbus. At first, Camp Benning housed less than 2,000 troops. On February 8, 1922, the name was changed to Fort Benning and the two world wars together have made of it a military post of 150,000 persons. Its construction cost over $35,000,000, and since Pearl Harbor alone payrolls of more than $125,000,000 have been disbursed. Today it embraces 227,000 acres, about 354 square miles, including 12,000 acres in Alabama. According to General Pershing and other military experts, Fort Benning has all the requirements for a military post. In addition to all activities performed by military personnel, civilian personnel amounting to more than two regiments of men are required to operate so vast a project.

Harris County, adjoining Muscogee on the north and Talbot on the east, is noted for its many strong leaders. My contemporary on the Supreme Court for many years, Marcus W. Beck, was a native of Harris. Today there is being carried on in that county a great agricultural project. Cason J. Callaway, a great cotton manufacturer, formerly of LaGrange, has acquired 28,000 acres in Harris on which to experiment in soil conservation and product diversification.

As a circuit-riding reminiscence, I recall an unusual incident in Harris. A visiting judge was presiding for me. During the week he had incurred the displeasure of some of the Pine Mountain "boys" by his strict sentences. Some of the mountain boys came riding down the mountain on horseback, firing pistols in the streets of the county seat. The visiting judge denounced them to the grand jury. Their repeating the performance brought from the Bench a caustic lecture. However, when the judge had left for his return home, the rowdy element came down the mountain in a "tin can procession," celebrating the judge's departure by beating **tin cans and buckets.**

Riding the Judicial Circuit

I relate the following story because of its very unusual nature, not so much because of any special appropriateness to my circuit-riding experiences as a judicial officer. One summer morning I was sitting on the front porch of my residence in Columbus, reading the morning paper. My eye fell upon a news item to the effect that one Judge Samuel Brewer of Tuskegee, Alabama, was to preside that week in the circuit court at Seale, Alabama, only twenty miles from Columbus. I was familiar with that section of Alabama, having operated a farm near Seale for more than ten years. The name Samuel Brewer carried my mind back to preparatory school days, for a Sam Brewer and I had been together in Park High School in Tuskegee. I did not know what had become of him, and I was satisfied he was my old friend. I was, of course, interested to know that he, like myself, had become judge; and immediately I decided to run over to Seale and renew my acquaintance.

Upon reaching the courthouse in Seale, I looked through the door only to find my friend a tall and handsome young man. Being acquainted with all the officials, I had no hesitancy in walking up to the bench and taking a seat beside by old friend. After brief greetings, my attention was attracted to the case on trial. It was a minor criminal case, the defendant being charged with buying stolen cotton seed at his public gin. I was startled upon recognizing that the defendant was another boyhood friend, one I had dearly loved. I watched the evidence. At its close, the court suspended a few minutes after argument of counsel. I acted upon an immediate impulse.

"Sam," I said to my jurist friend, "I would like to argue this case." Of course, I had not intimated that I knew the defendant.

"Well, Price," he answered, "having never heard you argue a case, I would like to have you do so, if agreeable to the counsel."

I replied that I knew both the lawyers and would consult them. I stepped down from the bench, went over to the counsel table, and made known my wish. Counsel for the defense asked, "Which side?"

"Your side," I answered. Then he and the prosecution counsel both said, "Go ahead."

I immediately stepped forward, faced the jury, and said: "Gentlemen of the Jury, as some of you doubtless know, I am a farmer in this county and not a lawyer. Indeed, I am not practicing law at this time anywhere, since I am judge of my circuit in Georgia. I am not going to discuss the law of this case at all, as I make no pretense of being versed in Alabama law. As a matter of fact, I am not even going to discuss the evidence."

This brought smiles all round, as they wondered what sort of argument I was going to make, possibly thinking I intended merely to tell some witty story.

"I merely wish to tell you a story," I continued, and the jury seemed to think I might be going to tell a joke of some kind.

"About thirty years ago," I went on, "there were two boys who lived in another state on adjoining farms. One was larger than the other, stronger, more robust. The strong boy always gave up to the little boy in everything. He gave the smaller boy the better of any task they were doing. The big boy always took the unruly animal when they played with their goats, or colts, or even steers as they grew up. Whenever they went to the forest or field or to the 'old wash hole,' the big boy was careful to watch over the little boy, to protect him. This friendship continued with the years, ripening into a deep affection. Finally, the parents of the little boy moved away from the farm to the city. The little boy never saw the big boy or even heard of him for many years. In the meantime, the little boy went through high school and college, entered the practice of law, and returned to his home in Columbus, Georgia. Years passed, and finally one day, even today, that little boy, now grown to manhood and after engaging in the law for years, made a visit to Seale, Alabama, and while there he happened to listen to the trial of a case about which he knew nothing until he entered the courthouse. Strange to say, he recognized in the defendant none other than his old friend, the big boy. He listened as the case proceeded, and somehow he could not get out of his mind the boyhood days when the big boy had been so kind and good to him. And now that little boy stands before this jury; and the case is one against the big boy who protected and befriended him. Gentlemen, I am that little boy, and . . .," pointing to the accused, "there sits the big boy."

I turned and patted my old friend on the shoulder and said, "Tommie, it is going to be all right. Goodbye!"

Tears were streaming down his face. I bowed to the two lawyers and to the judge and bade them good day. As I left the courthouse, I asked the sheriff, whom I well knew, to telephone me the verdict as soon as it was returned.

I was at home in an hour. The telephone rang almost as I was entering the house. It was the sheriff. He said, "Your friend was acquitted." I need not say that I was very, very happy. I may as well add here, as I look back upon the scene, that perhaps my conduct was somewhat irregular and might possibly not receive the commendation of every person who had not known my experience. I can only say now that, knowing what I knew then and feeling what I felt, I would do the same thing again.

CHAPTER VII

Old Columbus Days

THE City of Columbus, Georgia, was chartered by the General Assembly in 1827. It was my home town from the time my parents moved from Stewart County when I was a boy until 1916 when I moved to Atlanta as a Justice of the Supreme Court of Georgia. However, Muscogee County, of which Columbus is the seat, continued my legal residence, where I voted, until my retirement from the Supreme Court on December 31, 1936. In the preceding chapter dealing with my judicial circuit, I reserved mention of Muscogee County because I desired to devote an entire chapter to it and Columbus.

Many unusual features distinguish Columbus from other cities. First of all, Columbus was not selected by some person owning land which was thought to be available for a real estate speculation. It did not grow up merely because two or more railroads were built to that point. It was selected by the Legislature for a chartered municipality for very logical reasons. The site on the extreme western border of the state had long been an Indian trading post built on a level plateau on the banks of the Chattahoochee River. The river itself inspired a famous poem by Sidney Lanier who by many is regarded as the South's greatest poet, certainly Georgia's, and whose fame rests mainly upon his "Marshes of Glynn" and his "Song of the Chattahoochee." The latter poem, I think, perhaps is his best. A portion of it follows:

SONG OF THE CHATTAHOOCHEE

Out of the hills of Habersham,
   Down the valleys of Hall,
I hurry amain to reach the plain,
Run the rapid and leap the fall,
Split at the rock and together again,
Accept my bed, or narrow or wide,
And flee from folly on every side
With a lover's pain to attain the plain
     Far from the hills of Habersham,
     Far from the valleys of Hall.

All down the hills of Habersham,
   All through the valleys of Hall,
The rushes cried *Abide, abide,*
The willful waterweeds held me thrall,
The laving laurel turned my tide,
The ferns and the fondling grass said *Stay,*
The dewberry dipped for to work delay,
And the little reeds sighed *Abide, abide,*
     Here in the hills of Habersham,
     Here in the valleys of Hall.

High over the hills of Habersham,
   Veiling the valleys of Hall,
The hickory told me manifold
Fair tales of shade, the poplar tall
Wrought me her shadowy self to hold;
The chestnut, the oak, the walnut, the pine,
Overleaning, with flickering meaning and sign,
Said *Pass not, so cold, these manifold*
     Deep shades of the hills of Habersham,
     These glades in the valleys of Hall.

   . . . .

> But oh, not the hills of Habersham,
> And oh, not the valleys of Hall
> Avail: I am fain for to water the plain.
> Downward the voices of Duty call —
> Downward, to toil and be mixed with the main,
> The dry fields burn, and the mills are to turn,
> And a myriad flowers mortally yearn,
> And the lordly main from beyond the plain
> Calls o'er the hills of Habersham,
> Calls through the valleys of Hall.

There are many things in nature, inanimate as well as animate, that we cannot fully understand. Consider "Old Man River" as an example. The Chattahoochee channeled a path from the hills of Habersham, through the valleys of Hall, to the Gulf of Mexico. It should have cut its way right through what is now known as Five Points in Atlanta. Why not? Atlanta would have loved it, tamed it, fed it, and claimed it as its very own. Whatever it might have done, the Chattahoochee went right along the downward course; streams of water have a way of moving downward. This one does. It runs consistently and heedlessly on the outskirts of Atlanta about fifteen miles west of Five Points. It is deaf to Atlanta and its yearnings, though the said yearnings have been quite audible these many years. In fact, such overtures have become more and more audible. Uncle Sam is now being lovingly beseeched to come to Atlanta's aid and "do something" about the stubborn indifference of this "Old Man River" and its adamantine heedlessness. It just continues to run downward, and incidentally right by West Point and Columbus, giving them abundantly of her rich blessings. West Point and Columbus both know full well how King Nature has favored them. They know, too, that there is another city that has long been looking hungrily at these nature-given blessings that have builded solid, yea prosperous, cities. When they sleep, if they ever do, both Columbus and West Point keep one eye on Atlanta lest the latter's tremendous momentum, an accumulation of its entire young life of enterprise, shall really take over the waters, leaving only the disjointed skeletons of the river lying in its bed. Perhaps they should forego sleep and keep both eyes on Atlanta.

Well, you have guessed it. From the river's standpoint, there is a perfectly sound reason why it did not carve out its course via "Five Points." Atlanta had not been conceived until after the bed of the Chattahoochee had been made and occupied. But Atlanta is an enterprising aggregation of good Americans, and its citizens are intelligent, loyal, and apparently sleepless as to the welfare and growth of Atlanta. Indeed, Atlanta, while courting the help of Uncle Sam, has not overlooked the old maxim about self-help, or God helps those who help themselves. Atlanta has for years steadily grown toward the Chattahoochee River. That's something like going *to* the mountain. Beautiful residences have been constructed all the way to the very bluff of the river. The Chattahoochee supplies all of Atlanta and neighboring communities with an abundance of good water which the city clarifies and purifies. It is the belief of this writer that a good case can be and should be made for sufficient aid from the United States Government to increase the normal flow of water into the river by protecting and controlling its watershed, wisely regulating the use, and employing modern capable engineering to benefit not only Atlanta but all who reside along its route to the Gulf.

The Chattahoochee rises in Habersham County, Georgia, and winds its way to the Gulf of Mexico at Appalachicola, Florida. Near a point where the Florida line crosses it, the Chattahoochee joins with the Flint River, and the two then form the Appalachicola River.

Where the busy textile city of West Point spreads on both sides of the Chattahoochee, the river becomes the boundary line between the States of Georgia and Alabama. The post office in West Point is in Georgia, while the greater part of its cotton mills are in Alabama. From West Point to Columbus, about thirty miles, the river cuts through a rugged terrain. Cutting deeply through sloping hills and through the diminishing heights of Pine Mountain, tumbling over beds of great stone barriers, and threading its way by the wear of centuries, it becomes the head of navigation at Columbus. That facility of navigation is not fully available for use today. The clearing of forests and loosening of the soil over its rainshed have so choked the stream and checked its flow that large steamboats disappeared long ago. Only an occasional barge or smaller craft may now use it successfully. However, in my youth, the Chattahoochee was a regular thoroughfare of steamboat traffic. The boats carried not only an immense tonnage of freight but also innumerable passengers up and down the river between Columbus and Appalachicola and to distant points by transfer.

This river traffic was notable; it keyed the community's life. Often several hundred people met the boat on its passage up and down the river. Warned of its approach by the long blast of the steam whistle, crowds would gather at the river edge at each landing to see the boat tie up and to watch the descent of passengers and the unloading of freight. The unloading was superintended by one known as a "mud clerk." It was his duty to go to the landing and direct the loading and unloading, giving orders to deck hands who performed the heavy work. Such scenes were precisely like those on the Mississippi,

STEAMBOAT ON THE CHATTAHOOCHEE
The steamer *W. C. Bradley* mirrored in the Chattahoochee River

which gave to the world "Old Man River," the song unmatched for the Negro bass voice.

Looking back over those days, I recall that people for miles around used the river for transportation. Steamboat days were real days of romance because they were days of gaiety. Virtually the only mode of travel from Columbus southward was by steamboat. Every spring the young people of Columbus (of course chaperoned) made up parties for travelling to Appalachicola and return. At the Florida terminus of the river they feasted upon crabs and what they thought were the finest oysters in the world. Other young friends were invited to come from far and near to join in these trips. All varieties of amusements and entertainments were enjoyed. There was dancing to an Italian orchestra and singing on deck in the moonlight. The Negro deck hands, famous for their quaint songs, always obliged the young people when asked to sing. They often could be heard singing before the boat reached a landing, their voices drawing still greater crowds. These "roustabouts" were physical giants, and the way they unloaded bales of cotton while singing was a sight to behold.

These steamboat parties frequently had romantic sequels. Often inquiries about engagements or courtships brought out the information that the young people had been on a boat trip. It required one week for a round trip from Columbus to Appalachicola, and in those days there was plenty of time for Dan Cupid to play his part. Indeed, in one case I recall, a young lady from Kentucky, whose engagement had already been announced before she reached Columbus, met a Georgia boy on a boat trip and decided to throw overboard her Kentucky lover. The Georgia boy became her husband.

The site of Columbus was only some ten miles from

Coweta Town, the headquarters of the Creek Nation, a trading post on the Alabama side of the river. It is said on good authority that a steamboat came up the river and landed on the site of Columbus long before any settlement was there — or at least before a white settlement had been located there. When General Oglethorpe came from Savannah to treat with the Creeks at Coweta Town, he crossed the river at the site of Columbus. The point of his crossing is shown by a marble monument, which was erected by the Oglethorpe Chapter of the Daughters of the American Revolution.

Thus the foresight of the Georgia Legislature in chartering a municipality in Columbus has been borne out. It was the head of navigable waters at the time, and it was at the foot of continuous falls in the river stream from West Point thirty miles to the north. The plateau on which Columbus is located is surrounded on north, east, and west by hills and dales, affording wonderful locations for many homes. The business section, as was planned, is at the river bank level on the east side. On the south and east of this section are commons reserved for the public and controlled by a Board of Commons Commissioners. These commons could not be sold without legislative permission. In addition to this foresight, the charter provided for wide avenues and streets. The avenues run north and south and are each 132 feet wide, except Broadway which is 164. The streets, which cross at right angles, are 99 feet wide. All the city blocks are rectangular. The city maintains uniformly on each side of avenues strips of lawn which, when they are at their best and are viewed from the end of an avenue, look like bands of green ribbon.

The charter also reserved, at suitable places, blocks for building churches of the several denominations, a square for a jail, and one for the county courthouse. The residential part of the city grew so rapidly that the jail was pushed out of its reservation and sent to a spot on one of the commons. The old jail lot was sold and residences were built there. My wife's mother built one of these and was living there when I married her daughter, Miss Mary Howard, over fifty years ago on December 12, 1895.

Mrs. Howard was a charming, intellectual, and capable woman, both in the home and elsewhere. She had been left a widow some years before and had proven herself efficient in the management of her cotton plantation some twenty miles from Columbus where she also maintained an attractive country home. She was one of the rapidly disappearing class of outstanding women of the "Old South." Her dignity and bearing unfailingly won respect and deference on all occasions. It was in such a home and in such an atmosphere that Mary Howard and her brothers Thomas A. and Ralph O. Howard were reared. Mrs. Gilbert and I resided there for twenty-one years, until I was called to Atlanta by my appointment as Justice of the Supreme Court of Georgia. Our two children were born in that home. It was twenty-one years of happy home life for all of us. The break in that home life was a keen regret. We were singularly blessed in our two boys — our only children. Price, Junior, the elder, graduated from Georgia Tech in 1921 and has been a business success. In the summer of 1942, Price, at that time a vice president of the Coca-Cola Company in charge of its advertising, heard the call of duty and joined the United States Navy. He was immediately commissioned Lieutenant Commander, USNR. After months of service at various naval stations in the homeland and on the Hawaiian Islands, he was assigned to the staff of Admiral

Durgin, who commanded an escort carrier force. Since early in the fall of 1944 until the final surrender in Tokyo Bay, he served as logistic officer on Admiral Durgin's flagship, in its operations in the Pacific, around the Gilbert and Admiralty Islands, the Mariannas, Carolines, Philippines, Iwo Jima, Okinawa and others. He was promoted to the rank of Commander and after the war was honorably discharged.

Our younger son, Francis Howard, received a bachelor's degree from the University of Georgia in 1927, graduated in law at Yale University in 1930, and then began the practice of law in Atlanta. He married a charming and lovely Atlanta girl, Miss Mary Middleton, in 1932. Their happiness was cut short. Only one month after his marriage, Francis died after an illness of only five days.

Columbus has become a real city. Its rapid growth may be said to have really begun with the establishment of Fort Benning during the First World War. World War II further accelerated the city's growth. With its manufacturing plants in cotton, iron, and wood, and with its many and varied industries, it has a foundation so substantial that Columbus cannot fail to continue as a leading Georgia city. Since it is situated at the "Foot of the Falls" of the Chattahoochee River, from which much hydroelectric power is generated for Columbus and vicinity, no one can estimate the boundless future of this fair municipality. However, the foresight of man is limited. Suppose the entire thirty miles of falls below West Point had been reserved for Columbus when it was chartered in 1827; the size of the city today would be far beyond anything that could have been predicted. As a matter of fact, the Tennessee Valley is not superior in its possibilities for electric power, within the same limits of territory, to the thirty miles in the Chattahoochee.

MRS. GILBERT
For over fifty years my helpmate and inspiration

COMMANDER PRICE GILBERT, JR., USNR

FRANCIS HOWARD GILBERT

Among the city's distinctions must not be overlooked the fact that in Columbus the artificial manufacture of ice in this country was first realized. Not one of these points of excellence, however, is more to the city's credit than the uniform reputation of its citizens for high character, patriotic public service, advancement of education, and freedom from the taint of municipal corruption. I know of no city of which these things may be said with more confidence or pride.

The year 1892 saw an unprecedented depression throughout the country. A notable reminder thereof will always be the postponement of the celebration of the four hundredth anniversary of the discovery of America by Columbus in 1492. The Chicago World's Fair scheduled for 1892 was held in 1893, and other events were postponed because of the depression. An evidence of the widespread business "let-down" was the issuance throughout the land of clearing house certificates, by which it was hoped to float the large stores of idle goods which were packing warehouses everywhere. There was in Columbus at this time a young Bostonian, Frederick B. Gordon, a dry goods jobber. He was active in the Chamber of Commerce, where he advocated the remedy of building more factories. Naturally this was thought little short of madness, since the stocks of idle goods were already so great. But he urged the measure as a cure for unemployment. At first he received little encouragement. I can see him now tramping from door to door to discuss his idea with business men. He declared that his scheme would cause the purchase of hardware, brick, and innumerable items of manufactured goods if a large, new cotton mill were built. Of course, the city already had such mills. Nevertheless his earnestness prevailed, and he sold stock subscriptions for his new mill by the artifice of letting brick men pay in brick for the mill, lumber men pay in lumber, and so on. He secured subscriptions totalling $150,000 in this way. This seemed small but it was a start. Gordon was aided by W. C. Bradley who became one of the city's, and indeed the nation's, big business men. The mill increased to a $700,000 venture. Gordon went to New England for the machinery and paid for it with stock in the mill. He was succeeded as head of the concern by Bradley, who was succeeded by D. Abbott Turner. I procured the charter of incorporation for the company and later became a director. The capital stock increased to $1,400,000, because of increased earnings.

Columbus has been the home of many eminent people. It was the birthplace of the celebrated Southern novelist, Augusta Jane Evans, known after her marriage as Augusta Evans Wilson. The house in which she was born in 1835 was in Muscogee County but not then within the city limits, though it is today. One of the most beautiful of ante-bellum homes in Columbus is called "St. Elmo," for Augusta Evans' best known novel of the same name. This home is immortalized in the novel as "Le Bocage," the home of "St. Elmo Murray." Augusta Evans spent a portion of her childhood at this home, visiting her aunt, Mrs. Seaborn Jones. However, it is not true, as is commonly thought, that she was born in this house or that she wrote *St. Elmo* or any of her novels there. All of her books were written in Mobile, Alabama. She spent only a part of her childhood in Georgia, moving to Texas, then back to Alabama in her early years. Early in life she did live for a short time on a farm on the Alabama side of the Chattahoochee River. That farm today belongs to my son, Price Gilbert, Jr. There is a well-founded tradition that Augusta Evans came to Columbus from Mobile for a visit to her aunt just prior to completing her novel, *St. Elmo*, and while there, in the fine old home, she either completed the book or decided, with the advice of her aunt, on just how she would complete it. Of course, the home was not known as "St. Elmo" at that time, inasmuch as it was not until after publication of the book that this name arose at all. The home was named for the book; not the book for the home.

Another noted author, Dr. Francis O. Ticknor, lived in Columbus. He wrote the famous poem, "Little Giffen of Tennessee," as a tribute to a wounded Confederate soldier. It is reliably said that the soldier recovered, returned to war, and was killed. The home of Dr. Ticknor, known as "Torch Hill," is about five miles south of Columbus, situated on a very high point. Possibly the most admired residence in Columbus or vicinity is the old home of Early Hurt, known as "Dinglewood." It still stands. Hurt's daughter, Julia, a famous belle, married Peyton H. Colquitt, son of Judge Walter T. Colquitt.

The Colquitts of Georgia were a noted family. Columbus ranks them among her most renowned dwellers. Judge Walter T. Colquitt, father of Peyton H. Colquitt and of Alfred Holt Colquitt, held the first term of Muscogee Superior Court (the first term, in fact, of the Chattahoochee Circuit) in 1828, just one year after the City of Columbus was laid out. He afterwards became United States Senator, as did his son, Alfred Holt Colquitt. No other father and son have ever represented Georgia in that body. Alfred Holt Colquitt was a gallant Confederate general and also Governor of Georgia, before serving in the United States Senate. Shortly after marrying Julia Hurt, the famous beauty, Peyton H. Colquitt was killed leading his regiment into battle at Chickamauga.

Among other Columbus celebrities may well be mentioned United States Senator Alfred Iverson and Henry W. Hilliard who at one time represented Alabama in Congress and was, after the war, in the United States diplomatic service. His *Memoirs* was a notable contribution to the post-war era. There was also Hines Holt, relative of the Colquitts, one of Georgia's most famous lawyers. Thomas W. Grimes and Seaborn Jones, eminent Columbus lawyers, served terms in Congress. One of Jones' granddaughters (a daughter of Henry L. Benning) married Samuel Spencer, a native of Columbus who became connected with the banking house of J. Pierpont Morgan and was also the builder of the Southern Railway; his statue stands upon the plaza of the Terminal Station, Atlanta. Joel Hurt of Columbus moved to Atlanta and built the Hurt Building. Ernest Woodruff, born and reared in Columbus, spent all of his business career in Atlanta and became one of a small circle of eminently successful citizens, his special lines being banking and street railways. His career reached its climax, however, in the purchase with W. C. Bradley, also of Columbus, and other associates of the soft drink, Coca-Cola. Robert W. Woodruff, son of Ernest, born in Columbus, has established in the business world an outstanding reputation that is becoming international.

Another leading Columbus family, one of those having achieved success in cotton textile manufactures, is the Swift family. Edward W. Swift is the very capable senior member of the Swift clan. Both the Bradley and Swift families are of Massachusetts ancestry.

Other notable citizens of Columbus were James M. Smith, Georgia's first Governor after the dreadful military Reconstruction administration ended in 1872; Mirabeau Lamar, founder of the Columbus *Enquirer*, one of Georgia's earliest newspapers; and Theodore O'Hara, author of the renowned poem, "The Bivouac of the Dead," whose remains were first buried in Linwood Cemetery, Columbus, though afterwards removed to Frankfort, Kentucky. It has been said that more lines from O'Hara's poem than from those of any other author have been carved on stone monuments. They are seen in countless military cemeteries here and abroad.

Under the date of November 27, 1944, I received from James J. Gilbert, an outstanding citizen of Columbus of many years, a life-long friend of mine, though not a relative, a letter which relates much concerning the beginnings of newspapers in that city. Much of it is interwoven with the career of his father, Thomas Gilbert, who was brought to America from England when just a lad. The letter relates that Thomas DeWolf, an enterprising printer, had taken up early residence in Cahaba, Alabama, anticipating that the settlement would become the capital of that state; but when Montgomery was selected for the capital, he removed in 1855 to Columbus, having learned that this place of considerable size had no daily paper. The letter further states:

On July 30, 1855, he began the publication of *The Daily Sun*, the first daily newspaper ever published in Columbus. The other papers there, *The Enquirer* and *The Times and Sentinel*, were tri-weeklies. Coming back from England, my father was on his way through New Orleans to California, but decided to go to Columbus and see the DeWolf family. He went to Columbus, and DeWolf said: "Tom, stay here; I need you." So he decided to stay.

You doubtless know the remainder — how General Wilson, in 1865, destroyed *The Daily Times* and *The Daily Sun*. However, *The Daily Enquirer* was not disturbed. I have been told that it was because a Yankee spy was working there. *The Daily Times* was never revived. *The Daily Sun* got started again in the course of a few months.

It was in the latter part of 1873 that my father, having passed through the troublous times of Reconstruction, sold *The Daily Sun* to *The Daily Enquirer* and the paper became *The Enquirer-Sun* on January 1, 1874.

Thus is traced part of the history of early Columbus journalism and the establishment of that well known Georgia daily, The Columbus *Enquirer-Sun*.

During the early days of Columbus, Indian depredations and conflicts were constantly occurring. This made the town war-conscious and produced a number of military organizations. As has been said by Lucian Lamar Knight, "The town soon began to bristle with bayonets and to swarm with gay and brilliant uniforms." One of those conflicts was known as the Creek War of 1836. The vicinity was in constant alarm until that war ended by suppression of the Indians. Then followed the War with Mexico, for which three Columbus companies were equipped — the Columbus Guards, the Georgia Light Infantry, and the Crawford Guards. No other city in Georgia sent more than one company. Columbus sent a great number of soldiers to the War Between the States, the Spanish-American War, World War I, and World War II.

General Henry L. Benning, for whom Fort Benning is named, lived in Columbus. He was Solicitor-General of the Chattahoochee Circuit, a Justice of the Supreme Court of Georgia, and a Brigadier General in the Confederate Army. Others who claimed this city as their home were Martin J. Crawford, Justice of the Georgia Supreme Court, member of the Congress that formed the Confederate States of America at Montgomery in 1861, and later a member of the United States Congress; Mark H. Blandford; and William A. Little, whom I succeeded as a member of the General Assembly of Georgia, and who held the offices later of Superior Court Judge and Supreme Court Justice.

Old Columbus Days

While I was Judge of the Chattahoochee Circuit, still residing in Columbus, I was elected president of the Chamber of Commerce of that city in 1915. The Columbus Chamber was notified by the Chamber of Cincinnati, Ohio, that it was sending a good-will committee which would visit us that year. We held a special, called meeting to receive this committee from the North, at which a very unusual and unexpected event transpired. After the usual addresses of welcome and a formal reply, one of the visitors, a citizen of Cincinnati, arose and spoke in substance as follows:

"I have come not in search of trade or of anything of material value. I have come in obedience to a heart-yearn of many years' standing — to gather, if possible, information about a friend of many, many years ago, one who was a friend indeed. In fact, I am seeking that friend, himself, though I have no fact or circumstance by which I may be guided. I only know my friend was a Georgian and lived in Macon. My story, which will explain all, is this: When the War Between the States broke over the land I was a student at Ohio Western Reserve College. My roommate was from Macon, Georgia. His name was Neal. We were devoted friends; but upon the call to arms, each of us repaired to his own home, in order to join the forces of his own people. We were both under the age required for admission to the army, but we feared the war would end before we could be accepted if we waited to reach the required age. We bade each other an affectionate farewell, with absolutely no hope whatever of ever seeing each other again.

"I was at first admitted as a drummer boy in the Union Army, but was eager to win my way into the fighting ranks. After many months I was made a private and given a rifle. A night came when it was my turn to be sent out as a sentinel and to ferret out the location of the Confederates. It was a very dark, rainy night, and the enemy front lines were known to be very near. At one point between our lines and those of the enemy there was a potato patch, and it was, of course, a clearing and, due to the rain, very soft ground. My orders were to work my way across as far as possible. To keep from being seen, I crawled on my hands and knees. At length there loomed before me a very large object, discernible against the sky. What it was I could not guess. Crawling closer, I discovered the object to be a tree. Knowing it would afford some shelter from the rain, I crawled toward it. Presently there was a sound like some one coughing in smothered tones. I edged nearer until my body struck suddenly against the body of a man. We both demanded instantly: 'Who goes there?' I at once answered, giving my name. The other immediately answered: 'Neal, your old roommate!'

"In utter amazement, we grabbed each other, forgetting all in an ecstatic embrace. What a meeting! Of all places in the wide world, I would never have expected to see my friend here or under such circumstances. By accident, there in that pitch-black darkness met Yank and Rebel, boys who had roomed together in school and who loved each other devotedly but who had taken up arms against each other. I would rather have seen this boy that night than anybody else in the whole world. It was like a miraculous benediction.

"We chatted a while, and planned to meet again the next day. We designated a spring between the lines that both of us knew about. Each of us was to approach the spring with cap on bayonet, instead of on head. This was done so that we would know each other from the ranks of hundreds of encamped soldiers. He was to bring me some tobacco and I was to bring him some brandy. Our plans worked and we met. It was the last time we ever saw each other. I came on this trip to find him. Of course, I do not even know whether he is alive. I would like to renew the old days — we loved each other."

I do not know whether our visitor ever saw his friend again. He was told that prominent families, still in Macon, were numbered among the Neals of Georgia; that possibly a visit to Macon would locate his old friend. He said he would go there. He did not return our way. A half century had passed over the heads of those two young soldiers, one from the South and one from the North; so whether they met again we never knew. I do know that I was so profoundly impressed by his story that I hoped and prayed that they would yet meet again.

CHAPTER VIII

Appointed Supreme Court Justice

DURING forty-four years of service as a judicial officer of Georgia,[1] I was defeated only once. That was in the primary election of 1916, in which I was a candidate for re-nomination to a third term as Judge of the Chattahoochee Circuit. The First World War was engaging the attention of everyone, and, among other things, war conditions had caused business difficulties in many lines. The prohibition question was especially alive. The "blind tigers" were on the job, causing still more activity among the adherents of prohibition. The Anti-Saloon League was in flower, and both factions were making demands upon candidates for office.

Representatives of the Anti-Saloon League called on me and asked if, in return for their support of me in the Judge's race, I would agree to sentence all persons convicted of violating the prohibition law, including all who pleaded guilty, to terms on the chain-gang or in the county jail, instead of allowing them to pay fines. I replied that my oath of office required me to assess punishment according to the law and the facts, and that I could not know the facts until the trial had ended in each case respectively. Consequently, I would make no promise of this kind since such a promise would necessarily have reference to cases not yet laid before me. It would have been a pledge to fix sentences of punishment by imprison-

---

[1] The 44-year period is reached by counting my whole service under the Judicial Department of the State government; that is to say, service as Solicitor General, Judge of the Superior Court, and Justice of the Supreme Court—the three being consecutive, beginning with the year 1893 and closing with the year 1936.

Appointed Supreme Court Justice

ment at the behest of persons having no connection with the cases and no responsibility for their legal and just determination. I furthermore stated that, since I could not afford to have my position in the matter misunderstood, I would place a card in the newspaper to that effect; this I did. The card displeased some of the anti-liquor voters, and the record of firmness I had made on the bench with respect to violators had offended many of the anti-prohibitionists. The combination of votes, I presume, defeated me. Anyway, I was defeated.

The primary election of September 10, 1916, in which I was defeated for re-nomination as Judge of the Superior Court, was followed within a very few days by the death of Associate Justice Joseph Henry Lumpkin of the Georgia Supreme Court. He was the second eminent lawyer by that name to sit on that court, the first being Joseph Henry Lumpkin, having been also Chief Justice. Governor Nathaniel E. Harris sent me word by former Justice William A. Little of Columbus to come to see him in Atlanta. I responded at once, and upon my entering his office, the Governor said, "Price, didn't I tell you that if there was a vacancy on the Supreme Court while I was Governor I would appoint you?" I replied in the affirmative; for two years before he had made such a statement of his own accord. The subject had never been mentioned by me.

Governor Harris next said, pointing to a visitor seated in his office, "This gentleman wants me to appoint him. Would you be willing to step aside and wait for another chance?" I replied, "Of course not." The Governor, with a smile, declared, "That settles it." He immediately instructed his secretary to prepare a commission appointing me an Associate Justice of the Supreme Court of Georgia to succeed Justice Lumpkin, and to serve under such appointment until the next general election which would be in November. My commission was dated September 14, 1916. Thus I assumed office as a Supreme Court Justice four days after the primary election in which occurred my defeat for renomination as Superior Court Judge. There yet remained the period until January first of my Superior Court term; so there was no break in the continuity of my judicial service. In November, 1916, I was elected to the Supreme Court by the people of Georgia, and was re-elected in 1918, 1924, and 1930, always without opposition, the absence of which I owe largely to my brothers of the Bar. The Supreme Court term was six years. On January 1, 1919, I began my first full term.

When Governor Harris tendered me the Supreme Court appointment he had just been defeated for re-nomination as Governor in the same primary in which I was defeated for re-nomination as Judge of the Superior Court. Hugh M. Dorsey was the winner in the gubernatorial race. In handing me my commission, Governor Harris stated that he could not tell what the next Democratic State Convention would do about nominating a candidate to succeed Justice Lumpkin, as such conventions were dominated usually by the winner in the governorship race. He suggested that Dorsey men might cause a Dorsey supporter to be nominated for the Supreme Court. The convention's customary practice was simply to confirm nominees who had been successful in the preceding primary election by the people, the actual nomination of candidates being by the people themselves in such primary. Still, we did not know what the convention would do. Would it or would it not undertake to nominate a candidate for the general election in November to succeed Justice Lumpkin? All candidates in the primary had to run in the general election.

When the State Convention met in Macon in October of 1916, this question was perhaps the foremost one on the minds of all delegates. It created much debate in the convention hall as well as considerable discussion in the hotel lobbies. Some wanted the office for a Dorsey man. Others contended that there should not, and could not legally, be a convention nomination because no one had been nominated in the primary; that the proper course was to make no nomination but to leave the race in the general election open to any and all candidates. The lawyers in the convention naturally were looked to for a solution of the dilemma, for the laymen of the convention members did not know whether to nominate or not to nominate.

I owe it to Governor Dorsey to state that I recognized that he could have caused a convention nomination, in which case I would have had opposition in the 1916 general election. However, there was no nomination by the convention, and there is good reason to believe that Governor Dorsey agreed that there should not be. As already indicated, the reason there was no nomination of a candidate for that seat on the Supreme Court in the primary by the people was that at the time of the primary there was no vacancy. Justice Lumpkin died after the primary. Being elected for the two-year unexpired term of Justice Lumpkin, then for full terms of six years in 1918, in 1924, and in 1930 (my final term ending on December 31, 1936), I thus served more than twenty years on the Georgia Supreme Court.

Governor "Nat" E. Harris gave me, of his own volition, the appointment to the only Supreme Court vacancy that occurred during his term as Governor of the State. It came about very unexpectedly. His purpose to do so was announced to me and my wife before his election, while he was campaigning for the governorship. At the time I was judge of my judicial circuit. It was my fixed rule while serving that office not to attend political gatherings or take part in such contests except to cast my vote. "Nat" Harris had served as circuit judge and had a distinguished record as a brilliant trial lawyer. The latter talent made him particularly effective as a "stump" speaker who drew large crowds. He came to my home town to speak. It was at night and my court was not in session. My wife was urgent about hearing Judge Harris speak. Making an exception to my rule, we attended. Appearing a few minutes late and taking a seat near the rear of the auditorium for the purpose of being inconspicuous, we heard the captivating speech which obviously won the vote of the county in the election. Retaining our seats while many crowded around the platform to shake the hand of the speaker, we were recognized by him. Very soon he walked from the platform, grasped our hands, and expressed some complimentary words to Mrs. Gilbert. Then came the most unexpected and the most welcomed of words. Placing his hand upon my shoulder and turning to my wife, he said, "Mrs. Gilbert, if there is a vacancy on the Supreme Court while I am Governor, here's the man I am going to appoint." A surge of happiness and appreciation so filled by heart and mind that I cannot now recall my reply. That was happiness enough to fill my cup to overflowing. What put the thought in Mrs. Gilbert's mind to induce me to break a rule for "the one and only" time in my eight years of service on the Superior Court and more than twenty on the Supreme Court? The vacancy did not come until the last few months of Governor Harris' term of office were ending. He promptly made good his voluntary promise of more than two years before.

Appointed Supreme Court Justice

Governor Harris was a great Georgian, as a brief reference to his services and his life in Georgia abundantly show. His record and his life are a necessary part of my story; for although it was John B. Gordon who first fired my ambition for public service, it was "Nat" Harris who actually made possible the achievement of my life's ambition — to serve on our State's Supreme Court. His story is interwoven with mine and cannot be omitted. Within the necessary limitations of space, the high points are presented here as a labor of love.

Nathaniel E. Harris was born of an outstanding family on his father's plantation in East Tennessee, a section long distinguished for independence of thought and action. In highland sections, anywhere in the world, sharp clashes between bitter factions are noted. This was especially true of East Tennessee, as it was of Scotland in the days of the McGregors, the Douglases and the Bruces. It was true in the early political arena of East Tennessee and is still true there, as it was true when men's passions divided them in the bitter War Between the States, a war which produced for the Southern side from Tennessee's soil such great names as Nathan Bedford Forrest, Gideon J. Pillow and Felix K. Zollicoffer. Here lived, and still lives in history, Andrew Johnson, the tailor-President, and his satellites, among whom was the picturesque and influential "Parson" Brownlow. In truth, Tennessee history smacks much even of the legendary, for within its borders there rose and soon expired "the lost State of Franklin." And this state gave the world the illustrious John Sevier and, of course, Andrew Jackson (Old Hickory), James K. Polk, and Sam Houston who, though born in Virginia, led a romantic and spectacular political career in Tennessee. *The Raven* by Marquis James tells the thrilling story of Houston's career. Also might be mentioned Cordell Hull, James C. McReynolds, and Admiral David Glascow Farragut.

Dr. Alexander Nelson Harris, the father of "Nat" Harris, stood out as the champion of democracy and of the Southern viewpoint in the division that was rapidly leading to war. If ever in human history convictions called for courage, they did in that day in turbulent Tennessee. Divisions there still exist, growing out of the same strife. East Tennessee remains Republican, while all of the other portions of Tennessee are overwhelmingly Democratic. In the midst of this setting, at the age of fifteen years, our "Nat" followed his father's leadership under the Stars and Bars, and shouldered his musket as a soldier in the Army of Northern Virginia. He followed that flag throughout the war, engaging in numerous major battles until that fateful day at Appomattox. Then he led his regiment of cavalry into North Carolina to join General Joseph E. Johnston who had not yet surrendered. After that surrender, penniless, with his defeated comrades, he set his face toward his home in Tennessee, again to face another grim battle — the battle for existence. He was the last Confederate soldier to serve Georgia as Governor.

The following beautiful tribute is from an editorial in the Atlanta *Journal*, published upon the occasion of Governor Harris' death:

> Another gallant figure from the South's brave days of old is gone — Governor "Nat" E. Harris. A soldier, a statesman, a servant of humanity, his life was a romance of brave endeavor and liberal deeds .... His surviving comrades of the army of Lee remember him as a youthful soldier, radiant in the smoke and flame of battle. His neighbors and fellow citizens of Macon remember him as a scholar, "and a ripe and good one," as a lawyer at once profound and persuasive, as a Christian whose ruling passion was love of his adopted Georgia. "A great State to work for, my countrymen; a great State to live for; a great State to die for and be buried in her soil" — thus said the veteran Governor

Appointed Supreme Court Justice

— and today his words are those of one "who, being dead, yet speaketh." But if there be one virtue and one benefaction for which he will be remembered longest and most gratefully, it is that revealed in his labors for the Georgia School of Technology. In the forefront of its founders, he served it for well-nigh fifty years as a far-seeing counselor, as chairman of its board of trustees, as a never-failing friend to the legions of youths it has trained for Georgia's upbuilding. So he lived, fighting the good fight, keeping the faith, bettering the world; so he passes, as rich in honor as in length of days, and lifted high in the hearts of his people.

The Supreme Court of Georgia was established in 1845. On May 30th, 1945, the Georgia Bar Association sponsored a centennial celebration of its establishment. The exercises were held in the Supreme Court Room, the very able and beloved Chief Justice Reason Chestnut Bell presiding. All former Justices of the Court were invited to sit with the present members. A memorial address was read and presented to the Court, and a bronze plaque also was presented by Honorable Marion Smith, representing the Bar Association. The plaque contained the names of all who had ever served on that Court, including the present membership.

There was considerable opposition to the establishment of the Supreme Court in 1845, but the reply of the proponents that the Court would settle all of the law in ten years and could then be abolished seems to have been accepted as a sufficient reply to the objectors. In 1907 the Georgia Court of Appeals was established for the purpose of taking away some of the mounting labor of the Supreme Court. Both courts began with three members; both were increased to six; and the Constitution adopted in 1945 added another Justice to the Supreme Court.

The State Constitution declares that certain specified

classes of cases may be reviewed by the Supreme Court, and that all other cases may be reviewed by the Court of Appeals. All judgments of the Court of Appeals may be reviewed by the Supreme Court, by writ of *certiorari*, if such a petition is granted by the latter Court.

The Court of Appeals itself has the right to certify questions of law to be decided by the Supreme Court which are involved in cases pending in the Court of Appeals. The answers to such questions are binding upon the Court of Appeals. I have no design here to write a history of the Supreme Court, interesting as such might be. It is being written at this time in a most elaborate and painstaking manner by the Georgia Bar Association, acting through carefully selected committees from its own membership. In that work I am very much interested and am cooperating in it fully.

The Supreme Court's first term was held in January, 1846, at Talbotton in old Talbot County, which was then, and still is, in the Chattahoochee Circuit in which later I served as Solicitor General and Judge for some twenty-four years. Only two of the Judges were present — Hiram Warner and Eugenius A. Nisbet. The other, Joseph Henry Lumpkin, was absent for providential cause. Warner had formerly lived at Talbotton. Among lawyers attending this first session, some afterwards attained distinction. Alfred Iverson served in the United States Senate from 1855 to 1861.[2] James Johnson was Provisional Governor of Georgia by appointment during military occupation of the state in the Reconstruction era, being well respected thereafter despite such a handicap. And there was Hines Holt, noted in courts throughout the state. All of these were from Columbus. There were present nine lawyers who resided in Talbotton, among

---

[2] His Georgia contemporary in the Senate was Robert Toombs.

them Judge Barnard Hill, father of Walter B. Hill who was Chancellor of the University of Georgia during my time. Also there was Edmund H. Worrill, who became Judge of the Superior Courts of the Chattahoochee Circuit and whom I knew.

It is of still further interest to note that the first case appearing in Volume I of the *Georgia Reports* (published decisions of the Supreme Court) was not a case argued at the January, 1846, session at Talbotton nor at the next session in February that year at Macon. It was a case argued at the session held in March at Cassville. This town was the county seat of Cass County, Georgia, named for General Lewis Cass of Michigan, but the honor proved fleeting, as those bestowed on political leaders often do. The county name was changed from Cass to Bartow; and although the town's name is still Cassville, it is no longer the county seat. Today the seat is Cartersville. General Cass had been a member of the United States Senate, candidate for President on the Democratic ticket in 1848 when Zachary Taylor was elected on the Whig ticket, and he had been very popular in the South because of his leanings on the slavery question. After the war, Cass lost his popularity in the South because of his attitude during the war; and an effort was made to change the name of the town of Cassville to Manassas in honor of the first battle of the war which had been won by the South. But the Federal Government said it would not operate a postoffice for the town if it bore that name; so Georgians changed the name of the county instead. The county was named Bartow in honor of Francis S. Bartow, the great Georgian who fell at Manassas on July 21, 1861, the first Confederate officer killed in the war.[3]

---

[3] Lucian Lamar Knight, *Georgia Landmarks, Memorials and Legends.* Vol. I, p. 286 *et. seq.;* Vol. II, p. 588 *et. seq.*

In the year 1868, as it appears in the Code of Georgia Laws, 1873, the law requiring the Supreme Court to sit in designated counties was changed. Under that amendment the court was required to hold all of the sessions in Milledgeville, then the capital of the state. The law was again amended and has under all subsequent codes required the Supreme Court to sit "at the seat of the government." Atlanta being the capital, or seat of the government, all sessions of the court must be held in Atlanta. (See *Code of Georgia* - 24 - 3801.) They are held in the Capitol Building, and occupy nearly half of the third floor. Moreover, to provide for all contingencies or emergencies the *Code of Georgia* also provides: "When from providential cause the Supreme Court cannot be held at the time and place designated by law, it may be adjourned by order of the Justices . . . to some other convenient time and place." (*Code of Georgia* - 24 - 3803.)

CHAPTER IX

The Supreme Court of Georgia

DANIEL Webster, in his eulogy of Mr. Justice Story, second only to John Marshall among justices of the Supreme Court of the United States in learning and judicial eminence, said:

"Justice, sir, is the great interest of man on earth. It is the ligament which holds civilized nations together. Wherever her temple stands, and so long as it is duly honored, there is a foundation for social security, general happiness and the improvement and progress of the race. And whoever labors on this edifice with usefulness and distinction, whoever clears its foundations, strengthens its pillars, adorns its entablatures, or contributes to raise its august dome still higher in the skies, connects himself in name, in fame, and character with that which is and must be as durable as the frame of human society."

At a meeting of the Georgia Bar Association, May 31, 1923, it was my privilege to read a prepared address on "The Administration of Justice." On that occasion I made the statement that in the administration of justice, errors were made and had always been made, not only in Georgia but everywhere. The obvious reason is that courts are made up and decisions are rendered by human beings, and no human is so nearly perfect as to be immune from error. That is true, despite the fact that President Grover Cleveland said that L. Q. C. Lamar could not decide a question wrong; that his mind was so logical that given the facts, his mind would automatically turn out the correct answer on the given facts.[1] We should under-

---
[1] Wird A. Cate, *Lucius Q. C. Lamar*, pp. 473-74.

stand and remember how and upon what foundation court decisions are made, more especially those of reviewing courts. Such courts render judgments based upon the record made in the trial courts, either written or printed. Therefore, the reviewing court's decision is made according to the case shown by the record. That record may be incomplete or in some respects erroneous. The reviewing court cannot consider anything not a part of the official record. It is quite likely that Lamar was incapable of drawing an erroneous conclusion from the printed record. He had a great mind and was an unimpeachable public servant and statesman.

As to the administration of justice in Georgia, I said in the address to the Bar Association: "Of the departments of government, the judicial is criticized least, and never in history has the administration of justice been better . . . Georgia lawyers are abler and better prepared than ever before." It should now be added that the Georgia lawyers are abler, because they are better prepared before they are admitted to the Bar and licensed to practice law. I think that the process of improvement still continues and this is all to the benefit of the public. The importance to the public of licensing only lawyers of capacity and integrity cannot be overestimated.

It has often been said, and well said, that "ours is a government of laws and not of men." Yet all government is executed by men; no law, however wise and respected, can enforce itself; thus is shown the necessity of electing and retaining in office wise, honest, and courageous men. That applies with especial emphasis to the judicial department. Our judges must not only be learned in the law, not only be of impeccable honesty, they must also be impartial and independent of all outside influence and have the moral courage to maintain that independence

The Supreme Court of Georgia

in all judicial acts. Only thus may justice be judicially administered. The thought could scarcely be better expressed than in the words of Judge William Cranch, in dissenting from the court's judgment committing Bollman and Swartwout for treason in connection with the trial of Aaron Burr. He said:

"When the public mind is agitated, when wars and rumors of wars, plots, conspiracies, and treasons alarm, it is the duty of a court to be particularly watchful lest the public feeling should reach the seat of justice, and thereby precedents be established which may become the ready tools of faction in times more disastrous. . . . Dangerous precedents occur in dangerous times. It then becomes the duty of the judiciary to poise the scales of justice, unmoved by the armed power, undisturbed by the clamor of the multitude."

These words of Judge Cranch were written during a time of great popular excitement aroused by the arrest and trial of Aaron Burr on a charge of treason. The Supreme Court of the United States as now constituted would have performed a great service to our country in preserving the public reverence for that court for the last few years had they remembered the words of Judge Cranch. During these years, it must be said with deep regret, that court has rendered decisions *apparently* conceived and based upon other than sound non-political foundations. Friends of that court are disturbed by resolutions formally adopted and published, both by the American Bar Association (1944) and the Texas Bar Association (1944) severely criticizing that court. In making this statement, neither the personal honesty nor the sincerity of intentions is questioned. It does seem that the criticisms of the court are the result of minds biased by a determination to give new meanings to well-understood and previously construed provisions of the Constitution and laws of the United States.

My service on the bench, Superior and Supreme, with reference to personal contacts, was all that I could have wished and more than ever was preconceived by me. My relations with my associates were always the most agreeable. They were all able and fair. They desired above all things to render just decisions between all litigants. I loved judicial work; and if I could live my life over again, it would be my wish to follow the same calling. I have neither the inclination nor the physical and mental endurance to mention all or any considerable number of the more than twelve thousand cases in which I participated, nor the two thousand opinions that I prepared. They are included in the official records and the printed volumes of Supreme Court *Reports*. They — good, bad, or indifferent — speak for themselves. Some of my best work was done in preparing dissents. It is my settled conviction that in most cases the best opinions are formed where there are dissents. A strong dissent causes the first opinion to be either withdrawn or strengthened.

I have thought wise here to discuss briefly some of my own dissenting opinions which finally superseded the opinions from which they differed. For instance, there were the two cases of McIntyre and McEntyre. In the case of *McIntyre* v. *Harrison*, 172 Ga. 65, written by Justice Hines and decided by our Supreme Court on February 10, 1931, it was held that injunction was an available remedy to restrain the Georgia Public Service Commission from exercising the regulatory power over a private motor carrier which it exercised under an act of 1929 over a public or common motor carrier. Under the law, the Commission regulated motor hauling on public highways of the State by requiring carriers to secure a license for which they had to pay and which was, thus, a tax. The Supreme Court held that a private carrier, not engaged in the general business of hauling goods for the public, could transport goods over the highways by motor truck without taking out the license, on the ground that the act did not extend to the private or casual carrier. I dissented, contending that if the private carrier collected money for hauling the goods on public highways maintained by the State, he was subject to the license fee whether regularly in that business or not. The Legislature changed the law in 1931, after the decision was rendered. In the meantime, the Supreme Court of the United States handed down a decision enunciating the point I had made.[2] On February 16, 1933, the Georgia Supreme Court, in the case of *McEntyre* v. *Georgia Public Service Commission*, 176 Ga. 398, 402, adopted the view announced in my dissent, made a private carrier for hire subject to the act, and, in thus changing its ruling on the question, announced that the law itself had been changed by the Legislature and that the United States Supreme Court had held the doctrine which the Georgia Court now held.

In *City of Atlanta* v. *Stokes*, 175 Ga. 201, our Supreme Court held, on July 20, 1932, that property bought by a World War I veteran with money received as an allowance from the Federal Government was not subject to taxation. I dissented, announcing the contrary view in an opinion in which I said:

> The original thirteen States possessed all sovereign powers, and in forming the Federal Government, the United States, they created a government of limited powers. It was endowed with only such powers as were delegated to it, expressly or by neces-

---

[2] *Stephenson* v. *Binford*, 287 U. S., 251.

sary implication. The United States Constitution went into effect on March 4, 1789. The first ten amendments were submitted to the several States by a joint resolution of Congress on September 25, 1789, under a preamble reciting: "The conventions of a number of States having at the time of their adopting the Constitution expressed a desire, in order to prevent misconstruction or abuse of its powers, that further declaratory and restrictive clauses be added; and as extending the ground of public confidence in the government will best insure the beneficent ends of its institution," such clauses were now submitted in such amendments. The tenth amendment, intended to make clear that the States reserved all powers not delegated, is: "The powers not delegated to the United States by this Constitution, nor prohibited by it to the States, are reserved to the States respectively, or to the people." As other States were admitted, the powers of the Union remained limited to those delegated by the States.

One of the chief purposes of creating the new government, as declared in the Preamble to the Constitution, was "to form a more perfect Union." The last and concluding words of that great document, excepting only the date and the names of the signing patriots, are: "Done in Convention by the unanimous consent of the States present." Wherever, therefore, the power to tax is delegated to the United States, unless the grant is made exclusive, the States retained concurrent power to tax. Restrictions on the power of States to tax must be within the Constitution, State or United States, or they cannot possibly exist. See *United States* v. *Boyer*, 85 Fed. 430. "This government is acknowledged by all to be one of enumerated powers. The principle that it can exercise only the powers granted to it would seem to be too apparent" to require argument, and "We admit, as all must admit, that the powers of the government are limited and that its limits are not to be transcended." (*McCulloch* v. *Maryland*, 4 Wheat. 404, 420.)

The last cited case above, of course, is the celebrated decision of the U. S. Supreme Court, as written by Chief Justice John Marshall. I had deemed it wise to indicate the limits of the Federal Government in undertaking to say when a State could tax or when it could not. Naturally, the effect of my decision (being, of course, a dissent only) was to say that any law of Congress exempting veterans' property from taxation in any of the states on the ground it was purchased with government allowance, or in any other way, would be unconstitutional and void because the states had never granted to the Federal government, in any of its branches, that power. The power to say whether such property was to be taxed was state power only.

My dissent was upheld by the U. S. Supreme Court itself. That Court, in the case of *Trotter* v. *Tennessee*, 290 U. S. 354, held such property not exempt from state taxation. Strangely enough, the Court cited as one of its authorities for its ruling (as authorities of the same persuasion, of course) the *Stokes* case in Georgia, which had, of course, held directly the converse. I can explain this only by pointing out that the Court had reference to, or had in mind only, my dissent. When next the Georgia Supreme Court had a chance to pass upon the question (*City of Augusta* v. *Rawson*, 179 Ga. 179, decided July 12, 1934), it set aside its former ruling and adopted my dissent as the law of the State, pointing out that the first decision was not by a full Bench and, moreover, had subsequently been opposed in a ruling by the Supreme Court of the United States.

In one instance my dissent was adopted by the Supreme Court of the United States in reviewing and reversing a decision of the Supreme Court of Georgia. The U. S. Supreme Court decision was written by Mr. Justice Brandeis in the case of *John Hancock Mutual Life Insurance Company* v. *Yates*, 299 U. S. 178, decided December 7, 1936, shortly before my retirement from the Bench. The Georgia decision reversed was that of the same name, reported in 182 Ga. 213, my dissent being reported at page 221. Our State Supreme Court had upheld a judgment in Carroll County awarding to a widow $2,000 on a life insurance policy taken out by her husband in the State of New York where he had died. The Georgia Supreme Court held that the *lex fori*, the law of the state where the case was brought and tried, was controlling and sufficient to give Georgia courts jurisdiction. I dissented on the ground that the *lex loci*, the law of the state where the contract or obligation was executed (*Ga. Code*, 1933, Sec. 102-108), controlled and gave jurisdiction to that state; and that thus the widow's litigation belonged properly in New York courts, that Georgia courts did not have jurisdiction to try her claim. I contended that the *lex fori* applied only to the determination of *remedies;* whereas the question whether there was a *right*, whether there was an obligation or an indebtedness, as in this case, was controlled by the *lex loci*. The insurance contract was applied for, issued, and delivered in New York. However, it is proper for me to state that the U. S. Supreme Court did not mention my dissent, though it did adopt the doctrine therein set forth and did reverse the Georgia decision with which I had disagreed.

Naturally I have recorded these cases because they were germane to my career on the Bench, not because of my desire to make invidious comparisons between other members of the Court and myself. I do not overlook the fact that I also wrote a good number of dissents which remained such, never becoming law.[3]

It is doubtful if any member of the Georgia Supreme Court ever entered upon his duties under circumstances as agreeable to himself as those in my case. The Chief Justice, William H. Fish, resided in Macon County which

---

[3] Other Supreme Court of Georgia cases in which I dissented and was later upheld, however, were: *Bentley* v. *Bentley*, 149 Ga. 707 (See *Huley* v. *Huley*, 154 Ga. 321); *Chero-Cola* v. *May*, 169 Ga. 273 (dissent adopted on rehearing); *Powell* v. *Columbia*, 175 Ga. 738 (See 177 Ga. 508); *Axtell* v. *Axtell*, 181 Ga. 24 (See 183 Ga. 197).

The Supreme Court of Georgia

was adjacent to Taylor, one of the counties in my old circuit, and I had known him for years. Besides, he had been a contemporary on the Supreme Court of my esteemed friend, William A. Little, who became a member of the high Court following our association in Columbus. Chief Justice Fish was in every way a cultured, genial, and scholarly gentleman, learned in the law, a former Superior Court Judge, and an excellent presiding officer for the Supreme Court.

The next ranking member was Presiding Justice Beverly D. Evans, also a learned lawyer, former Solicitor General and former Superior Court Judge. I have already referred to our days together at Yale. Then there was Marcus W. Beck, born in Hamilton, near Columbus. We had served together in the General Assembly. We had formed a close friendship there which followed us, since our careers had been quite similar. We had hailed from the same region; he had been Solicitor General and Superior Court Judge as I had. Justice Beck was probably the most widely read member of the Court, in literature as well as in law. He was a linguist of some note.

Another member I came to know and admire greatly was Justice Samuel Carter Atkinson. He had been City Court Judge at Brunswick, was a well grounded lawyer and a man of fine judicial temperament. He was patient, thorough, and concise in what he wrote. Judge Samuel Atkinson, doubtless unconscious of it, closely adhered to the ideal expressed by the learned Chief Justice Bleckley in an address delivered at a meeting of the Georgia Bar Association in 1894: "If I could realize my own ideal, whatever I produce would be in volume a fragment, in thought a volume. My model for all things that involve expression is condensed headnotes rather than expanded opinions. The labor of production should be on the producer and not thrown upon the consumer. By labor I mean thought-work, not handicraft or alternate contraction and expansion of muscles. A problem of first importance for the intellectual artist to solve is how to put the most soul into the least body, how to represent the immaterial by the smallest mass of material." His unique distinction is that he served longer on the Supreme Court of Georgia than any other member to the present time (1906-1944). A remarkable characteristic in his case was that he could remember what was read to him in consultation better than what he read or wrote himself. I do not recall ever hearing him read one of his own opinions to the Court; he always asked another Justice to read it for him. In this way he could better decide whether he was satisfied with what he had written.

Then, there was Justice Hiram Warner Hill, grandson and namesake of one of our most famous and revered Chief Justices, Hiram Warner. Chief Justice Warner was born in Northampton, Massachusetts, later the home of President Calvin Coolidge. It was not surprising that his namesake went to Harvard for his law degree. I have already referred, with fondest recollection, to the days when Hiram Warner Hill and I were in the General Assembly, occupying adjacent seats; and our offices on the Supreme Court, fittingly enough, were adjacent, though this was quite unplanned, since I took the office vacated by Justice Lumpkin which was next to that of Hill. We were close, very confidential friends. I greatly admired him; in fact, the entire Court and the general public as well held him in highest esteem. He was gentle in manner, but firm as Gibraltar in his convictions of right and wrong. He was industrious, amiable, judicial in temperament, and his one determination was to live up to his oath — to stand for justice judicially administered. When he passed away, it was my privilege to speak for the Court in response to the eulogy prepared by a committee of Georgia lawyers and read to the Court on the occasion set apart for his memorial.[4]

Justice Hill's home was in Greenville; mine was at Columbus only fifty miles away. We belonged to St. Mark's Methodist Church in Atlanta, and it had been my privilege to bring his church letter there, where he became teacher of the Men's Bible Class. It grew very rapidly under his leadership; and though he has been in that better land some years now, his memory has not dimmed in that class. It is still called by his name, the "Warner Hill Bible Class," and still foregathers each Sunday from one to three hundred men. No vestal virgin ever more zealously watched her sacred altar fires than did Warner Hill guard the good name of our Supreme Court and his own honor. Not long before his death, without thought of its ever being published, he wrote some lines entitled "Plant a Violet" that bespeak his fine nature and sweet regard for mankind. I quote a stanza:

> When I am dead and calmly lie
> Beneath the sod and Southern sky,
> Plant a modest violet nigh
> And let its fragrance reach the sky.

Justice Hill died in 1934 and was succeeded by Judge John B. Hutcheson of the Stone Mountain Circuit, by appointment of Governor Eugene Talmadge.

Thus, when I went on the Supreme Court in 1916 there were four former Judges of the Superior Court, including me, one former City Court Judge and three former Solicitors General. Within a year after I became a member, Justice Evans resigned to accept appointment

---

[4] Held before the Supreme Court on April 18, 1934. See *Georgia Reports*, Vol. 180, pp. 873-888.

as United States Judge for the Southern District of Georgia. Walter F. George, who was former Solicitor General, Judge of the Cordele Circuit, and Judge of the Georgia Court of Appeals, was appointed by Governor Hugh M. Dorsey to succeed Justice Evans. Justice George carried on the excellent record he had already made as a judicial officer. Of quiet manner, thoughtful methods, his great ability was soon recognized as a notable asset to the judicial system of the state. But he did not long remain on the Supreme Court. He resigned to take up again the practice of law, but he was soon pressed into public service. In 1922 he was elected to the United States Senate, where he still serves, having been re-elected time after time. His election in 1944 gave him a tenure in that great body until 1951. He is of outstanding Presidential caliber, and it is a pity that such men are overlooked in the selection of Presidents. In the meantime, no state is better represented in the Senate than is Georgia by her two Senators, Walter F. George and Richard B. Russell, Jr.

When Justice George resigned from the Supreme Court, James K. Hines was appointed by Governor Thomas W. Hardwick to succeed him. Here again was an appointee of outstanding ability — so recognized by the entire Bar of Georgia. The reader will recall that he is not only referred to in this chapter but also in the opening chapter of this work in connection with the John B. Gordon campaign. Justice Hines brought to the Supreme Court a vast legal experience. He had entered the practice at the age of 21; had served as Solicitor General, riding the Middle Georgia Circuit with Judge Herschel V. Johnson from whom he learned much about American history; had been Superior Court Judge himself; and had again been in the practice for some thirty years before being called to the Supreme Court at the age of 69. The law is exacting upon the physical constitution of any man, for it is hard, confining work. Justice Hines enjoyed remarkable health. He told me he had never been ill since his youth, not even with so much as a cold. He served on the Supreme Court exactly a decade, breaking rather suddenly at the age of 79 and dying in 1932.[5] In a sketch of Judge Hines' career published in the Atlanta *Journal* one year after his demise (issues of May 15, 16, and 17, 1933), written by William W. Brewton who was his secretary both before and after his entrance upon the Supreme Court, we find, in the first article, the following:

When Judge Hines' term as Associate Justice began on January 1, 1922, he brought to the Supreme Court of Georgia exactly a half-century of legal experience. It was in 1872 that he entered the Harvard Law School. Admitted to the Bar of Georgia in Savannah on December 17, 1873, he was in the practice only three years before his marked ability brought about his election at the age of 24 as Solicitor General of Middle Judicial Circuit, which included Washington County to which he had moved. He held this office four years and then resumed the practice. In 1884-5 he represented Washington County in the Legislature, which body elected him Judge of the Middle Circuit in 1886 to succeed the Hon. R. W. Carswell. He was Superior Court Judge for the four years intervening until the end of 1890, and removed the next year to Atlanta where he immediately entered upon a very active practice lasting more than thirty years. So vast an experience in the actual trial of all kinds of cases had therefore given him an insight into the situation which had necessarily arisen in trial courts but which the papers or record on appeal could not show.

Judge Hines' truly phenomenal industry added to his admirable legal equipment could not fail to produce outstanding results. He, too, was a decided asset to Geor-

---

[5] See report of Hines Memorial, held before the Supreme Court on March 20, 1933, in the *Georgia Reports*, Vol. 178, p. 881 *et. seq.*

gia's judicial system. He was succeeded by Judge R. C. Bell of the Georgia Court of Appeals, by appointment of Governor Richard B. Russell, Jr.

Richard Brevard Russell, Sr., was elected to succeed Chief Justice Fish in November of 1922, and began his duties on January 1, 1923. He had served as Representative in the General Assembly of Georgia. When he was barely of voting age, 21 years, he was chosen by Clarke County, which embraced the classic city of Athens with the University of Georgia, as a member of that body. "Dick" Russell, as he preferred to be called, was next elected Solicitor General of the Western Circuit, from which he became Judge of that Circuit. He continued to advance, being elected to the Georgia Court of Appeals of which he later became Chief Judge. He then retired to the private practice of law until 1922 when he ran against Chief Justice Fish of the Supreme Court, defeating Fish as he was rounding out 26 years of service on that Court. However Judge Russell had been defeated in the meantime for several offices: for Congress, for Chief Justice in a former race, and for Governor. While serving as Chief Justice he ran against Senator George for the Senate in 1926 but was defeated. It will thus be seen that, although Judge Russell coveted political office, it was always to judicial office that the people elected him. The electorate thus compelled him to build, if not wiser than he knew, then wiser than he wished. After all, his career was remarkable. After graduating from the University of Georgia in 1879, he was at once given public office where he remained until his death in 1938, save for seventeen years. He retained until old age much of the classical knowledge which most men forget in the struggle for material things. He remained a scholar in English literature, in the dead language, Latin, as well as in the principles of law. He was a fluent speaker with excellent diction. He often stated to his colleagues that he was happier in political than in judicial activity — as Walter T. Colquitt had said. How serious he was in this cannot be known.

Chief Justice Russell, with whom I served on the Supreme Court of Georgia, told a unique story of a member of the Georgia Legislature with whom he had formerly served. It illustrates the resourcefulness of a "politician" (used in the colloquial sense) to escape from an obligation rashly made during his campaign for office. In the earlier days of Georgia, especially in rural sections, all lawyers indiscriminately were addressed as "Colonel." The story told by Justice Russell was about Colonel Tyke who was a candidate for the Legislature. As frequently happened, there was a voter in one of the country districts credited with enough influence among the voters of his neighborhood that his support was usually enough to insure a majority. So Colonel Tyke made an early visit to "Squire" Luke, as we may call him, and succeeded in securing his support. This resulted in the Colonel's carrying the district and, in turn, his being elected to the Legislature; but to do so he had promised in a general way that, if elected, the "Squire" had only to come to Atlanta when the Legislature was in session and the Colonel would see that he received anything that he asked from the Legislature. The two houses of the General Assembly, familiarly called the Legislature, always required, and each elected, several door-keepers. These stood at the several doors more or less to turn away the idle curious. "Squire" Luke conceived an ambition to hold the office of "Door-keeper." Accordingly, he promptly appeared when the Legislature convened and, seeking out the "Colonel" whom he had substantially aided in the election, reminded him of his campaign promise and told him that he very much desired to be a "Door-keeper" of the House of Representatives. Usually there are many more applicants than there are doors to be "kept," and the Colonel saw no possibility of fulfilling his promise, so the following method of evasion was tried out successfully.

"Yes, Squire, I am for you above all else. I'm for you for anything you want. I remember my promise and it affords me a great pleasure to back you to the limit. But, there are certain qualifications that a 'Door-keeper' must possess or he is quite likely to get himself into serious trouble, and I must guard you against getting into serious trouble. You understand, don't you, Squire?"

"Is that so?" said the Squire. "I never thought about that."

"Yes," said the Colonel. "Now, let's see about your qualifications. Were you ever a Door-keeper?"

"No," said the Squire.

"Well," replied the Colonel, "it might be very serious if, while you were holding that high office, you violated any of the rules of the House; for instance, if you allowed any unauthorized person to get into the House."

"To be sure, Colonel. I never once thought about that sort of thing, or I certainly would not have come here."

"Another thing, Squire," said the Colonel, "did you ever study the 'Rules of the House'?"

"No," said the Squire.

"Did you ever read any of the many printed books on 'The Duties of a Door-keeper'?"

The Squire admitted that he had not, and to the Colonel's great relief he announced the withdrawal of his candidacy until he could read up on the question and feel competent for the place.

While Judge Russell was Chief Justice, his son, Richard

B. Russell, Jr., was Speaker of the Georgia House of Representatives. He later became Governor, and is now United States Senator. Another son, Robert L. Russell, is now U. S. District Judge, Northern District, Georgia.

Soon after 1930, when I was re-elected for another six years on the Supreme Court, I began seriously to consider the matter of retirement. I had noted the course pursued by other men who had occupied similar judicial positions. It had seemed to me that some of them had retained their offices too long for the public good and for their own reputations. One conclusion especially determined my course: I had observed that as men grew older they became less vigorous physically and that their minds followed the same trend, although often the latter weakness was not realized. In such a case the nature of the mental work performed would grow less creditable. Of course, it would be easy to point out exceptions to this rule, such as John Marshall, but no man can ever know that he is an exception. The Federal Government fixes the age at which its Supreme Court Justices may retire at 70 years, though retirement is not compulsory. Many Justices of this Court have continued thereon after passing that age, notably Justice Holmes. That, however, does not disprove the rule, and it may tend somewhat to prove its soundness since it is exceptional. Georgia's own Chief Justice Logan E. Bleckley retired at about the age of 67 but did not die until he was 80. He was Judge (later called Associate Justice) from 1875 to 1880, and Chief Justice from 1887 to 1894. The fact that during his service the Georgia Supreme Court consisted of only three members rendered the task of deciding all the cases extremely difficult, especially in view of the constitutional rule limiting the time within which the cases might be decided by the Court. If the Court had not made its decision within the time limit, the case would be affirmed by operation of law. However, Judge Bleckley was not the man to cling to office when conditions prevented the performance of duty according to his standard of excellence. His first retirement as Associate Justice caused an immediate amendment to the Constitution, adding three Justices to the Court, as mentioned above.

Chief Justice Bleckley — in addition to being a philosopher, a profound logician, a learned lawyer, a poet, all self-taught — had some unique characteristics. All of these attracted and held the admiration and affection of the people of Georgia.

There was a story that bears the earmarks of truth, though I was a student at Vanderbilt University at the time and not yet old enough to have been a participant in the occasion. It sounds Bleckleyan, and I relate it with the above explanation. It may be entirely without foundation.

In the year 1880, Governor Alfred H. Colquitt was a candidate for re-nomination by the State Democratic Convention. He had a clear majority of the delegates, but not two-thirds. The minority based their strong opposition upon the contention that Georgia Democrats historically had required nominations for the office of Governor to be made by a favorable vote of two-thirds. Admittedly there had been exceptions, but the debate raged with much eloquence and heat and the convention remained for days firmly deadlocked.

At length a group of delegates, representing all factions, agreed that the convention should and would nominate a compromise man, who commanded the respect and confidence of the party. The group finally agreed that Bleckley was the ideal man, whom all could accept.

The Supreme Court of Georgia 143

The group contacted Bleckley, explained the situation, and requested his permission to report his willingness to serve. The following conversation, in substance, ensued:
Bleckley: "Are you sure that I would be nominated, if proposed?"
The Group: "Of course, we made sure of that before coming to you."
Bleckley: "Are you sure, gentlemen, that I am fully qualified in every way to fill the office to the satisfaction and welfare of the people?"
The Group: "Of course, everyone knows that you have every qualification and would grace the office as no one else could."
Bleckley: "Well, gentlemen, I am profoundly grateful to you and to those whom you represent, but if all you say is true, I could not wish for higher honor. The office of Governor could add nothing to my happiness; therefore, I must decline your flattering offer."

As an evidence of his modesty and to support the probability of the truth of the above story, the following is a matter of state records. In January, 1880, prior to the meeting of the Democratic Convention mentioned above, Bleckley, then an Associate Justice of the Georgia Supreme Court, sent the following letter to Governor Colquitt tendering his resignation.

ATLANTA, GA., JAN. 22, 1880
HIS EXCELLENCY, ALFRED H. COLQUITT:

Dear Sir, — I hereby resign the office of Associate Justice of the Supreme Court for the following reasons: —
First, I am not sufficiently learned in the law to be qualified on a large and liberal scale for judicial functions. In consequence of this deficiency I rarely know how to dispose of difficult cases until after a degree of labor which exhausts me in mere preparation for deciding. It follows that I am generally

behind in writing out my opinions. At present I am much behind.

Second, my health threatens to fail unless I change my mode of life.

This resignation is designed to take effect on the first day of the approaching February term.

Very respectfully, your obedient, humble servant,

L. E. BLECKLEY

Governor Colquitt accepted the resignation, but wrote as follows in reply:

EXECUTIVE OFFICE, Jan. 26, 1880

Judge LOGAN E. BLECKLEY, Associate Justice
   Supreme Court, Atlanta, Ga.

DEAR SIR: — Your resignation as Associate Justice of the Supreme Court of Georgia has been received, and I hereby give you official notice of its acceptance, to take effect on the first day of the approaching February term.

Permit me to express regret that you should feel it due to yourself to close your official duties and retire voluntarily from the high trust you have so faithfully discharged. I must beg to dissent from your modest estimate of your qualifications, and to assure you that I would not feel justified in accepting your resignation based alone on that ground. The consideration of your health, however, leaves me no alternative.

With high respect for you personally and officially, I am, very respectfully,

Your obedient servant,
ALFRED H. COLQUITT.

On his retirement as Associate Justice, Bleckley read from the bench the following lines from his own pen, which have become a gem in the legal literature diadem of our state:

IN THE MATTER OF REST

Rest for hand and brow and breast,
  For fingers, heart, and brain;
Rest and peace! A long release
  From labor and from pain;
Pain of doubt, fatigue, despair —
  Pain of darkness everywhere
And seeking light in vain.

Peace and rest! Are they the best
  For mortals here below?
Is soft repose from work and woes
  A bliss for men to know?
Bliss of time is bliss of toil;
  No bliss but this, from sun and soil,
Does God permit to grow.[6]

I am sincerely grateful for having known Logan E. Bleckley, both as Chief Justice of this state and as a private citizen. I have argued cases before him and have sat at his feet in casual groups at meetings of the Georgia Bar Association. The knowledge of him, of his purity of character and greatness of mind, has been a real asset to me in my everyday labors as citizen, lawyer, and jurist. One does not need to be distinguished or to hold public office in order to find a guiding light by studying the life of this great man.

This chapter began with "Justice" and it ends appropriately with "Justice." "Justice," it has been wisely said,

---

[6] See the Bleckley memorial in Volume 128 of the *Georgia Reports*, p. 849 *et. seq.*, where several of his poems are quoted. The memorial was held before the Supreme Court on July 3, 1907.

"embraces all the virtues, bar none. Without it the universe would be chaos." Said Sydney Smith: "Truth is its handmaid; freedom is its child; peace its companion; safety walks in its steps; victory follows in its train; it is the brightest emanation from the gospel; it is the attribute of God. It is the center around which human passions and interests turn, and Justice, sitting on high, sees Genius, Power, Wealth, and Birth revolve around her throne, and marks out their orbits and teaches their paths and rules with a strong hand and warns with a loud voice, and carries order and discipline into the world, which, but for her, would be a wild waste of passions."

CHAPTER X

The U. S. Constitution and The Supreme Court

IT has been the boast of the ethical lawyer that our judges, on assuming judicial duties, cast off all political and other ties and influences. There can be no dissent from the accepted "Canons of Judicial Ethics." The American Bar Association is looked upon by the legal profession as being a body of lawyers who represent the highest standards. They maintain the keenest interest in judicial ethics. Their own standing, welfare, and pride of calling demand no less.

On July 9, 1924, that Association adopted the "Canons of Judicial Ethics." The chairman of the committee preparing and presenting it for adoption was William Howard Taft, former President of the United States and afterwards Chief Justice of the United States Supreme Court. It can truthfully be said that he was universally respected and affectionately regarded, regardless of political affiliations. These same Canons were adopted by the Georgia Bar Association on June 6, 1925. One of the Canons is: "Judges ought to remember that their office is *jus dicere*, not *jus dare;* to interpret the law, and not to make it." No informed judge will dispute the rule that courts are never concerned with what ought to be the law. Their concern is to correctly rule what the law is.

As one who for sixty years reverenced the United States Supreme Court as next to the United States Constitution, I have ever been unvarying in my effort to defend its dignity and wisdom. In every step of life it has been pointed to by me as the greatest judicial tribunal ever created in the history of the world. As one who has spent a long life as lawyer and judge, I have held it my duty as well as wish to uphold the legal profession, especially the judiciary, from lowest to highest. It has been plain to me that the judiciary is the last bulwark of our liberty and the palladium of our rights. No matter how complete the words of our laws and constitutions, they are not self-executing. It is to the judiciary that the poor and weak must appeal for life and liberty in the last resort.

No words of mine can adequately portray the disappointment and grief which have been mine during recent years when evidences of decay in judicial life have appeared—evidences that dignity and rigid disregard for political and other pressure had waned.

Another Canon is: "That ours is a government of laws and not of men, and that he violates his duty as a minister of justice under our system if he seeks to do what he may personally consider substantial justice in a particular case and disregards the general law as he knows it to be binding upon him. Such action may become a precedent unsettling accepted principles and may have detrimental consequences beyond the immediate controversy."

A third Canon is: "He should avoid making political speeches, making or soliciting payment of assessments or contributions to party funds, the public indorsement of candidates for political office, and participation in party conventions."

There are a number of others, but these three are pertinent to the matter about to be disclosed here. The third Canon is too often violated by Georgia judges other than members of the two appellate courts.

The preceding discussion arises by reason of two resolu-

The U. S. Constitution and the Supreme Court 149

tions recently adopted by such responsible organizations as the Assembly and the House of Delegates of the American Bar Association and the Texas Bar Association, to-wit:

RESOLUTION

Adopted by the Assembly and the House of Delegates at the Annual Meeting of the American Bar Association
September 11-14, 1944

WHEREAS, changes in the settled meanings of the provisions of the Constitution affect and prejudice a great many persons who are not parties in any given sense; and

WHEREAS, a minority of Justices cannot speak for and bind a majority of the whole Court should the same issues presented arise again, so that any decision by a minority purporting to change the meaning of Constitutional provisions as previously settled will not actually change them but will merely create uncertainty and confusion as to the enforceability of Constitutional provisions of settled meaning, and will thus foment additional and otherwise unnecessary litigation by such third persons in a prudent effort to protect their interests,

RESOLVED, That the American Bar Association approves the practice of the Supreme Court of the United States, established by Chief Justice John Marshall in 1834 in the case of *Briscoe v. Commonwealth Bank*, 8 Peters 118, and followed invariably until June 5, 1944, of never deciding a case involving a proposed change in Constitutional doctrine unless a majority of the whole Court concurs in the change.

At its 1944 meeting, the Texas Bar Association adopted a resolution as follows:

1. That the Supreme Court of the United States is losing, if it has not already lost, the high esteem in which it has been held by the people, an esteem created by their belief that it had always remained free of political, personal, and unworthy motives and had interpreted and declared the law as it is written, according to tradition and precedent and agreeably to the provisions of the Constitution and the Bill of Rights.

2. Lately it has repeatedly overruled decisions, precedents and ignored landmarks of the law, of long standing, without assigning any valid reason therefor, and contenting itself with the assertion that these precedents have been eroded by the processes of the years; or basing its decision on casuistry and sophistry rather than logic.

3. Unless cases be disposed of by application of known principles and previously disclosed courses of reasoning, our common law process would become the most intolerable kind of *ex post facto* judicial law-making.

4. By disregarding these principles and these processes and by vacillations and uncertainties and the inconsistencies of its decisions, the Supreme Court has created such a state of uncertainty as to what the law is, that it has rendered it impossible for even the practicing lawyer to advise his clients as to what the law is today, or even offer a guess as to what it will be tomorrow. Its decisions reflect the governmental philosophy and political purpose of the Administration by which appointed and of which many of them have recently been a part, rather than an application of established law.

5. The American Bar Association cannot ignore these conditions and feel it their public duty to call them to the attention of the country and to return to the application of known principles and previously disclosed courses of reasoning, so the country may be delivered from the most intolerable kind of *ex post facto* judicial law-making. To that end we direct that a copy of this resolution be forwarded to the President of the United States, the Vice President of the United States and to the members of the Congress of the United States.

As reported in the Macon *Telegraph* of September 22, 1944, Attorney General, now Justice, Supreme Court of Georgia, T. Grady Head of Georgia, "acting for Georgia and thirty-seven other states, has applied for a rehearing in the Federal Government's case against the Southeastern Underwriters Association, in which the Supreme Court held fire insurance business to be interstate commerce and therefore under the regulations of the Federal Government, as in violation of the Sherman anti-trust law. Declaring that the court had destroyed the foundation on which state regulation is based, the petition asserted that by a four to three majority the Supreme Court Justices had overthrown precedents of seventy-five years' standing in a case of vital interest not only to the defendants but to all forty-eight states."

My natural impulse, of course, is to denounce the critics and demand a retraction in the name of all lawyers and judges in America who are devoted to our great profession. I am, however, reminded of numbers of things that have taken place. I recall that not so long ago a school of thought became quite vocal in its demand for new blood on the court. They denounced the "nine old men" who were, they said, "too feeble-minded to bear properly the tremendous burdens of the court. Gradually Father Time reduced the "nine old men" to a minority of the court, and the new school could congratulate itself that they now had a majority of brilliant young men capable of saving the country. Soon a decision was rendered by this brilliant majority on a great Constitutional question, but there was one old man still "carrying on" who had not lost his loyalty to the Constitution despite his constant persecution by newspaper Constitutionalists. This old man felt outraged at what he adjudged to be an overthrow of the Constitution by adjudication or construction, and in a dissent he cried out: "The Constitution is gone!" Newspaper ridicule, of course, followed; none was too severe. Even his personal manner and voice were subjects of ridicule.

In regard to the 1943-44 term of the Supreme Court, the Bureau of National Affairs, Washington, D. C., recently issued a bulletin stating that "more dissents were registered than in any recent term, and only 33 of the court's 135 opinions were unanimous. Five-to-four decisions were numerous; some were four-to-three. In several instances precedents were toppled over by a sharply divided court." That is the court's recent history; yet such was the very criticism brought against the "nine old men." It was charged against them that they rendered too many five-to-four decisions. For myself I see nothing formidable in such decisions — the so-called "split" decisions. There is nothing like a dissent to bring out the weak points in the majority opinion; for nothing more true could be said about it than that a majority opinion is more likely to contain a defect when it does not have the critical eye of a dissent placed upon it.

Admittedly, new developments in science and invention and industry, also perhaps in other fields, present issues that were not and could not be known far in advance. Some contend that the broad language used in the Constitution should be interpreted to fit such new facts. To my mind, that gives to the power of *discretion* much too wide a range. Our reverence for the Constitution is not an idle, fleeting matter; it is grounded in the fact that it was submitted to the people of the states and ratified. If new developments have come to light which should be controlled or limited by the Constitution, it would be far better for the court to so declare than to distort the plain meaning of the *present* Constitution into fitting those new developments. The courts are not to *change* the law, no matter what conditions exist.

I am aware of the fact that there are able lawyers who disagree with the above view. There are those who take the Constitutional terms, "general welfare," "due process of law," "liberty," "interstate commerce," etc., as a basis for making the Constitution become what they call "workable." Courts may, and should, examine all pertinent facts for the purpose of deciding whether the issue is one controlled by the plain words of the Constitution

The U. S. Constitution and the Supreme Court 153

as it was written and ratified by the people; but no such examination should be undertaken to determine if new conditions, new developments, "changing times," and the like have altered the *meaning* of the Constitution as it stands.

"Sociology, political morals, policy and that convenient refuge of loose thinking which is vaguely called the 'spirit of the constitution' are excluded from consideration. They have already received too much attention from legislators and judges, to the beclouding of constitutional doctrine."[1]

Instances may be cited where it has been asserted that a legislative act was unconstitutional and void because it conflicted with "the spirit of the Constitution," or the "spirit of our institutions," or our "inherent and inalienable right," or because the law is unjust or oppressive. In the case of *Plumb* v. *Christie*, reported in 103 *Georgia Reports*, p. 686, *et seq.*, may be found the answer by the Supreme Court of Georgia. The opinion, learned and unanswerable, was written by Mr. Justice Lewis and has the concurrence of a unanimous bench. The opinion and the decision are in accord with the great majority of courts. Obviously, those terms are utterly without prescribed limitation, leaving every judge and every court to change their meaning which would destroy all means of protection afforded by the Constitution and laws to which a citizen is entitled. The following was said in that opinion: "It is worse than useless then for the courts to undertake to pass upon the validity of a statute by an inquiry as to whether or not it is unjust or oppressive. To enter upon such a field of investigation would be like embarking upon the sea without rudder or compass. A law is not necessarily unconstitutional or otherwise invalid because it is unjust. We live under a

---

[1] Thomas J. Norton, *Losing Liberty Judicially*, p. ix.

constitutional government and written laws; and the courts can enforce only such rights as they protect, and remedy such wrongs as they redress."

When a Constitutional issue is presented to the court, the court has but one duty. That duty is to lay the statute attacked by the side of the clause of the Constitution invoked, and if from the actual words of the two there is a conflict, the court should, after allowing all reasonable deductions in favor of the validity of the statute, strike down the statute. Possibly there is only one exception to this rule, and that is in cases where the power to tax is raised, the power is resolved in favor of the sovereign; but where the question is as to amount or the method of arriving at the amount, the reverse is true and the doubt is resolved in favor of the taxpayer. But if there is one rule in existence that has no exception it is that courts have no concern as to the need for laws or their desirability and should not substitute their judgment for that of the law-making body.

To permit a court — any court — to change the law by construction, merely because of the "changing times," would be simply to destroy the Constitution. This is true with respect to the Federal Constitution, and it is equally true with respect to any state constitution. The law-making bodies, the Congress of the United States and the State Legislatures, are the recognized authorities in determining the will of the people.

Moreover, amendments to a constitution do not destroy contracts previously made, while construction by a court might do so; but a court has no right to do so by construction since such action would itself be unconstitutional. The reason is that when any statute or constitution is duly amended, the change applies only to contracts made subsequently to such amendment. When a court changes the meaning of a law or a constitution that action necessarily means that all former constructions were wrong, albeit under those former constructions many persons have contracted and risked their rights. Such a change in meaning simply rules that the new meaning is the only one that ever had the legal right to be recognized. The new meaning may enrich one party while bankrupting another — whereas neither had before even thought of the new construction and interpretation. Legal advisers must necessarily adopt the construction placed upon the writing by the parties. Such has heretofore been the universal rule of construction by the courts. It is fairer to all parties and sounder for the courts as well. Prior decisions which have long stood and have been acted upon should be followed until the law has been changed by statute or by the Constitution. That is called the doctrine of *stare decisis, et non quieta movere* — to abide by things decided and not to disturb settled points. Such a rule ought to apply to the courts because it applies even to legislative bodies under all our constitutions. If even the Legislature, or the Congress, seeks to change past contracts or obligations by statutory enactment, such enactment would be stricken down as *ex post facto* by the very courts themselves.

George Washington said in his Farewell Address: "In proportion as the structure of a government gives force to public opinion it is essential that public opinion should be enlightened." Who better than he should know, and who more than he held the welfare of America uppermost in a patriotic heart? That great patriot also said:

> Toward the preservation of your government, and the permanency of your happy state, it is requisite, not only that you steadily discountenance irregular oppositions to its acknowl-

edged authority, but also that you resist with care the spirit of innovation upon its principles, however specious the pretexts.

One method of assault may be to effect in the forms of the Constitution alterations which will impair the energy of the system, and thus undermine what cannot be directly overthrown....

Liberty itself will find in such a government, with powers properly distributed and adjusted, its surest guardian.

And again he said:

If, in the opinion of the people, the distribution or modification of the Constitutional powers be in any particular wrong, let it be corrected by an amendment in the way which the Constitution designates.

But let there be no changes by usurpation; for though this, in one instance, may be the instrument of good, it is the customary weapon by which free governments are destroyed.

In a great and fateful moment of our national history Patrick Henry said: "I have but one lamp by which my feet are guided; and it is the lamp of experience." The lamp of experience sheds its light through the printed pages of history. It is a universally accepted rule that a contemporaneous construction, when the founders of our government and framers of our Constitution were actively engaged in public affairs, is of the highest weight in fixing a construction of its powers. Following that guide, let us see what the great men who lived contemporaneously with, or soon thereafter, have said with reference to construing our Federal Constitution.

Chief Justice John Marshall (*Gibbons* v. *Ogden*, 9 Wheaton 1) said: "As men whose intentions require no concealment generally employ the words which most directly and aptly express the ideas they wish to convey, the enlightened patriots who framed our constitution, and the people who adopted it, must be understood to have employed words in their natural sense and to have intended what they said."

One of the most powerful arguments in favor of construing the Constitution as it was written will be found in the Padelford case, 14 Ga. 438. The opinion was written by Judge Henry L. Benning, afterwards a brilliant Confederate General who, because of his dauntless bravery, was by his soldiers called "Old Rock." He said that the Constitution is to be construed "in the sense in which it was understood by the makers of it at the time when they made it."

The case, *Cunningham* v. *Campbell,* 33 Ga. 625, 632, involved the question of the accumulation of supplies by impressment under an act of the Congress of the Confederate States which provided that in such a case prompt and just compensation should be made. The court, in answering the suggestion that fatal consequences might result from judicial interference with the war measures of the Government, said:

> Much has been said, and eloquently said, of the imperiled condition of the country, and the fatal consequences likely to result from judicial interference with the *war* measures of the Government; but let it be remembered that by a provision of the instrument itself, Judges as well as legislators, are sworn "to support the Constitution," and this they are to do in war, as well as in peace. We yield to none in respect for the Congress of the Confederate States; we would at all times, and especially in times like the present, most reluctantly dissent from their construction of the Constitution; we would, in cases of doubtful meaning, incline to give them the benefit of the doubt, for the safety of the country. Beyond this point of concession, not even war, with its attendant horrors, may rightfully impel the judiciary. Positive conviction of constitutional obligation may not be yielded under any circumstances.

In the Minnesota mortgage moratorium case, 290 U. S. 398, Chief Justice Hughes said:

Emergency does not create power. Emergency does not increase granted power or remove or diminish the restrictions imposed upon power granted or reserved. The Constitution was adopted in a period of grave emergency. Its grants of power to the Federal Government and its limitations of the power of the States were determined in the light of emergency and they are not altered by emergency.

Justice Sutherland in a dissenting opinion in the same case said:

A provision of the Constitution, it is hardly necessary to say, does not admit of two distinctly opposite interpretations. It does not mean one thing at one time and an entirely different thing at another time.

Supporting his view, he quotes from *Ex parte Milligan*, 4 Wall. 2, as follows:

The Constitution of the United States is a law for rulers and people, equally in war and in peace, and covers with the shield of its protection all classes of men, at all times, and under all circumstances. No doctrine, involving more pernicious consequences, was ever invented by the wit of man than that any of its provisions can be suspended during any of the great exigencies of government. Such a doctrine leads directly to anarchy or despotism.

He also quotes from *South Carolina* v. *United States*, 199 U. S. 437, as follows:

The Constitution is a written instrument. As such its meaning does not alter. That which it meant when adopted it means now . . . . Those things which are within its grants of power, as those grants were understood when made, are still within them, and those things not within them remain still excluded.

Mr. Thomas M. Cooley, formerly a Justice of the Supreme Court of Michigan, Professor of Law in the University of Michigan, and Chairman of the Interstate Commerce Commission and author of *Constitutional Limitations*, says on pages 123-124, Vol. I, 8th Edition, of his admirable work:

A cardinal rule in dealing with written instruments is that they are to receive an unvarying interpretation, and that their practical construction is to be uniform. A constitution is not to be made to mean one thing at one time, and another at some subsequent time when the circumstances may have so changed as perhaps to make a different rule in the case seem desirable.[1] A principal share of the benefit expected from written constitutions would be lost if the rules they established were so flexible as to bend to circumstances or be modified by public opinion. It is with special reference to the varying moods of public opinion, and with a view to putting the fundamentals of government beyond their control, that these instruments are framed; and there can be no such steady and imperceptible change in their rules as inheres in the principles of the common law. Those beneficent maxims of the common law which guard person and property have grown and expanded until they mean vastly more to us than they did to our ancestors, and are more minute, particular, and pervading in their protections; and we may confidently look forward in the future to still further modifications in the direction of improvement. Public sentiment and action effect such changes, and the courts recognize them; but a court or legislature which should allow a change in public sentiment to influence it in giving to a written constitution a construction not warranted by the intention of its founders, would be justly chargeable with reckless disregard of official oath and public duty; and if its course could become a precedent, these instruments would be of little avail. The violence of public passion is quite as likely to be in the direction of oppression as in any other; and the necessity for bills of rights in our funda-

---

[1] *Scott* v. *Sandford*, 19 How. 393; *South Carolina* v. *United States*, 199 U. S. 437; *Corry* v. *Carter*, 48 Ind. 327; *Murphy* v. *Com.*, 172 Mass. 264, 52 N. E. 505; *Ex parte Woods*, 52 Tex. Crim. Rep. 575, 108 S. W. 1171.

mental laws lies mainly in the danger that the legislature will be influenced, by temporary excitements and passions among the people, to adopt oppressive enactments. What a court is to do, therefore, is *to declare the law as written,* leaving it to the people themselves to make such changes as new circumstances may require.[2] The meaning of the constitution is fixed when it is adopted, and it is not different at any subsequent time when a court has occasion to pass upon it.[3]

The object of construction, as applied to a written constitution, is *to give effect to the intent* of the people in adopting it.

Those of you who have examined the original *Documentary History of the Constitution* deposited in the Archives at Washington could not fail to observe the evidence of the painstaking care in its wording. Probably no body of men ever devoted more meticulous caution in expressing the exact meaning which should be conveyed. In almost every sentence words were added or stricken, or probably both, for the purpose of clarity of meaning. And remember that the Convention was composed of men who knew history. They knew the mistakes and evils of the governments of the old world. Imagine, if you can, someone rising in that Convention in Philadelphia and declaring to such men as George Washington, Benjamin Franklin, James Madison, James Wilson, Oliver Ellsworth, Alexander Hamilton, the two Pinckneys, Iredell and others like them that they were wasting time over needless detail; that it was useless to devote so much time on the shades of word meanings, because as conditions change, the courts would expand or contract the limitations to suit such changes; that the instrument should be flexible, *not* a strait jacket. Can you make a mental picture of such a scene? Can you picture a joyous wel-

---
[2] *People* v. *Morrell,* 21 Wend. 563; *Newell* v. *People,* 7 N. Y. 9; *Hyatt* v. *Taylor,* 42 N. Y. 258; *Slack* v. *Jacobs,* 8 W. Va. 612, 650.
[3] *People* v. *Blodgett,* 13 Mich. 127, 138; *Scott* v. *Sandford,* 19 How. 393; *McPherson* v. *Secretary of State,* 92 Mich. 377, 52 N. W. 469.

The U. S. Constitution and the Supreme Court 161

come for such a release from serious, laborious duties? Or would the picture be one of consternation? How many of those delegates, think you, would have voted to adopt a Constitution which permitted any court to change the meaning as conditions change? My judgment is that not a corporal's guard would have voted to accept such a worthless document. In such an alternative, I think it certain that there would have been no United States Constitution.

So intense was the purpose of leaving no possibility of increasing the Federal powers or decreasing the powers of the states that vigilance did not cease with the adjournment of the Convention and the transmission of the adopted Constitution to the Congress. The Congress, as it was bound to do, then submitted it to each state for ratification. Conventions composed of leading men, many of whom had been members of the Constitutional Convention, assembled in every state to consider ratification. Great difficulties were encountered in the states because of apprehension that the document was not sufficiently guarded against the grant of powers to the United States not intended by the framers. The debates show intense feeling on both sides. In most cases delegates feared that by some sort of construction Federal powers other than those expressly granted were being delegated. Judge Benning in the Padelford case, 14 Ga. 438, has performed an invaluable service to all future students of the question by collecting the history of those state conventions and inscribing them as an imperishable record. No one can dispassionately read that record and fail to be convinced that the Constitution would never have been ratified without assurances from leaders that ten amendments would be immediately adopted to prevent the evils of such misconstruction. These amendments are known as the "Bill of Rights." The Constitution went into effect on March 4, 1789. The first ten amendments were submitted to the several states by a joint resolution of Congress, September 25, 1789, under a preamble reciting: "The conventions of a number of states having at the time of their adopting the constitution expressed a desire, in order to prevent misconstruction or abuse of its powers, that further declaratory and restrictive clauses should be added. And as extending the ground of public confidence in the Government will best insure the beneficent ends of its institution." The tenth amendment, intended to make clear that the states reserved all power not delegated, says: "The powers not delegated to the United States by the constitution, nor prohibited by it to the States, are reserved to the States respectively, or to the people." In the light of that history, how can it be contended that the Constitution would have been ratified had it been thought possible by the people who created and ratified it that any court at any time could by construction change the meaning because of emergencies or changed conditions? To so declare is to charge them with insincerity or a willingness to commit a fraud on their posterity, when their chief purpose was to "secure the blessings of Liberty to ourselves and our Posterity." One who reads the Padelford Case, Elliott's *Debates* and the *Documentary History of the Constitution* with other than a closed mind will not doubt that the Constitution is to be construed "in the sense in which it was understood by the makers of it at the time when it was made."

Whenever the rule is established that the meaning of the great American charter of liberties shall, chameleon-like, change with the tide of popular passion or party supremacy, then Tyranny is enthroned and Liberty is but a name. The pages of history are replete with the cruel injustice inflicted by both majorities and minorities who have seized supreme power. The innocent and the blameless have shed rivers of blood at hands of prejudice and ignorance, incited to passion by brutal and selfish leaders. In clarion tones the voice of Washington rings down the corridors of time against these very excessive mistakes. Organized "blocs" already beset with permanent lobbies our representatives in the Congress, and boldly demand, not the general welfare of the republic, but partiality for their own business, class, or minority organization. The greatness of our country was not achieved by any of these blocs, or by all combined, or indeed by the present generation. The very life of this Republic depends upon respect for the Constitution by every citizen. If it can be said that any class owes a greater allegiance than another, it must be those who as judges are sworn to support the Constitution. That duty must not be evaded by construction or otherwise.

In the face of every selfish interest or attempted usurpation let us renew our resolute support of the Constitution. May it endure forever, its glory undiminished, its limitations unchanged save by the act of the people, effected in the constitutional way.

When our Constitution was formed men were seeking protection against government. Generally the king, by whatever name he ruled, sought more and more power and gathered unto himself more and more of the things that increased his power. When we keep this in mind, we can fully understand why the chief purpose of the Constitution is to restrain and prevent the government from oppressing the citizen. The same tendency on the part of centralized government demands local self-government. It is a basic issue and a pressing one at the present hour to oppose centralization of power when it is a detriment to the states. Thomas Jefferson saw clearly the tendency in its infancy when he wrote: "I believe the states can best govern over home concerns and the General Government over foreign ones. I wish, therefore, to see maintained that wholesome distribution of power established by the Constitution for the limitation of both, and never see all offices transferred to Washington."

Jefferson contended that the Constitution should be construed to mean what its framers and ratifiers understood it to mean. These are his words: "I do with sincere zeal wish an inviolable preservation of our present Federal Constitution according to the true sense in which it was adopted by the states; that in which it was advocated by its friends, and not that in which its enemies apprehended who therefore became its enemies." He called our Federal Constitution "the ark of our safety, the grand palladium of our peace and happiness."

We should never forget that the framers in their wisdom placed in that great Magna Charta a provision for adopting amendments. At the same time it is of the utmost importance to remember that public opinion and popular clamor, fickle and variable as they are, are least dependable among all things as a basis for just judgment. Our own experience demonstrates that truth. The Supreme Court declared unconstitutional the levy of an income tax by the Federal Government. The Constitution was quickly amended to permit such a levy. Now we find that we have given the Federal Government power to levy an income tax so high that the states are restricted to a levy of a similar tax at a rate so low that the yield is distressingly small. The fact is that the Federal Government has unrestricted power as to rate and could make it so high that no state could levy any income tax at all.

Again, at a time when we were at war and patriotic sentiment was above everything else, we adopted an amendment prohibiting the sale and manufacture of intoxicating liquors. Almost immediately it became a football of politics. A large portion of the public refused to respect it; the "bootlegger" became familiar and tolerated, if not respected. Politicians had ridden the prohibition bandwagon into office. It became more and more unpopular, for various reasons; politicians rode repeal into office and quickly caused another amendment repealing the eighteenth. In obtaining the latter, they made strong promises about correcting the worst evils. Little if any effort has been made to carry out these promises.

Speed is desirable in any undertaking, provided it does not impair the result or cause loss of direction. Too much speed might cause a complete wreck of the entire purpose and lead to disastrous results. Certainly in amending the most important document affecting a free government, we should take abundant time for calm consideration. Indeed, the effects that may follow from such amendment, from every point of view, should be carefully weighed, *before* it is made a part of our supreme law.

We are deeply indebted to John H. Wigmore for his *Panorama of the World's Legal Systems*. There we read that from the earliest recorded time men have striven for progress in law and in the administration of justice. Enduring fame has come to those who have been eminent in contributing to advancing the cause. Their names and achievements are found in printed books as well as on parchment and stone. Always justice has been the chief desire of man. We now have records of the Egyptian legal system as old as 4000 B. C. "Maat" was their goddess of justice. "Maat" meant "straight" or "true," hence "just." Ramses III was king and as Wigmore remarks, the philosophy of Ramses III, as to justice, may be gleaned from his statement: "I have made the land safe, so that a lone woman could go on her way freely, and none would molest her. I rescued the humble from their oppressors. I have made every man safe in his home." And again: "Gibbon says, of the Emperor Timour, 'Timour might boast that, at his accession to the throne, Asia was the prey of anarchy and rapine; whilst under his prosperous monarchy a child, fearless and unhurt, might carry a purse of gold from the east to the west'." So it has been said: "Justice is a natural instinct among the inhabitants of India and they hold nothing in equal estimation." Ulpian expressed the lofty Roman conception: "Justice is the constant and perpetual will to allot to every man his due." On down the centuries in every age and clime we find the same idea and the same yearning. It is only natural that we should find the sentiment in the Preamble to the Federal Constitution and in the organic law of Georgia. The Georgia "Bill of Rights" says in the second paragraph: "Protection to person and property is the paramount duty of government, and shall be impartial and complete." In *Penal Code* (paragraph 1008) we find the age-old conception of justice: "The object of all legal investigation is the discovery of truth." In *Lyons* v. *Planters Loan & Savings Bank*, 86 Ga. 485 (5), Judge Bleckley said: "In contemplation of law, justice is not a cardinal, but the pontifical virtue." The sentiment has lost none of its beauty and purity by reason of its antiquity.

CHAPTER XI

Retirement

EARLY in 1936 I gave notice to the press that I would not seek another term on the Supreme Court. I took this course in order to throw open equally to every lawyer in the state the opportunity to offer for my place with full knowledge that the incumbent would not be a candidate. My successor turned out to be Presiding Judge W. Frank Jenkins of the Georgia Court of Appeals who, being duly elected in November, 1936, took his seat on the Supreme Court on January 1, 1937. No one opposed Judge Jenkins, his fitness for the Supreme Court being so generally recognized.

I am very happy to record that when my friend, Justice Jenkins, assumed office as my successor, he found no part of my work unfinished. My slate had been wiped clean, and he had no case awaiting until new cases had been assigned.

I trust it will not be considered immodest for me to set out here the words expressed by my associates on the Supreme Court on December 17, 1936, just a few days before my actual retirement on the last day of that year. No public honor could have so filled my heart with gratitude as this evidence of friendship on the part of my own colleagues on the court. I copy from the Court's Minutes:

Whereas the Honorable Stirling Price Gilbert declined to offer for re-election this year as an Associate Justice of the Supreme Court, choosing to retire at the expiration of his present term, December 31, 1936; and whereas the current and last term of the Court for the year 1936 is now about to adjourn, thus concluding the actual service of Justice Gilbert in the work of the Court, be it therefore resolved by his five associates:

1. The retirement of Justice Gilbert and the resulting loss of his delightful companionship, together with his invaluable counsel and assistance, are matters of deepest concern and regret to the other members of this Court.

2. Having been appointed to this Bench in September, 1916, he has served for more than twenty years as an Associate Justice. During this time he has participated in more than 12,000 decisions, and has actually prepared the opinions in more than 2,000 cases. Previous to this, he served his State successively as member of the General Assembly, Solicitor General of the Chattahoochee Circuit, and Judge of the same circuit, from which last office he was promoted to this Court. Accordingly, his voluntary retirement at this time marks a period of nearly fifty years of continuous service to the people of this State.

3. During all of this period his conduct and official action have been characterized by the utmost patriotism and fidelity as well as by an exceptionally high order of ability and wisdom.

4. His record upon this Court is distinguished not only for the number of decisions made, but for their clarity, force, and soundness, thus constituting a living contribution to the Law and Jurisprudence of this State. For such record, the State will ever be indebted to him as to few of its public servants.

5. Naturally agreeable and considerate in his relations with others, he has, through his tireless industry and willingness to serve, constantly assisted other members of the Court far beyond what might be considered his quota of the Court's work. For this and numberless other courtesies, he merits and has the sincere gratitude of each of his colleagues.

6. As Justice Gilbert retires, he will carry with him the profound affection and esteem of his associates, together with their best wishes for his continued success and happiness.

Unanimously adopted by his fellow-members of the Court, Richard B. Russell, Chief Justice; Marcus W. Beck, Presiding Justice; Samuel C. Atkinson, R. C. Bell, and John B. Hutcheson, Associate Justices.

Retirement

Mr. Justice Gilbert made the following response:

My much beloved friends and comrades: Your more than generous expressions so fill me with gratitude that I can summon no words adequate to thank you. With full knowledge that you far over-value my services, I nevertheless love you for the friendship that prompted you. Looking backward over the pathway which we together have trod, and at times with such difficulties and laborious effort, I can now see nothing but the sunlight of helpful companionship that cheered and guided me. The knowledge that my efforts fell so far short of what I hoped and strived to accomplish humbles and gives emphasis to the abiding gratitude which I owe you, to the Bar, and to the people of Georgia who aided and permitted me to serve the State. May the choicest blessings of our all-wise Creator be yours forever.

It was then ordered by the Court, Justice Gilbert not participating, that the foregoing proceedings be spread upon the Minutes and be printed in the *Georgia Reports*.[1]

The following resolution was adopted by the Atlanta Bar Association:

Whereas, at this, the 1936 meeting of the Atlanta Bar Association, we are honored in having as our guest the Honorable Stirling Price Gilbert, Associate Justice of the Supreme Court of Georgia, who voluntarily retires on January 1, 1937, after twenty years of active service on that Bench; and

Whereas Judge Gilbert's long service has been that of an upright and conscientious Judge, ever loyal to duty, firm in his adherence to the highest principles of justice, an indefatigable worker faithful to the principles and noblest traditions of the Supreme Court, erudite in the preparation of opinions; and

Whereas it is with regret and sorrow for us to realize that he will no longer be a member of the Supreme Court, which is assuaged somewhat by the hope that he will continue to live among us and that we may have the benefit of his friendship and counsel; and

---

[1] See Vol. 183, pp. 889-890.

Whereas it is our purpose not only to honor him by our presence but to leave with him a written opinion of our respect and love.

It is now Resolved by the Atlanta Bar Association as follows:

We are proud, Mr. Justice Gilbert, that our highest Court has had the good fortune to have had twenty years of your devoted service. Your career is written in an indelible record in the official *Reports* of the Supreme Court. Your opinions as a member of that Court are living examples of your knowledge of the Law, your deep learning, and of an understanding heart. Your work as a lawyer, Solicitor General, Circuit Court Judge, Justice on the Supreme Court of Georgia, as Code Commissioner, and your work to improve the administration of justice are a tribute and monument to which we can add: "Well done, good and faithful servant." Now as you retire from the active service and return to the quiet pursuits of private life, may the knowledge of a rich service which you have rendered your State in the morning and noontide course of your life be a sweet benediction and a kindly guide through lanes of peace and happiness as the shadows of evening lengthen.

It was during the latter years of my service on the Supreme Court that I became a member of the Code Commission under whose direction the *Georgia Code of 1933* was produced. This Commission was set up under a resolution of the General Assembly approved August 27, 1929.[2] It provided among other things that "Said Commission shall have authority to determine the form and manner in which all manuscripts shall be submitted, so as to secure an accurate, concise, plain, and comprehensive revision and codification of the laws of this State; and that to that end said Commission may require that all useless, contradictory, and confusing language shall be omitted, changes in arrangement, wording and phraseology made, statutes digested and inconsistencies reconciled." The law provided that the personnel of the Commission

---

[2] *Ga. Laws*, 1929, p. 1487.

should include a member of the Supreme Court, a member of the Court of Appeals, the Reporter of the Supreme Court, the President of the Senate, and the Speaker of the House of Representatives. The Supreme Court designated me as its member, while the Court of Appeals designated Judge Nash R. Broyles as its member. The other original members were Richard B. Russell, Jr., Speaker of the House; and W. Cecil Neill, President of the Senate. The Commission met in my office in the State Capitol, where most of the conferences were held. I was elected its chairman. Because of his removal from the House and election as Governor, Speaker Russell was succeeded on the Commission by Speaker E. D. Rivers, and President Neill was succeeded by Hamilton McWhorter.

Pursuant to law, the Commission submitted the *Code* to the General Assembly for its adoption, after the manuscript had been prepared under the editorial supervision of Orville S. Park and Harry S. Strozier, of the Macon Bar, assisted by Harry B. Skillman and Henry H. Cobb. The General Assembly adopted the work as the *Code of Georgia of 1933* in an act approved March 24, 1933.[3] This act directed that legislation at the 1931 and 1933 sessions of the General Assembly be included in the codification, and this action made necessary its going into effect later. The act provided that the *Code* should become effective at a date fixed in a proclamation by the Governor, and that it should be published under contract negotiated by the Commission. The Harrison Company of Atlanta were the publishers, and upon their delivery of the specified number of printed and bound copies, the Commission made its report to the Governor, Honorable Eugene Talmadge, on November 22, 1935, and he issued his proclamation on December 14 next, making the *Code*

---

[3] *Ga. Laws*, 1933, p. 31.

effective as of and upon the first day of January, 1935. It was officially designated the "Code of 1933," however, since the legislation of that year was the last embraced within it.

The Commission served without pay. No action was taken on any of the compilation in block, but every section was considered separately. Mr. Park, the distinguished annotator of *Georgia Law*, read the manuscript in my office at conferences of the Commission and a stenographic record was made of the deliberations of the Commission. The official *Code* is in one volume, but the compilers later produced through the same publisher an annotated edition of the work with the several subjects or titles bound separately. Some very valuable annotation appears in the official edition also. It may be safely said of the *Georgia Code of 1933* that it is unsurpassed in editorial excellence by the codified law of any other state in the Union. Notable with respect to it is the altogether new system of section numbering, which interlocks with each section the chapter and the title under which it falls. This system was a distinct invention for this *Code*.

During the entire time of my service on the Supreme Court of Georgia I continued to live in Columbus, Muscogee County. At the end of the service, having almost arrived at the age of 75, I determined not to undertake the practice of law. It was my settled wish to enjoy complete retirement for the remainder of my life — a life which had been full of labor as well as enjoyment. I had enjoyed the friendship of my fellow men and I had been singularly blessed with friends. Now my days could be devoted to home life and the wife who had been helpmeet and inspiration for half a century.

The words of Thomas Jefferson express well my thoughts: "There is a time for all things; for advancing and for retiring; for a Sabbath of rest as well as for days of labor; and surely that Sabbath has arrived for one near entering his 80th year. Tranquillity is the *summum bonum* of that age. I wish now for quiet, to withdraw from the broils of the world, to soothe the enmities, and to die in the peace and good will of all mankind." He also wrote what seems on the surface to be a contradiction but which, on examination, is seen to be true: "*A mind always employed is always happy.* This is the truest secret, the grand recipe, for felicity. The idle are the only wretched. In a world which furnishes so many employments which are useful, so many which are amusing, it is our own fault if we ever know what *ennui* is, or if we are ever driven to the miserable resource of gaming, which corrupts our dispositions, and teaches us a habit of hostility against all mankind."[4]

Long before the time set for my retirement, the matter of where and how Mrs. Gilbert and I would spend the days of our old age had been a subject of frequent discussion between us. I had not engaged in active practice for more than forty years. Moreover, the practice as I remembered it had a feature that was ever distasteful to me — that of fixing and collecting fees. This included, of course, the estimate of what my professional services were worth to any client. When that time arrived in the course of employment, my mental attitude was such as to impel me to a drastic reduction from what I had first had in mind. Sometimes my charges disturbed my law partner, who once remarked when I told him what fee I had named to a client: "We cannot make a living and pay office rent on fees like that."

I had practiced law with several partners. The partnership that lasted longest was with Charlton E. Battle, under

---
[4] Edward Boykin, ed., *The Wisdom of Thomas Jefferson*, pp. 132-133.

the firm name of Battle and Gilbert. He was an able lawyer, untiring student, and especially resourceful in the trial of cases. With him, as with all of my several partners, my associations were agreeable and of close friendship, personally and otherwise. Charlton was born in Stewart County as I was, and our fathers were co-partners at one time in the ownership and operation of a Chattahoochee River plantation.

Sometimes a situation similar to the following developed when I was on the trial bench. Often during the trial of a criminal case, when the evidence disclosed a particularly atrocious crime, the thought would run through my mind that a very severe sentence would have to be meted out upon conviction. When the jury had returned a verdict of guilty, and the time had arrived for pronouncing sentence, the convicted man would be told to stand up, and I would then ask what, if anything, he had to say before sentence; or what did his counsel have to say. As soon as this procedure had been gone through, a new picture would present itself to my mind. It would then be the picture of the convict in prison, with days, perhaps years, behind bars. If there were a wife and children, and if they were present in court, the thought of severity would "dim out" in my mind and thought of mercy would take its place. Little wonder, then, that after I had become 75 years of age and had retired from the Appellate Bench, I had no desire to go back to active participation in law, either in the practice or on the bench.

Several years before my retirement, I had been invited to join one of the leading firms of Atlanta lawyers. The financial features were entirely satisfactory, indeed quite attractive, and the personnel of the firm was all that could be desired, all of them being my old friends. However, after a week of serious consideration, I concluded that

I had been out of the practice and in judicial office too long to make a successful return to the practice of law. I accordingly declined the offer, frankly giving the above reasons.

My mind now constantly dwelled upon tranquillity, a far removal from the city with its hurrying traffic and local controversies. I wished to be near the ocean and in a warmer climate than that of Columbus or Atlanta. After I had spent forty-eight years of official life in Georgia, naturally my only desire was to spend the remainder of my days in Georgia. Removal from Georgia would have been unthinkable. Sea Island, on Georgia's Atlantic Coast, was the only spot that filled the specifications. It seemed to have more attractions to offer — the climate, the beautiful natural growth of the trees and flowers, the birds and their lovely songs, and the people, many of whom, like myself, had reached the *summum bonum* of age.

Sea Island always has a pleasant climate. During the eight years already past since retirement, we have not had a hard freeze at our winter home. The coldest weather we have had there brought only a thin coat or ice in the bird bath. Flowers may occasionally be "nipped" or killed by cold, but plants are not injured. The beautiful indigenous trees are nearly all evergreen; the live oak and the pines are evergreen wherever they grow. There are the palms, the sweet bay, the fragrant sea myrtle, the beautiful redberry cassima, and the orange and grapefruit trees. There is an abundance of lovely flowers whose perfumes fill the air. The grapefruit tree bears delicious grapefruit; the oranges are not extra fine.

The Island is a bird sanctuary. The birds are numerous, some quite friendly and unafraid. This is especially true of the red-winged blackbird and the mocking bird. The cardinal is not so friendly; he seems by nature to be very wary, not only of human beings but also of other birds. My inclination to cultivate mocking birds and cardinals and, to some extent, flowers is necessarily held in check by the fact of our months of absence during the summer. It would seem cruel to make friends with birds for just long enough for them to lose their resourcefulness and then leave them to their fates by moving away. So we have abandoned the regular feeding of birds.

Our garden of azaleas and camellias is a never-failing source of interest and pleasure. The fact that camellias are the object of continued attacks by all kinds of insects and also scale seems to endear them to us. Azaleas are less so. In our garden we grow camellias and azaleas in two units. Camellias require some shade, and, accordingly, some trees are left standing. We also have a few roses, wisteria, and yellow jasmine climbing on trees. In such surroundings, I receive with undisguised affection my neighbors' little children with their happy faces and cheerful voices. They, with the flowers, the birds, and the constant roll of the ocean's waves, complete the happy scene and fragrant atmosphere.

Some of the other features making Sea Island attractive are the ocean with its beach and surf-bathing; an excellent hotel, The Cloister, with its great variety of entertainment always open to those of us living in cottages; the harmonious style of buildings; and chiefly the people who are found here. There are ever at Sea Island some attractive, agreeable, and often distinguished public figures, such as Governors, United States Cabinet members, and members of the United States Supreme Court, as well as many former members. Often they are found spending vacations at The Cloister. Lastly to be mentioned are those who reside in their own cottages. Many of the

Retirement

"cottages" are real homes. The owners are from many states and even Canada. It may be of interest to add that at present there are the following cottage owners: From Georgia, 29; Virginia, 2; Pennsylvania, 7; New York, 10; Florida, 2; Michigan, 2; New Jersey, 4; Ohio, 4; Canada, 1; Connecticut, 2; Massachusetts, 4; and 1 each from Illinois, New Hampshire, Delaware, and the District of Columbia. Of course, warm friendships develop from constant contact with these estimable people. Companionships are agreeable; and, because of the fact that most of these people are men and women who have been successful in life, they are persons of intellect and wide travel. Coming, as they do, from widely separated sections, they have broad viewpoints which make for respect and tolerance. The life at Sea Island is ideal for elderly people.

My selection of Sea Island has proven to be singularly fortunate. It would be extremely difficult, if not impossible, to find a location so well fitted for a home for anyone in my situation. Certainly for a Georgian who had spent his whole life in this state and who for fifty years had been honored by his fellow Georgians with positions of trust, there is no comparable place. Here at Sea Island, eleven miles from the mainland and connected thereto by a causeway which crosses five bridges (two being drawbridges), we have found living conditions ideal. The marshes of Glynn stretch away as far as you can see to the northwest and to the ocean, southeast. Then as your eyes travel out to sea beyond the "marshes," made famous by Sidney Lanier, you can see no end — no end save the blue sky. Whether you take your stand on the ocean shore near the restless waves or on the brink of "the wide sea-marshes of Glynn," you become conscious of Infinity.

Yes, Infinity; that must have been the thought which filled the mind of Sidney Lanier. The world and its Creator, who was Creator of all things. This must have been the thought of Sidney Lanier as he pondered under the Brunswick oak which bears his name. For there he wrought the lines on "The Marshes of Glynn" which brought to him deathless fame, which, indeed, would have been his had he wrought nothing more than his "Song of the Chattahoochee." It is quite significant that the extreme western and extreme eastern borders of his beloved Georgia supplied the inspiration for his immortal verse. In Chapter VII a glowing sample of the western border poem is given. I could close the present chapter in no better way than by quoting lines from the poem of Georgia's coastal plain.

> Aye, now, when my soul all day hath drunken the soul of
>   the oak,
> And my heart is at ease from men, and the wearisome sound
>   of the stroke
>   Of the scythe of time and the trowel of trade is low,
>   And belief overmasters doubt, and I know that I know,
>   And my spirit is grown to a lordly great compass within,
> That the length and the breadth and the sweep of the marshes
>   of Glynn
>   Will work me no fear like the fear they have wrought me
>   of yore
> When length was fatigue, and when breadth was but bitterness sore,
> And when terror and shrinking and dreary unnamable pain
> Drew over me out of the merciless miles of the plain,—
> . . . .
> Ye marshes, how candid and simple and nothing-withholding and free
> Ye publish yourselves to the sky and offer yourselves to the sea!
> Tolerant plains, that suffer the sea and the rains and the sun,
> Ye spread and span like the catholic man who hath mightily won
> God out of knowledge and good out of infinite pain
> And sight out of blindness and purity out of a stain.

LANIER OAK
Located on the edge of the marshes in Glynn County near Brunswick

As the marsh-hen secretly builds on the watery sod,
Behold I will build me a nest on the greatness of God;
I will fly in the greatness of God as the marsh-hen flies
In the freedom that fills all the space 'twixt the marsh and the skies;
By so many roots as the marsh-grass sends in the sod
I will heartily lay me a-hold on the greatness of God:
Oh, like to the greatness of God is the greatness within
The range of the marshes, the liberal marshes of Glynn.

. . . .

And now from the Vast of the Lord will the waters of sleep
Roll in on the souls of men,
But who will reveal to our waking ken
 The forms that swim and the shapes that creep under the waters of sleep?
And I would I could know what swimmeth below when the tide comes in
On the length and the breadth of the marvelous marshes of Glynn.

CHAPTER XII

Georgia's Coastal Paradise

ON June 9th, 1732, a charter was granted on petition of an imposing list of "lords and gentlemen" to colonize Georgia land. Under the leadership and management of General Oglethorpe it succeeded. This grant purported to include territory to the "South Seas" (the Pacific Ocean). This charter provided that no trustee could own any land in the colony or receive any compensation. Their efforts were purely patriotic and unselfish, many of them contributing funds toward the venture. The true reason was military — to afford protection to colonies already founded against a threatened Spanish invasion from the south in Florida and probably one also by the French from the west. Thus Georgia required a capable military leader, and this requirement Oglethorpe filled. But the success of the venture also required a good administrator and executive. Oglethorpe combined those qualities with the first named. He had shown his military capability in the British army, and he had been for some time a member of the British Parliament. That he was not indifferent to the spiritual necessities of his settlers was proven by the fact that he brought with him the two Wesleys — John and Charles. They served as Chaplain and Secretary respectively. They preached in a small chapel under a giant live oak near Fort Frederica — now in Christ Churchyard, St. Simon's Island. The decayed trunk of the tree now bears, and has borne for some years, a wooden sign indicating that it was the tree under which John Wesley preached.

Several years ago the Council of Bishops of the Meth-

Georgia's Coastal Paradise 181

odist Church met on Sea Island to consider the creation of a Methodist Shrine on land offered by the Sea Island Company, consisting of eighty acres, or more if desired, just across the Frederica road from the Wesley Oak. Thus, on the opposite side of the road from the Shrine would be Christ Episcopal Church, with its ancient graveyard. Services are regularly held at Christ Church, which has also a Sunday School building. Visitors of all denominations attend these services, since there are always many sojourners from far and near on the island. The inscriptions on tombstones reach far into the past, so long ago that many are worn away and others greatly dimmed. These are graves of English naval officers, Georgia colonials, including the earliest citizens of St. Simon's Island, and of more recent members of the church. Among the comparatively recent burials are Howard E. Coffin and his wife, of whom I speak at some length further on. The Episcopal Church and the adjacent Methodist property acquired for an international shrine to Methodism are separated at a point where there is a fork in the road, one branch leading to old Fort Frederica, now established as a national monument, and the other to an historic place called West Point where are found the ruins called Pink Chapel, a chapel which had belonged to a single family.

Before the Georgia Colony had begun to establish its settlement, Spain had often been a menace to the Colony of South Carolina, and that colony rendered some aid to the newly arrived forces of General Oglethorpe. As time rolled on, South Carolina became desirous of merging the Georgia territory with her own domain. Georgia's refusal caused a cooler feeling toward the younger colony by South Carolina. Then came the momentous year of 1742. General Oglethorpe had already made a return trip to England to obtain reinforcements and funds with which to defend his settlement against the Spaniards. He had clearly seen the necessity. There had been rivalry for the friendship of the Indians. From the first landing at Yamacraw, today included within the limits of the splendid City of Savannah, Oglethorpe had rapidly won the Indians' loyal friendship by his just and trustworthy dealings with them. He even made a horseback trip from his settlement across the uncharted wilderness to Coweta Town, the capital of the Creek Nation. That town was about ten miles from the present city of Columbus, Georgia, on the Alabama side of the Chattahoochee River near what is now the railroad station of Fort Mitchell. Oglethorpe travelled with only a few soldiers and a small group of friendly Indians as guides through a territory supposed to be infested with a number of Indian tribes in the pay of Spain. None, however, molested him. At Coweta Town he was received with every manifestation of friendship, and obtained a treaty from the Indians granting many thousands of square miles of land which are today a part of the State of Georgia.

While in England, General Oglethorpe had arranged for reinforcements and had obtained ten thousand pounds for the building of a fort, so necessary for the defense of St. Simon's Island where he had made his home, the only home he ever had in America. Accordingly, Fort Frederica was built on St. Simon's Island on the Frederica River. The village where the soldiers camped—I would not designate them an army — was called Frederica, after Frederick, Prince of Wales, son of King George II. The location for the fort was not selected without thorough examinations of its surroundings by General Oglethorpe and his scouting party of fourteen white men and two Indians.[1]

Oglethorpe's preparations for defense were begun none too soon. The Spanish fleet, consisting of 51 warships and from three to five thousand men, anchored off St. Simon's bar on July 4, 1742, and the attack was soon begun. The decisive Battle of Bloody Marsh was fought on July 7, 1742. It is interesting to note that the attack came just 34 years, lacking three days, before our Independence Day. General Oglethorpe, with less than one thousand ill-clad and ill-supplied soldiers, so completely defeated more than five thousand Spaniards (according to some estimates) that the survivors fled on fifty or more warships, never to return. The battle was fought on St. Simon's Island. A granite monument, erected by the Society of Colonial Dames, marks the site. On its face are these words, credited to General Oglethorpe: "We are resolved not to suffer defeat. We will rather die like Leonidas and his Spartans if we can but protect Georgia and Carolina and the rest of the Americans from desolation." The story of that battle is unsurpassed for heroism in our colonial history.

The granite block marking the site of the Battle of Bloody Marsh was not the only patriotic service looking to the preservation of the memory of Fort Frederica and the heroism of General Oglethorpe's intrepid band of English, Scotch, and friendly Indians. The Georgia Society of Colonial Dames obtained title to the ruins of Fort Frederica and a small plot of ground adjacent thereto, caused such repairs as were deemed necessary to preserve the ruins from destruction, and placed thereon a

---

[1] For a thrilling story in detail of Frederica, the fort and the village, as well as the Battle of Bloody Marsh, see the article by Margaret Davis Cate in *Georgia Historical Quarterly*, Vol. XXVII, No. 2 (June, 1943).

tablet indicating that the Society was the owner. The moat, which still could be filled with the water of Frederica River, may still be seen, though time has somewhat obscured it. Fort Frederica has now been made a National Monument and has been taken over for maintenance and development by the United States Government through the National Park Service.

After the Battle of Bloody Marsh there was no further need for the strategically located Fort Frederica, and it was deserted and unused for military purposes for nearly two hundred years. During that time the waters of Frederica River unceasingly for every moment of every day and night washed its western side. The dusts of all those days settled on the scene, gradually covering the surrounding area on the north and east until the features of the whole were lost to sight, save a small ruin, just enough to remind the passing stranger that *there* in that place had occurred an event of inestimable value to Georgia and to all of the English colonies.

After more than a century and a half, Mrs. J. J. Wilder, a daughter of Thomas Butler King of Retreat plantation on St. Simon's Island, conceived the idea that something should be done to save the crumbling ruins from complete oblivion. That was in 1903, when the Fort and surrounding property belonged to Mrs. Belle Stevens Taylor who resided thereon. Mrs. Wilder and Mrs. Taylor were friends, and the former was a member of the Georgia Society of Colonial Dames. Mrs. Wilder's plan was to induce Mrs. Taylor to convey the Fort to the Colonial Dames, provided the Dames would preserve it for historical purposes. The plan elicited the interest of Mrs. Taylor, and accordingly, in 1903, the latter conveyed the property to the Dames. Some small repairs were made, which arrested further decay, but the Dames were unable to finance a complete restoration. Appeals to the State Legislature proved unavailing, and the matter so remained until U. S. Senator W. J. Harris of Georgia undertook to obtain help from the Federal Government. After the War Department had declined to approve any appropriation of money for the purpose by Congress, Senator Harris in 1925 introduced a bill in the Senate seeking to have the United States accept the property as a national park or monument, but the United States consistently refused on the ground that it could not maintain the project without special funds for the purpose and such had not been made available. The government contended it had no authority to use other funds already appropriated for this historical purpose. Senator Harris renewed his effort in 1928, but again met failure.

Subsequently, bills were introduced in the Congress by Representatives Deen and Gibbs of the Eighth Georgia District, providing that the Fort and a small area of land adjacent be acquired by the government for a public park or monument, and for the appropriation of funds to be used for that purpose. The Congress passed the required legislation for acquisition but turned down the appropriation of funds.

Some years later an unsuccessful effort was made locally in Glynn County to raise the funds necessary to carry out the project. Thus the matter remained until the fall of 1940. Then began a renewal of the effort begun in 1903 by the Dames. Mrs. W. Walter Douglas of Savannah, then President, and Mrs. Frank Jones of Clinton, Chairman of the Committee on Historic Activities of the Georgia Society of Colonial Dames, assigned Mrs. Price Gilbert to that Committee with special request to examine conditions and advise as to what could be done at Fort Frederica.

In January, 1941, there was a meeting of the full committee, called by Mrs. Price Gilbert, chairman of the subcommittee, at Frederica. The Fort was inspected, and then the committee had a full discussion of the entire subject. It soon became apparent that quite a sum of money needed to be raised by private subscription if the plans of the Society were ever to succeed. It also became apparent that it would be useless to undertake to raise the necessary amount within the membership of the Colonial Dames. The Society had other undertakings, and World War II was rapidly drawing on all American resources. The government insisted that the Fort and considerable adjacent land be donated to it. Thus a considerable sum of money had to be raised for acquiring land titles. The Dames acted through their Board of Managers, with headquarters in Savannah; frequent meetings of the entire Society were not convenient. The plain need was for a small, compact body with power to act. So the Fort Frederica Association was formed and duly chartered as a purely eleesmosynary body with the special object and purpose of assisting in the Fort Frederica project. The Association was formally organized on June 3, 1941.[2] It succeeded in raising sufficient funds with which to purchase about eighty acres of land which had been surveyed and designated as acceptable to the government for a national monument. Also a hundred acres of marsh land were purchased and deeded

---

[2] Officers elected were: S. Price Gilbert, president; Judge C. B. Conyers, Brunswick, vice-president; and B. N. Nightingale, secretary-treasurer. An executive committee was formed, composed of these officers and Mrs. Frank Jones, mentioned above; Alfred W. Jones of Sea Island; and Harold Friedman of Brunswick. Later Mr. Nightingale was inducted into the army and P. F. Gould of St. Simon was chosen in his place. See *Georgia Historical Quarterly*, Vol. XXVII, No. 2 (June, 1943), p. 175 *et seq*. Glynn County made the largest contribution to the needed fund.

to the United States as protection on the north, though this was not required by the government.

The property was purchased with the funds raised by the Association through subscription — some from within the Dames, but largely from without. The titles were duly registered as vesting in the United States Government to which the property was conveyed as a national monument, and the government accepted the property as such national monument to be maintained through the National Park Service. The national monument was officially established on August 30, 1945. The government's archaeologist, the historian, and the Superintendent of National Parks in the Southeast have given much time to studying the locality, the walls of the citadel ruins, and other remains, and to making excavations. The prospect is that the project will ultimately become one of much larger range than originally contemplated. Of course, all that remains of Frederica is included in the government project: the citadel, the soldiers' barracks, the cemetery, and the town of Frederica site, even also the visible remains of the moat. While only small portions of these remain, there are enough to permit the archaeologist and his assistants to reconstruct almost the entire group of historical points, including even the streets of the village of Frederica. Excavations have already been carried forward sufficient to warrant this assertion.

We who have labored so earnestly in the matter hope that the name of the reconstruction will be changed from the contemplated Fort Frederica National Monument to Fort Frederica National Restoration. We think the word, monument, not sufficiently suggestive, since it is usually associated with the idea of a mere stone shaft or marker. The project is one to call travellers to the region, for it is extensive, and the idea of a monument alone would be little calculated to raise the proper anticipations in the minds of tourists; and unless these visit the place, much historical planning will have been lost. A vast restoration like that now going on deserves to be known far and wide. It may be easily taken care of by amending the existing law merely in wording.

On July 7, 1942, the two hundredth anniversary of the Battle of Bloody Marsh was celebrated under the aged spreading live oaks, near where stands the stone marker erected by the Georgia Society of the Colonial Dames of America. It was a notable occasion. Because the battle was fought under General Oglethorpe and by colonial, Scotch, and English soldiers, an invitation was extended through U. S. Senator Walter F. George to Lord Halifax, British Ambassador to the United States. Called to London on matters of state, Lord Halifax was unable to attend, though he sent personal representatives and a personal message. Lord Carrick and British Consul Majoribanks represented Halifax and brought also greetings from His Britannic Majesty. Speaking for Lord Halifax, Lord Carrick brought from him this message: "Two hundred years ago today Englishmen in America were fighting to secure for the newly-founded colony of Georgia a future in which men could lead a life of freedom and constructive work. Today, Georgians and Britons stand again in the forefront of the battle for the selfsame ideals by which our two peoples have been guided through the intervening centuries. We did not fail then: we shall not fail now or in the future."

Mr. Majoribanks said: "In celebrating the Battle of Bloody Marsh we celebrate the independence of the South from foreign influences. Had Oglethorpe been defeated, the whole history of the Southern States would have been changed and it is probable that this continent would have been the battleground for an Anglo-Saxon war for supremacy. Had the Spaniards been successful, the Old South, with its traditions of culture and independence, might never have been born."[3]

Being the presiding officer of the Association, I made the address of welcome. I took pains to point out our debt to Howard E. Coffin in these words: "I feel that no patriotic occasion could be celebrated on these islands without grateful mention of the man who thirty years ago came from Ohio and surpassed all native Georgians by recognizing the richness of our heritage from the noble deeds of our ancestors. He valued the Golden Isles, and he saw how their history had been overlooked. It was Howard E. Coffin who set us to work to preserve that history for future generations."

Coffin came to Georgia in 1909, just after launching the Hudson Motor Car Company. In 1910 he bought Sapeloe Island. There he found the old Thomas Spalding house, which was built about 1800 and which had been turned into a club house by a Macon group in 1907. This famous old mansion Coffin turned into a modern residence of magnificent appointments. Furthermore, he made extensive improvements on St. Simon's Island and on Sea Island, among them the palatial Cloister Hotel on the latter. The Coffin Recreational Park in Brunswick was one of the developments established by his admirers to perpetuate his name. He died at Sea Island in November of 1937.

As has been so indicated in *Flags of Five Nations*, a brochure issued by the Cloister Hotel, Sea Island, Georgia, the islands off the coast of Georgia, jutting inland, were centuries ago known to Spain, France, and England

---

[3] *Georgia Historical Quarterly*, Vol. XXVII, No. 2 (June, 1943), pp. 193-197.

as the Golden Isles of Guale. An Indian chief named Guale, encountered on St. Catherine's Island, thus furnished the first name Georgia ever had so far as researchers know. The word, Golden, is believed to have denoted the rich loot buried on these islands by pirates operating off the Spanish Main, of which they were then a part. The Islands of Ossabaw, St. Catherine's, St. Simon's, and Sapeloe were thus given this general name, with which came to be associated also the Islands of Jekyll and Cumberland. In a foreword to this brochure, Howard E. Coffin says: "Among these islands and winding waterways — nature's hiding places — lurked the picturesque pirates of the Spanish Main in the romantic days of treasure galleons and of high adventure under the black flag. On the Florida passage at Frederica was built England's largest and most important American fortress from which she launched her successful campaign against the Spanish in the first decisive battle of the Western World (Bloody Marsh). Nearby, under the moss-hung oaks the Wesleys preached and sang to Oglethorpe's garrison and first gave Methodism a name. Here German Salzburgers sought religious freedom and founded settlements whose names still endure. Here refugeed French nobility fleeing the guillotine and Santo Domingan planters escaping massacre at the hands of their slaves. In the ancient churchyard at St. Mary's, once Spanish Santa Maria, lie buried many Acadians exiled with Evangeline, immortalized by Longfellow. Here flowered later England's proudest colonial aristocracy, and the rich and colorful slave-owning plantations of the Old South."

The five nations whose flags successfully flew over the Golden Isles were Spain, France, England, the United States of America, and the Confederate States of America. No isles are richer in history or legend. It was among them that Aaron Burr, Vice President of the United States, roamed after slaying Alexander Hamilton in a duel; and it was from live oak timbers of St. Simon's Island that the frigate *Constitution* was built, in part, into that sturdiness that caused her to be named "Old Ironsides."

Interesting history clings to Cumberland Island. It was first called Missoe, an Indian word meaning sassafras. It is some thirty miles long and ranges from two to four miles in width. It was an Indian, one Toonahowie, who changed the name to Cumberland. Accompanying Oglethorpe along the Georgia Coast, Toonahowie, the nephew of Tomochichi, on reaching the island said to the General: "I will name this island in honor of the Duke of Cumberland who gave me a gold watch when I visited England." It will be remembered that on Oglethorpe's return to England seeking aid in men and money, he took with him his ever faithful friend, perhaps the best of all Indian chiefs, Tomochichi, who had first met and welcomed General Oglethorpe at Yamacraw. With them went Scenauki, wife of Tomochichi, his nephew, Toonahowie, and a number of other chiefs. Oglethorpe was so impressed with Toonahowie's spontaneous expression of gratitude respecting the Duke of Cumberland that he established a hunting lodge on the southern end of the island, naming it Dungeness after his country seat in the shire of Kent, England.

After the Revolutionary War, Cumberland Island was granted to General Nathaniel Greene in recognition of his services and his loyalty to Washington. General Greene did not live to occupy the island, but died at his home (Mulberry Grove) near Savannah on June 19, 1785, but the island became the home and last resting place of his widow. In February of 1813, Henry ("Lighthorse Harry") Lee, returning from Cuba where he had gone to regain his health, stopped at the island and went to Dungeness, then the home of General Greene's widow. He was too ill to continue on to Virginia, and died at Dungeness on March 25, 1818. His great son, Robert E. Lee, just before his own death in 1870, paid a visit to his father's grave at Dungeness. In 1913 the elder Lee's remains were disinterred and transported to Lexington, Virginia, where they now repose beside those of the great son. "Lighthorse Harry" Lee had served under General Greene and he was beloved of Washington himself. It was Lee who said of the father of his country that "He was first in war, first in peace, and first in the hearts of his countrymen." Cumberland Island, the beauteous, looks out upon the broad Atlantic across the expanse of a sound bearing its name; and from it are seen, too, renowned St. Mary's River, the mainland of Georgia of which state it is a part, and the mainland of Florida.

Indeed, all of that narrow strip of Georgia's coastal border, from the South Carolina to the Florida state lines, is steeped in history of heroic deeds of the early Georgians. Augusta, Savannah, and St. Mary's all furnish rich material for historic mention; but this work must have a limit somewhere and leaves them as "out of bounds." Savannah and Augusta each merit a book, or several books, as does St. Mary's, concerning which my information is too limited. That ancient town, along with the Okefenokee, would make another story. The narrow strip bounded on the east by the Atlantic and, rather generally, by the Atlantic Coastal Highway, embracing Midway, the vanished town of Sunbury, Darien, and Brunswick, together with the Golden Isles, is all within the scope of this limited narrative.

In the very midst of this coastal paradise is the city of Brunswick, established by Mark Carr, himself an historic character in the story of that section. Brunswick and Glynn County were among the first towns and counties, after Savannah, to be established by the English in the thirteenth colony, the youngest. At first there were parishes which were changed to counties. Brunswick still clings to its English names. Wherever you go you see names of streets, such as Newcastle, Gloucester, Richmond, Norwich, London, Prince, Egmont, and Halifax. All streets are straight and they cross at right angles. Its port is reached by sailing up the sound between St. Simon's and Jekyll Islands. It has a natural, excellent harbor, which has been neglected. However, in 1945, by legislative act, a Port Authority was created with power to raise $15,000,000 to restore the port and harbor to make them available to larger ships. It is the ambition of Brunswick business leaders to make it a thoroughfare of ocean shipping, possibly for important trade with South and Central America.

Darien is another town inseparably linked with the Golden Isles and Brunswick, from which it is only eighteen miles distant. A canal was cut through the marsh lands to enable boats to have a direct route rather than follow the winding path of the river in going between Frederica and Darien. This canal, still in use, is known as "General's Cut." The first settlers in Darien were Scotch Highlanders, who arrived in the spring of 1736 under the leadership of General Oglethorpe. From Darien these same Highlanders rushed to Fort Frederica to the aid of Oglethorpe and his small band of English and Indians. They gave a good account of themselves in the heroic Battle of Bloody Marsh. Some historians say the Scotch Highlanders first named the town New Inverness, but that assertion is vigorously, if not resentfully, denied by the editor of *The Gazette and McIntosh County News* of May 24, 1945. Darien is strategically situated on the north bank of the northern branch of the Altamaha River, twelve miles by water from Sapeloe Island Bar which is located at the entrance of Doboy Sound. There are four branches of the Altamaha, all navigable. All four are traversed by modern concrete bridges, but the two branches between the North Altamaha and the South Altamaha, namely Butler's River and Champney's River, are spanned by bridges that have no movable sections. Both the North and the South Altamaha bridges will permit the passage, without movable spans, of vessels carrying top rigging of not more than 45 to 50 feet in height. The bridge of the north branch, sometimes called Darien River, is so constructed that if it ever becomes necessary, it can be converted into a movable span. Traffic over the Atlantic Coastal Highway passes over all four of these rivers on wide, modern, concrete bridges over a course of two to three miles. It has been definitely planned by the Georgia Highway Department to make the Coastal Highway a four-lane, comparatively straight thoroughfare from, possibly, the South Carolina to the Florida line. The new bridges were built with that plan in view.

The Atlantic Coastal Highway in Georgia has a history entirely different from any other thoroughfare of the state. The Coastal Highway between Savannah and the Florida line is in large part built upon the roadbed of the oldest road in Georgia, for in the early colonial days the road was laid out by General Oglethorpe to connect Savannah and Darien. Oglethorpe's engineers "were assisted by Indian guides, no doubt following an Indian trail." In most instances, roads have been paved by local pressure on the Highway Department, but in the case of the Coastal Highway, the six counties through which it passes worked together in order to have uniform paving

OGLETHORPE OAK.
Traditional site of Oglethorpe's shelter in 1736 upon occasion of his visit to Darien

from Savannah to the Florida line. A Coastal Highway District was organized with a Board of Commissioners who were given the power of issuing bonds to defray the costs of the highway through the counties. It was necessary to pass a constitutional amendment before highway district bonds binding the property and incomes of the six counties equally could be issued. A contract was made on February 6, 1926, whereby the Coastal Highway District would undertake to issue $900,000 in bonds for the purpose of contributing one-fourth of the cost of construction of this highway, and upon such bonds being made available, the State Highway Commission would undertake to construct the highway, furnishing three-fourths of the cost from State and Federal funds. In 1931 a constitutional amendment was passed by which the costs of constructing highways of the State as paid to the Highway Department by the counties of the state and the Coastal Highway District, were ordered refunded to the counties by the issuance of highway certificates. The bonds, principal and interest, have been paid promptly. The amount remaining was held to pay the principal and interest on the remaining bonds, the last due in May, 1946, and the sum remaining will be used for the purpose of paying the expense of the future operation of the Coastal Highway District of Georgia which will continue to function. The chief objective now is to make this highway four-lane — the main highway on the East Coast to Florida. The old road laid out by Oglethorpe is now U. S. Highway No. 17.

Possibly the most interesting object at Darien is Old Fort King George at "Lower Bluff," about a mile from town. There one may see the ruins of the Indian ceremonial house which were uncovered while graves of soldiers were being excavated, the old blockhouse which is the only one of its kind in the country, and the colonial and English military cemetery. Among these ruins lies buried romance as well as history. Now owned by the State of Georgia, these sites are expected to become a State Park. This modest little village was once an important center of water transportation when as many as one hundred sailing vessels were in and about Darien loading with lumber for foreign trade. The Bank of Darien, with its branches in several Georgia cities, was the largest bank in the state. The walls of its building stand yet, a few feet from the river bridge. The story of its retrogression teaches a lesson Georgians were slow to learn. That is the fact that transportation is the chief factor in the building of a city, no matter how many other natural advantages may be possessed. Railroads soon were seen to be essential, as water transportation had been, then even bus lines. It has been said that the throb of the locomotive is the heartbeat of commerce. In the past that statement was a truism, and the railroad has not yet become obsolete or completely superseded by other modes of transportation. Darien failed to attract railroads, and water transportation soon almost ceased because there were no railroads to complete the shipments. It now has busline transportation. Tradition, but not history, has it that when the Central of Georgia Railroad was contemplating the construction of a rail line to the coast, Darien was chosen as a terminus, only to be objected to by influential citizens who said: "As long as the Altamaha flows, and it will flow forever, Darien does not need a railroad. The bosom of the Altamaha can and will bear the commerce."

Men have always sought new lands and advanced frontiers. Human nature seems to have run true to form through the centuries, both in the old countries and in the new. The State of Oklahoma furnishes a modern example of how thousands of people can make a "rush" for new territory. And remember the "gold rush" to California, across the Rockies and sandy deserts in covered wagons, defying death at the hands of savage Indians; and later the "gold rush" to the Klondike. Group after group from England, Scotland, France, Nova Scotia, and other countries drifted into Georgia. As usual, some remained to enrich the strain of our blood line, some others to wither on the stalk, and some merely to disappear in the process of the "melting pot." Of the last two may be mentioned the ill-fated Margravate of Azilia, and the Acadians from Nova Scotia, cruelly driven from their homes and "dumped" on Georgia soil, the objects of charity of a colonial treasury. Let it be said to the credit of these early Georgians that they received and gave food and shelter to these unfortunate "Papists" who were the objects of persecution because of their religion. They landed in Georgia in January, 1756, and like some others, left no "footprints on the sands of time" or elsewhere.

The charter of the Georgia colony was granted in 1732, to expire in 1753. In the latter year in which the charter was surrendered, a group of settlers appeared at Midway, Liberty County, which was to exert an influence for good that has continued until this day and is incapable of being fully realized. It is of this, the Midway Settlement, that we are here concerned. The people were descended from those who suffered persecution at the time of Charles I and came from England to America in search of religious freedom. First settling in Massachusetts and naming their settlement Dorchester, they subsequently moved southward and settled another Dorchester in South Carolina, then removed to Georgia where they established the noted Midway settlement. They were a remarkable group, whose history is worthy of anybody's time and research. The fame of their school teachers and preachers remains upon the pages of history. Abiel Holmes, father of Oliver Wendell Holmes, the poet, and grandfather of Justice Oliver Wendell Holmes (The Yankee from Olympus), preached there at Midway, before being called to preach at Cambridge, Massachusetts. At least seven Georgia counties are named for men who descended from Midway ancestors and who were renowned for character and patriotism. Among those leaders was Daniel Stewart, whose grave in Midway Cemetery is marked by an imposing statue. The Midway Church and Midway Cemetery, historic spots, are separated by the Atlantic Coastal Highway which fills the space between them. The custom of holding an annual celebration at Midway Church is still maintained.[4]

Not far from Midway, located on a high bluff overlooking Midway River from which may be seen Ossabaw and St. Catherine's Islands, the vanished town of Sunbury once was prominent. There lived Dr. Lyman Hall, a signer of the Declaration of Independence. Button Gwinnett, another signer, whose life of usefulness was cut short by his death in a duel with Lachlan McIntosh on May 15, 1777, lived on St. Catherine's Island. His grave is unknown and has been the object of historical quest for many years. Surely this region is hallowed ground — Midway, Sunbury, Darien, the Golden Isles — all that great coastal region of Georgia. Its atmosphere must ever remain worthy of a pause for renewal of love of country and reflection upon the great men and women who made the land itself great by a consecration of their lives to their country and their fellow men. May the

---

[4] Walter G. Cooper, *The Story of Georgia*, p. 348 *et seq.*

descendants of all those who lived there and made great, historic names prove worthy of such an ancestry.

How rich is Georgia in history and legend! How great were its forbears, the English, the Scotch, the Irish, the devout Salzburgers—many other immigrants from Europe, made up its early population; and these mingled on the coastal paradise. Even the Georgia Indians were a noble people. Even they, the original people, recognized the exalted spirit of James Edward Oglethorpe and united with the immigrants just named to follow him in building a great colony. A noble poem has been written commemorating this sentiment. Its author's name seems to be lost, but I am indebted to Mrs. Peter W. Meldrim of Savannah, formerly President of Georgia Society, Colonial Dames of America, whose husband so long shed lustre on the Bench and Bar of Georgia, for their preservation:

> The land that owes to you its birth,
>   Oglethorpe!
> Now calls your spirit back to earth,
>   Oglethorpe!
> To broad Savannah's tawny tide,
> Where Altamaha's waters glide,
> Where Stewart sleeps, his sword beside,
>   Oglethorpe, our Oglethorpe!
>
> You gave the prisoners liberty,
>   Oglethorpe!
> To find a land forever free,
>   Oglethorpe!
> From Scotland's hills, from Salza's dales,
> To Darien's beauty, haunted vales,
> The ocean bore their swelling sails,
>   Oglethorpe, our Oglethorpe!

From persecution, grim and harsh,
    Oglethorpe!
To Yamacraw and Bloody Marsh,
    Oglethorpe!
They followed you through storm and calm,
With McIntosh and Habersham,
Till Peace was won with Victory's palm,
    Oglethorpe, our Oglethorpe!

You call us now to braver deeds,
    Oglethorpe!
To nobler lives and loftier creeds,
    Oglethorpe!
By Telfair's faith, by Tattnall's grave,
Where Bonaventure's mosses wave,
By Screven's death, our land to save,
    Oglethorpe, our Oglethorpe!

CHAPTER XIII

Wars

THE War Between the States was less than a year old when I was born in 1862. The first I heard of that war was just after its close in the spring of 1865 in Virginia. But that was not the close in Georgia. The last battles of the war in this state were fought in Columbus and West Point on April 16, 1865, following Lee's surrender at Appomattox on April 9th. These engagements were brought on by Wilson's Raiders, a detachment of Sherman's army which had left Atlanta in ruins. These raiders were operating in Alabama and Middle Georgia with the design to re-join Sherman in Savannah. I was too young to understand the exact facts. But I well recall the fear entertained by the Negro children on our farm that Yankee soldiers might be expected at any moment to step forth from any hiding place. My parents were living on a farm and there were no white children except my sister and me. Thus all the rumors came from the Negroes. From these rumors I thought it prudent to look under the house and behind trees, outhouses, and everywhere else whenever I came out of doors. But I never saw one of those soldiers. Wilson and his raiders made a wreck out of Columbus, destroying all cotton mills, iron foundries, and bridges.

After I was old enough to enjoy the stories of the war and had become a resident of Columbus, the following story became current. A prominent Columbus citizen had seen distinguished service in Virginia, winning the rank of major. He was at home on furlough when news of the approach of Wilson's Raiders was received. They were approaching from Alabama and would necessarily cross the Chattahoochee River bridge. The people hurriedly collected all soldiers, ex-soldiers, and everyone who could be induced to join in the city's defense. The Major was the highest ranking officer, and he had boasted of his defiance of the "damyankees," as he was pleased to call the expected invaders; so he was placed in command of the nondescript collection of defenders. He had a brother named Charles Henry, and a Negro "bodyguard" named Dick. The Major addressed his troops thus: "Fellow Soldiers, follow me! You need not fear those rascals. Charles Henry, Dick, and I can whip a thousand of them." When the "damyankees" had reached the Alabama side of the river, behind some hills about half a mile from the stream, the Major's outfit had also crossed over to that side and soon heard the enemy's approach. Suddenly, his horse began to show fright and the Major appeared to have great difficulty in retaining his seat on the animal's back. He called out to his brother: "Charles Henry, take care of thyself and Dick; my horse is running away and I cannot control him." He rapidly clattered across the wooden bridge (the old covered type of bridge with plank floors), causing great clouds of dust and marvelous noise. The whereabouts of the Major thereafter fell into great mystery, inducing the theory that he and his horse were still running.

After the War Between the States came the Spanish-American War, which was a very small affair compared to its predecessor. It liberated Cuba, our close neighbor, from the galling yoke of Spain. Also it demonstrated, we hope for all time, to all persons that the South was back in the Union and anxious to fight for and with the United States of America. All that most people knew or cared to know was that the Spanish general in Cuba was called "The Butcher." They had heard, of course, the slogan "Remember the Maine." Perhaps some soldiers thought that meant "Remember the State of Maine." The war, however, afforded President McKinley the opportunity, which he seized upon, to appoint some former Confederate officers to commands in our army and navy. Among them were Brigadier General W. W. Gordon of Savannah, Major General Fitzhugh Lee, and Major General Joseph Wheeler, one-time commander of the Wheeler cavalry. Theodore Roosevelt took the war quite seriously and collected groups of young men from all parts of our country who undoubtedly became inspired by the patriotic "Teddy." His gallant charge on San Juan Hill at the head of his "Rough Riders" won for him and them the acclaim of the whole land as heroes. Moreover, it helped elect Colonel Teddy to the office of Governor of New York, Vice President, and then President of the United States, in which offices he rendered splendid service to his state and country.

From the outbreak of World War I in 1914 to September, 1916, I was serving as Superior Court Judge; and from the latter date to the close of that war in 1918 and on, until January 1, 1937, I was serving as Justice of the Supreme Court of Georgia. Soon after my service on the latter Court began, I sought, through the Governor of Georgia, the Honorable Hugh M. Dorsey, to obtain some assignment overseas in the armed service. I had served in the old Columbus Guards early in my years in that city, and although this was an organization of state troops only, I thought my experience from private to captain in those forces had enabled me to fit in somewhere. The Governor was entirely sympathetic, but at once assured me that my age would be an insuperable barrier to the success of my application. But he said promptly: "There is a service that you can perform, and at the same time continue in your present office, in winning the war." This was to take over his duties as chairman of the State Council of Defense. By statute the Governor was chairman of that body, but a different title was given me under which to perform the same service. I accepted and derived great comfort from being of some possible service in the great struggle. There was considerable correspondence with the National Council in Washington, and it was necessary to attend its meetings there. The last meeting was called for November 10, 1918. On our assembling at 10 o'clock, a. m., the chairman, the Honorable Grover Clarkson, announced that there would be no business transacted until the next day, the 11th.

On the morning of November 11, 1918, the meeting being "in order" and the roll called, the chairman made the startling announcement that at 11 o'clock an armistice would be signed and all fighting would cease in France. It was also announced that the President would immediately advise the Congress. The thrill that ensued there in Washington and all over the land can scarcely be imagined. It seemed that everyone immediately started to the Capitol. Pennsylvania Avenue was quickly filled from sidewalk to sidewalk, streetcars and all other transportation service being blocked. The Capitol quickly filled and overflowed. Everyone was deliriously happy.

Even wars have their amusing as well as pathetic incidents. After the long strain and tension on mind and body, the sight of dead and wounded comrades, it is well that such occasions arise to bring blessed relief. One such amusing incident came just after the end of World War I. Our army was being returned, and a shipload of soldiers had landed in New York City; the men were dispersing to their homes all over the United States. It was not an incident, at such a time, to attract wide notice in the great city of New York, but it was, to newspaper reporters, deemed worth considerable space in the great metropolitan papers. It was of supreme importance to one lone Negro soldier from a coastal Georgia county.

The soldier had served faithfully and well as a truck driver and in similar duties from his arrival in France to the surrender of Germany. He had served without pay, because in some unaccountable way his name had been omitted from the payroll. As a result, although he had received food, clothing, and other necessaries, he was without cash money, and in that condition returned to New York. To make matters worse, he lost contact with his command. There he was a stranger in New York, without funds, walking the streets, hoping to find someone of his army friends or acquaintances. He could not find a familiar face, and, with nightfall approaching, he became alarmed. He was wandering aimlessly, still in the uniform of the army, and his bewildered expression attracted the attention of a New York policeman. Naturally, suspicion or curiosity led the policeman to investigation. Approaching him the policeman inquired as to his name, where he lived, what he was doing, and where he was going. According to the New York papers, as I remember it, the soldier explained:

"Boss, I come fum down in Georgy, and I wants to git home, but I ain't got no money and I ain' know nobody. I live in Liberty County, and I been in de army all de time, but dey ain' give me no money to git me back to home in Georgy."

When asked where he was staying in New York he replied, "I ain' stayin' nowhar but here on the street, and I ain' got no place to sleep tonight, and I ain' got no place to eat, cause I ain' got no money to pay fur hit."

"Well," said the policeman, "what were you doing in France?"

"Fightin'," said the perplexed soldier.

"Who?" asked the policeman.

The soldier replied: "I was fightin' dem damyankees."

By this time, as would be expected, quite a crowd had gathered around and was greatly amused by the queer colloquy between the policeman and the soldier. The gathering had attracted a newspaper reporter who quickly sensed a good story and a case of deserving human need. A collection was quickly suggested to bridge over the emergency, and the crowd as promptly relieved the immediate requirements. The story appeared in the newspaper, and thus the facts found their way to Georgia and to the home of the soldier. His friends and neighbors, quick to sense the sentimental feature as well as their neighborly duty, soon raised sufficient cash and transmitted it to New York for necessary expenses of transportation, and in addition secured enough money to purchase a farm for the soldier in his home county.

It is safe to assume that upon proper presentation of the facts Uncle Sam promptly rectified the mistake and forwarded all back pay in perfectly good coin of the realm.

This is in no sense an effort to write a history of the first World War, nor indeed of the second. Nevertheless, it may not be out of place to state in a brief manner the chief steps which led to the great conflict which has been brought to a close in Europe. In 1931 Germany began building an armed force (though in defiance of the Versailles Treaty) which was thought to be invincible. Adolph Hitler, the fanatic, crazed Austrian who had been residing in Germany since World War I and who had in some inscrutable manner become dictator of Germany, ruled under the name of "Fuehrer." He had become

Chancellor and at once disfranchised all opposition and began the persecution and ruthless murder of German Jews. Instigating the annexation of Austria and agitation in Czechoslovakia and in the "Polish Corridor" by German residents, he hoped to annex sections in those areas to Germany. The agitation in Danzig, free city in the corridor, at once aroused Poland with the fear of aggression. Great Britain and France, both having treaties with the threatened countries binding them to render assistance in such circumstances, also became aroused. The Prime Ministers of Britain, Neville Chamberlain, and of France, Deladier, flew in 1939 to Germany for a consultation with Hitler in the hope of avoiding the outbreak of war which would spread, they knew, all over Europe and possibly also to this country. Their reception was insulting. Hitler, arrogant, scolding and confident of his power, was determined to pursue his plan of conquest. Efforts to appease him were futile from the first. Utterly base and blood-thirsty, while protesting that he had no desire to acquire territory, in 1939 he invaded Czechoslovakia, Danzig, Poland, and Austria, even Denmark and Norway. Then Britain and France declared war on Germany in 1939. Germany added Belgium, Holland, and France to those countries already overrun; and at Dunkirk, having destroyed the Allied armies, drove the remnants into the Channel, capturing an immense store of British munitions. However, about 300,000 Allied soldiers, mostly British, escaped to England. The escape of so many troops, while the victorious German army with all of its might was crowding on their heels, was an achievement outstanding in the history of warfare. It evidenced the resourcefulness and sturdiness of the English people.

Then came a series of the finest and bravest acts of

leadership the world has ever seen. Winston Churchill, as the new Prime Minister, declaring the determination of the British to fight on to the last man, and warning his people that they must gird themselves to withstand a life of "blood, sweat, and tears," led the way. From that day Churchill led gloriously through the more than four years of gloom and suffering to the unconditional surrender of the Germans and our day of victory and joy. The United States, without a declaration of war, began at once to aid the British. Then came the treacherous attack of the Japanese on Pearl Harbor on December 7, 1941, when great destruction was inflicted on our fleet and death inflicted on our soldiers and sailors. That was the spark that kindled a fire in the hearts of Americans. One thing America will not calmly accept is the sinking of our battleships. "Remember the Maine" had been once the cry, and now that cry could be multiplied over and over. Our giant vessel, the Oklahoma, had been capsized at Pearl Harbor, while others were sunk; and there had been over three thousand soldiers and sailors and over a hundred officers killed. Our government at once went to war with Japan, while all political differences as to waging war were suspended "for the duration." All our resources in men and materials were at once organized and a wonderful work was done. At the darkest hour for us, the German General Rommel drove his army to a point within sixty miles of Alexandria, Egypt; but, for some reason, he stopped there as the Germans had stopped at Dunkirk. Then the English General Montgomery drove Rommel all the way back to Tunis, capturing nearly all of Rommel's army.

The Allies invaded Europe by landing on the Island of Sicily on July 10, 1943. Quickly Mussolini was ousted and was no longer "Duce." General Montgomery and

General Clark, respectively commanding British and American armies, soon liberated Italy as far north as Rome. There, or nearby, these armies remained with only small gains until the early spring of 1945.

In the meantime, on June 6, 1944, a tremendous force of Americans made an amphibious landing on the beaches of Normandy and soon chased the Germans all through France into Germany. Mussolini was killed by Italians in the vicinity of Lake Como, and his body was taken to Milan where it was treated with indignities in revenge for his leading Italy into war and into the wreck of defeat.

The Allies, American and British, soon crossed the River Rhine and, having destroyed the means of transportation, prevented reinforcements and supplies reaching the Germans. The Allied armies then quickly overran all sections. Russia, after a rest, launched a full scale offensive in the east and reached Berlin. The Allied troops reached the vicinity of Berlin before Russia, but at the latter's request permitted Russia to enter first. It was agreed to assist Russia if help were needed, but the eastern ally did not have to make the call. Many German officers were taken – Goering among them; but Hitler and Goebbels eluded the Allied grasp. It is of no consequence what became of them. Unconditional surrender signed May 9, 1945, brought peace again to Europe. Fighting continued a short time in Czechoslovakia and Austria but soon died out. After seven years of chaos Europe is at peace, but the marks of indescribable suffering are upon her everywhere. Many of these marks are proofs of warfare waged against the very canons of war itself.

President Franklin Delano Roosevelt died April 12, 1945, of cerebral hemorrhage at Warm Springs, Georgia. After a courageous and valiant fight against infantile paralysis, and without complete recovery, he was elected and served as Governor of New York four years (two terms), and was then elected President of the United States in 1932, 1936, 1940, and 1944. He had just begun serving his fourth term as President when the final blow struck him down. He was a veritable war casualty. It was truly remarkable that one having his affliction could have served four years as Governor of New York and twelve years, or more, as President of the United States, especially with war virtually on his hands during his entire third term and as much of his fourth as he lived to serve. It was a global war, too, and he had to travel over the world to confer with Prime Minister Churchill and Joseph Stalin of Russia. He was the only President of the United States to serve more than two terms. He died the idol of millions over the world, and unfortunately incurred the dislike and opposition of numerous people making a strong minority. We cannot know now what history will say of him. One thing stands out clearly — his death saved him from the fate of Woodrow Wilson, whose fondest hope was killed by the United States Senate's rejecting the League of Nations. Wilson poured out his whole strength for his reform and undoubtedly was a casualty of the peace after World War I.

Since Germany's unconditional surrender there remains in the European theater only the punishment of the war criminals and the occupation and indefinite policing of Germany. No one can say when the occupation will end, for it must be continued until Germany has re-established an orderly government capable of maintaining peace at home. The New York *Times*, in a leading editorial on the fall of Berlin, said the German government of recent years was begun in anarchy and ended in chaos. The occupation must, for the salvation of Germany as well as for the peace of the world, continue until there is satisfactory evidence that Germany has repented of her sins of war and has been converted to the bona fide belief in the virtues of peace and friendship with her neighbors.

On July 26, 1945, the radio broadcasts surprised and shocked this part of the world. The defeat of Prime Minister Winston Churchill's party by the electorate of England was announced. The later news as brought by the newspapers showed that the Prime Minister's party lost to the opposition by a landslide — the Labor party electing about two members of the House of Commons to one for Churchill's party. Churchill himself, his foreign minister Anthony Eden, and a few others of his party were returned by their constituents. Churchill obviously met the fate so often experienced by great men at the hands of ungrateful constituents. Popular favor, however well founded, has ever been fickle. Often there is no known explanation to justify it. To persons at this distance and with admittedly very limited knowledge of England's internal affairs, the resounding refusal to return Churchill's majority in Parliament seemed like base ingratitude. We shudder to think what would have happened to England and to the civilized world five years ago but for Winston Churchill.

It was in June, 1940, when Hitler reached the pinnacle of his march to conquer or destroy the world. It was on June 17, 1940, that Petain, Marshal of France, "with a broken heart," had asked the Nazi Fuehrer, as one soldier to another, for an honorable armistice. The cause for which England and the United States stood adamant was at its lowest ebb. To many it seemed that not a glimmer of hope remained for England — and perhaps for America. England had lost nearly all of her guns, tanks, and munitions; the R. A. F. was no match for the devastating air power of Germany which soon began the destruction of London. That great and historic city seemed doomed to become a gigantic pile of scrap. It was then and under those despairing circumstances that a leader of great brain and matchless courage was the only hope. Fortunately, England had such a man — Winston Churchill. Promptly he was made Prime Minister, gathering such arms and forces as were obtainable. The man and the occasion, under Providence, had met; Churchill, as some writer has said, "hunched his head down between his great shoulders and said: 'We will fight on the beaches and the landing grounds, in the fields, in the streets, on the hills. We will never surrender....' " It was Britain's time for "blood, sweat, and tears."

Under such leadership Britain's utmost was thrown into the common cause of the "United Nations" to preserve liberty against slavery. The limitations of space will not permit the tracing of events from then until the utter defeat and unconditional surrender of Germany. It will suffice to say that Germany has been completely shorn of military power and is now occupied by the Allies. It seems to be generally agreed that Churchill still retains the love and admiration of his country, that the defeat of his party was due to the long endurance of sacrificial suffering of the English people and, to some extent, to the ill-abused campaign of bitterness and "mud-slinging" which displeased the electorate. Finally, human nature down through the ages has remained much the same, at least underneath the surface. Great praise and laudation centered on any individual for a considerable space of time often themselves engender a reaction. From jealousy or other motives, such reaction brings opposition and hostile criticism. Aristides, an Athenian whose equity and integrity gained for him the glorious appellation of "The Just," lived some five centuries B. C. He had been a great hero in Athenian wars and a wise and patriotic chief magistrate. He was leader of what was called the "democratical party" and was thus the opponent of Themistocles. "His patriotism and self-denial were strongly manifested by giving up his share of the command to Miltiades before the Battle of Marathon; and his conduct after the battle, when entrusted to divide the spoils, was equally praiseworthy. Themistocles succeeded in having him sentenced to banishment for ostracism. On this occasion a voter . . . explained his opposition. When asked if Aristides ever injured him he replied: 'No, but I am tired of hearing him called the Just'."

On the next day after the world was apprized of the political defeat of Churchill's party and his automatic removal as Prime Minister, our own learned and beloved Senator Walter F. George said of him on the floor of the United States Senate:

> A great man has fallen in Britain. A great man who revived and bolstered the moral courage of the British people and of nearly all the free people of this earth in that dark hour when the Axis powers stood in battle array across the narrow channel which separates French territory. . . .

A radio broadcaster expressed this opinion: "To Americans Churchill is the greatest Englishman of all times." Certainly, I think that is true of Americans who have closely followed world events for the last five years. And, it must be remembered that we view those events through our own glasses and from our viewpoints. This is nowise a criticism of the English voters who were guided by their own lights and by their own political influences. The world is fortunate in the assurance that the new English Prime Minister, Clement Attlee, is so well qualified by experience, education, and mental balance that war and post-war affairs will not suffer to any great extent.

If there is a Valhalla for heroic statesmen, Winston Churchill will find in that abode among the truly great a merited repose for the aeons beyond our ken.

Friday, August 10, 1945. At 7:30 this morning the Tokyo Broadcast announced the offer of surrender and acceptance of the Potsdam proclamation *provided* that Emperor Hirohito's sovereign prerogatives are not disturbed. Well, that's a pretty large proviso; and the offer has not yet been accepted by the Allies. However, it has brought jubilation and joy throughout most of the world. Here, in our country, there has been little or no demonstration of hilarity. The country is awaiting definite conclusion of the negotiations. Our Government, through President Truman and Secretary of State James F. Byrnes, is conferring with Britain, Russia, and China on the proper response to be made to Japan.

Saturday, August 11, 11 o'clock, a. m. The radio has just announced that the Allies have replied to the Japanese conditional offer of surrender, stating that Japan might retain its Emperor, *but* he must rule subject to strict military supervision of the Allies. That seems to be both a statesman-like solution and a humanitarian one as well. We await now Japan's reply.

Sunday, August 12. The great hoax! From seven o'clock, a. m., this writer sat for hours beside the radio hoping to receive the joyous news of Japanese surrender according to Allied terms. At intervals came announcements that there had been no reply received in Washington nor in Bern, Switzerland, through which neutral country the negotiations have been conducted.

Monday, August 13. The same rumors and some apparently reliable announcements were made, only to be denied. The suspense of the world grew in intensity but remained unrelieved.

Tuesday, August 14. Early this morning it was announced that the Japanese reply to our ultimatum had been received in Switzerland and was believed to be an acceptance of our terms. At noon this was totally denied. Finally, at 6:00 p. m., Central War Time, President Truman permitted the announcement to be made on his authority that the reply had been received by him. Here are his words:

> I have received this afternoon a message from the Japanese Government in reply to the message forwarded to that government by the Secretary of State on August 11.
>
> I deem this reply a full acceptance of the Potsdam declaration which specifies unconditional surrender of Japan. In the reply there is no qualification.
>
> Arrangements are now being made for the formal signing of surrender terms at the earliest possible moment.
>
> General Douglas MacArthur has been appointed the supreme Allied commander to receive the Japanese surrender. Great Britain, Russia, and China will be represented by high ranking officers.
>
> Meantime, the Allied armed forces have been ordered to suspend offensive action.
>
> The proclamation of V-J Day must wait upon the formal signing of the surrender terms by Japan.

All over America and the Allied countries the people demonstrated their happy relief from the strain of years in unrestrained impromptu celebrations. In the midst of our overflowing joy we are sobered by the thoughts of our beloved heroes who have suffered and bled and of those who have paid the supreme sacrifice by which the victory has been achieved.

Wednesday, August 15. The morning after our triumph on land, in air, and on the seas — Blessed Peace! One thinks of Kipling's classic "Recessional."

> God of our fathers, known of old,
>   Lord of our far-flung battle-line,
> Beneath whose awful Hand we hold
>   Dominion over palm and pine —
> Lord God of Hosts, be with us yet,
> Lest we forget — lest we forget!
>
> The tumult and the shouting dies;
>   The captains and the kings depart;
> Still stands Thine ancient sacrifice,
>   An humble and a contrite heart.
> Lord God of Hosts, be with us yet,
> Lest we forget — lest we forget!

While the war was over except in a few isolated areas in the far flung islands, peace had actually arrived on the main fronts. The unconditional surrender had not been formally and officially signed. That required some negotiation between representatives of Japan and General MacArthur, the officially designated representative of the United Nations. These consultations and negotiations were held in Manila and were strictly according to orders of General MacArthur and the approval of President Truman. The program adopted and substantially executed (a severe tropical storm or typhoon caused a few hours delay in some details) was fully carried out with military ceremony. The entire program was completed with cooperation and exceptional courtesy by the Japanese. As announced, August 27, 1945, through the Associated Press the program was as follows:

Here is the MacArthur time table for occupation and surrender of Japan (dates given in Japanese time, one day in advance of U. S. time):

MONDAY, Aug. 27—Third Fleet spearhead anchors in Sagami Bay, 24 hours ahead of MacArthur's schedule.
TUESDAY, Aug. 28—Advance fleet units enter Tokyo Bay; preparatory air force lands at Atsugi Airfield.
THURSDAY, Aug. 30—Ten thousand marines and sailors begin occupation of Yokosuka Naval Base; MacArthur lands at Atsugi with first wave of airborne occupation troops.
SATURDAY, Sept. 1—Lieut. General Robert L. Eichelberger's Eighth Army scheduled to begin landings for occupation of Tokyo and Yokohama areas.
SUNDAY, Sept. 2—Formal surrender ceremonies aboard U. S. S. *Missouri* in Tokyo Bay.
MONDAY, Sept. 3—Advance airborne party lands at Kanoya preparatory to occupation of Kyushu Island; by-passed island garrisons, including Truk, scheduled to begin surrendering.

General MacArthur has landed, on schedule. Admiral Nimitz is on the *Missouri* in Tokyo Bay. General Wainwright, the hero of Bataan, who had spent many weary months in Japanese war prisons, and other heroes flew to Japan on invitation of General MacArthur to witness the final and formal surrender.

The scenes were impressive with thousands of our war machines fully manned on the Japanese homeland. Every branch of the service was included, led by marines. One scene was most pathetic — that of our sick and wounded men, delivered from prisons and placed on mercy ships to be transported to our hospitals and to their homes. General MacArthur soon after his landing at Yokohama, his temporary headquarters, issued a statement of which the following is a part:

> Melbourne to Tokyo was a long, hard road. But this looks like the payoff. The surrender plan is going on completely according to previous arrangement. . . .
> The Japanese seem to be acting in complete good faith and there is every prospect of the success of the capitulation without undue friction and without unnecessary bloodshed.

Saturday, September 1, Atlanta time, 8 o'clock p. m. The radio gave us the news of the signing of the unconditional surrender of Japan. The signing had actually occurred a short time earlier in the day and was recorded. The broadcast was from the record. It was one of the most momentous occasions in the world's history. It was impressive, dignified and inspiring. The proceedings on board the *U. S. S. Missouri*, flagship of Admiral Nimitz, were conducted by General MacArthur, who opened them by a few well-chosen words, fully equal to the occasion. He spoke in part:

> It is my earnest hope and indeed the hope of all mankind that from this solemn occasion a better world shall emerge out of the blood and carnage of the past — a world founded upon faith and understanding — a world dedicated to the dignity of man and the fulfillment of his most cherished wish — for freedom, tolerance and justice. . . .
>
> As supreme commander for the Allied Powers, I announce it my firm purpose, in the tradition of the countries I represent, to proceed in the discharge of my responsibilities with justice and tolerance, while taking all necessary dispositions to insure that the terms of surrender are fully, promptly and faithfully complied with.

The representatives of the Emperor of Japan and the Japanese Government and the Japanese Imperial Government quickly signed, followed by General MacArthur representing the nations at war with Japan. Then followed the representatives of the United Kingdom, the Union of Soviet Socialist Republics, Australia, Canada, the Netherlands, and New Zealand.

General MacArthur then said: "Let us pray that peace be now restored to the world, and that God will preserve it always. These proceedings are closed." This was followed by an eloquent radio address of the President from the White House.

General MacArthur's concluding speech by radio to the American people was in part:

Today the guns are silent. A great tragedy has ended. A great victory has been won. The skies no longer rain death — the seas bear only commerce — men everywhere walk upright in the sunlight. The entire world is quietly at peace. The holy mission has been completed and in reporting this to you, the people, I speak for the thousands of silent lips, forever stilled among the jungles and the beaches and in the deep waters of the Pacific which marked the way. I speak for the unnamed brave millions homeward bound to take up the challenge of that future which they did so much to salvage from the brink of disaster. . . .

And so, my fellow countrymen, today I report to you that your sons and daughters have served you well and faithfully with the calm, deliberate, determined fighting spirit of the American soldier and sailor, based upon a tradition of historical trait, as against the fanaticism of an enemy supported only by mythological fiction; their spiritual strength and power has brought us through to victory. They are homeward bound— take care of them.

An American who does not thrill with pride in our men and women who have achieved the glorious victory, and who fails to feel an abiding sorrow for those who have bled and died is unworthy of his priceless heritage. Surely these are very, very few. Two thousand years ago, when Rome was at the zenith of her power, it was the proudest boast to claim "I am a Roman citizen." Indeed St. Paul himself found refuge in his Roman citizenship. May an overruling Providence so continue to guide us along the difficult days ahead, at home and abroad, that American citizenship shall afford an open-sesame all over a friendly world. May our forces of occupation in all subjugated countries adopt and apply the motto on the Great Seal of Georgia — "Wisdom, Justice and Moderation." Thus, and thus only, may we educate conquered peoples into our conception of our way of life.

Henry Van Dyke called Alfred Tennyson "the poet of the endless life." That was because, as Van Dyke said, the poetry of Tennyson reflects a profoundly religious spirit. His faith in God and in goodness is evident in his treatment of the world and nature. An atheist or an agnostic could not have written such poetry. At such a time as this, these words from "Locksley Hall" come to mind, and appropriately find place – a rightful place:

> Men, my brothers, men the workers, ever
>   reaping something new;
> That which they have done but earnest of
>   the things that they shall do;
>
> For I dipt into the future, far as human eye
>   could see,
> Saw the Vision of the world, and all the
>   wonder that would be;
>
> Saw the heavens fill with commerce, argosies
>   of magic sails,
> Pilots of the purple twilight, dropping down
>   with costly bales;
>
> Heard the heavens fill with shouting, and
>   there rained a ghastly dew
> From the nations' airy navies grappling in
>   the central blue;
>
> Far along the world-wide whisper of the
>   south-wind rushing warm,
> With the standards of the peoples plunging
>   through the thunder-storm;
>
> Till the war drum throbbed no longer, and
>   the battle flags were furled
> In the Parliament of man, the Federation of
>   the world.
>
> There the common sense of most shall hold
>   a fretful realm in awe,
> And the kindly earth shall slumber, lapt in
>   universal law.

CHAPTER XIV

Travels

WHEN in October, 1944, while enjoying my breakfast, I read on the front page of the Atlanta *Constitution* this large headline — "Russian Troops in Arctic, Reach Norwegian Border" — a flood of delightful recollections came to mind — recollections that are still fresh and cannot be forgotten. In 1935 Mrs. Gilbert and I were members of a party that filled the Swedish-American liner *Kingsholm* which took the cruise to the "North Cape, Russian and Lands of the Vikings." There were seventeen Georgians, most of whom were our personal friends of many years' standing. The term "Lands of the Vikings" included for this cruise, if not strictly so, the following: Iceland, Norway, Sweden, Finland, Denmark, Latvia, Estonia, and Lithuania. The word "Viking" does not apply, so far as I have been able to ascertain, to any definitely prescribed territory. So I use it as it was used by the officials of the Swedish-American Line. That tour increased our interest in World War II whenever in Norway, Russia, Finland, Denmark, there were happenings reported in the press; and it also increased our interest in German pressure on Sweden. When our morning newspaper said in part: "Russian troops, driving the Germans out of the valuable nickel mine country in Northern Finland, have smashed the Norwegian border along a fifty-four mile front to stand within three miles of Kirkenes," that was good news. Even to know that one of our allies, Russia, had ousted the Germans from those nickel mines was good news. But to learn that they had crossed the border into Norway was really heartening.

Looking at the map, you will find an unusually ragged and uneven boundary line to Norway. It is a very long, very narrow strip of land, nearly all mountainous from its southern tip to the northern, about eleven hundred miles. About three to four hundred miles are within the Arctic Circle. Norway reaches around and over the north line of Sweden and almost across the north line of Finland. Except for the harbor and the villages of Petsamo, that small strip is useful only to Laplanders. Parenthetically, while there are Laplanders, not so many, there is no Lapland. What is called Lapland is that very cold stretch of land across the top of Norway, Sweden, and Finland where Laplanders and no one else want to or can exist. They are a roving tribe, with a language of their own, who are harmless and are permitted to go about as they wish. Kirkenes is approximately twenty-five miles below the seventieth degree, thus not as far north as North Cape by probably around one hundred miles.

The cruise begins at New York, making its first stop at Iceland. There we see something entirely different from any other country. Its name Iceland is misleading. That wonderful Gulf Stream turns the trick and makes it habitable. First we are surprised, the moment that we are on the docks, that we do not need a topcoat on a clear, sunny day in August. We are warned, if we are going inland, to take along a sweater, just in case. We anchor a quarter mile off shore. Why? Possibly, because the boat is large, the dock is small; the charge for docking is saved; we transfer in small boats over rather rough water (on our day there), everyone taking the waves hilariously. It is soon over. We are on the docks, in

Reykjavik, capital of Iceland. Reykjavik (steaming bay) gets its name from a flowing well or spring of hot water two miles from the bay. It is pronounced, as nearly as I can indicate, "Reek a veek." You walk about the streets of a city of 26,000 to 27,000 people, friendly and intelligent — no beggars, no illiteracy, negligible crime, a small but nice hotel, some shops of various kinds, chiefly offering souvenirs of Iceland. They are loosely governed by the King of Denmark, but actually are independent. Iceland has now formally declared itself an independent republic. The principal mode of making a living is fishing and canning fish. The chief agricultural products are turnips, potatoes, and hay. The natural covering of the ground, seemingly everywhere, is boulders of all sizes — but almost no trees. You would have to search for a tree — there are a few on the island. There are a few shrubs in the city of Reykjavik, protected by the buildings.

In the winter months daylight lasts only a few hours and the nights are long. For about nine months a year little work requiring daylight can be accomplished. The people are friendly, especially to Americans. They number, throughout the island, a little more than 100,000. Leaving Reykjavik, we are soon across the Arctic Circle and we remain on deck, waiting to see the midnight sun. We are rewarded by clear weather and read from a newspaper at midnight without any artificial light.

On shipboard is a post office where all letters mailed while the ship is in Arctic waters are stamped with the words, "Arctic Circle," with date. Hammerfest is the town farthest north of all settlements in the world. In August it is quite a busy little place with a number of stores and residences. We see numbers of window sills decorated with growing, bright flowers. It is about 300 miles north of the Arctic Circle. North Cape, from which the cruise takes its name, is about fifty or seventy-five miles north of Hammerfest, and it is the extreme northernmost point to which commercial vessels penetrate the Arctic. At that point there is not one house; there is one covered shack to protect from rain those who stop to buy souvenirs — mainly post cards. The only living object in sight, save those on the ship, was one lone Laplander with his reindeer. He is friendly and grateful for any gifts, especially tobacco in any form. No one could understand his language, but he could indicate his thanks by motions and smiles.

The Cape is reached by sailing up the fjords for most of the approximately 1100 miles along the coast of Norway. It is not just one fjord. There are numbers of them connecting, so that there is a continuous inner water course. There is an occasional break, showing a village or inhabited area, very green and peaceful. On the other side the break shows the ocean, which is very rough and dangerous to sailing. The elongated pieces of land next to the ocean, which form the fjords between them and the mainland as seen from the ship's deck, are apparently just islands. For almost all of their course, except the breaks, these islands have abrupt banks and perpetual snow. In summer when cruises or navigation are attempted, the snow on both sides is melting, causing immense waterfalls which look like milk, as white as the snow itself. These waterfalls are so numerous they are constantly in sight. These islands act as breakwaters and the sailing is as smooth as on an inland lake.

John L. Stoddard, in his beautiful and interesting lectures, wrote: "Of all countries on our globe, Norway, in some respects, must rank as the most wonderful." To describe adequately the scenery of Norway, one must be a Stoddard and possess his power of description. I will only add that all of Norway is a continuous exhibition of mountains, water-courses, waterfalls, verdant valleys, clean villages, towns, and cities of fine, hospitable, lovable people. I think no one, having traversed Norway, will take issue with Stoddard. A nation must be guided by the instincts of barbarism to invade and despoil that peaceful and lovable people. They are a people devoted to the beauties and inspiring influences of their own scenery. Their music reflects the imagery that the God of nature has bountifully bestowed upon them. In their streets they have erected monuments to Ole Bull and Edvard Grieg. Norway is proud of its other native sons and daughters who have attained distinction in the arts and in letters, such as Ibsen, Bjornson, Dahl, the painter, Ludwig Holbert, the poet, and Flagstad, one of the real stars of opera. The country has a small population, only some 3,000,000 people before World War II, probably less now.

With these brief glances at Norway as a whole, we return to the cruise and make our first stop on the return from North Cape at a small village called Lyngen. The attraction causing the stop is the Lapp village just outside Lyngen. This village consists of some less than a dozen canvas tents, spread over two or three acres of vacant cleared land. There are Lapps of all ages, whose pictures can be had for a consideration paid in advance. They have a few trinkets for sale. All wear animal skins in winter, and whatever is obtainable to supplement them. Their appearance gives little hint of acquaintance with soap and water. They really seem to be a useless and purposeless race. On the other hand, they are not depriving anyone else of territory—no one else will occupy it. At Lyngen we ride to the Lapp village and return in a "stolkjaerre" — a four-seated vehicle drawn by small, ill-kept horses.

At one point, as we come down the fjord, we slow down but do not stop, while a large drove of reindeer are led out from the shore, swim around the boat and return to the shore. Next, we reach Trondheim. As explained above, we do not travel a single fjord, but a number of them, as one might travel several streets in a city to go from one point to another. Trondheim is approached through the beautiful Trondheimsfjord. It is Norway's third largest city and has a population of fifty or sixty thousand. It is a rather up-to-date city. The old Royal Palace is there. It is called "Stifsgaarden." The city was founded in A. D. 996 by Olav Tryggvesson, whose statue stands in the main square. Its chief attraction is the Cathedral, built in the Middle Ages and still being "repaired" when we were there. After a lengthy drive over the heights overlooking Trondheim, we return to the Brittania Hotel for an excellent lunch and the dance afterwards.

Only Bergen and Oslo, two beautiful, modern cities, can be mentioned, as full justice may not be done in limited space to our entire trip in this wonderful land. In these cities the shops are up-to-date, and the points of interest are many. Oslo is the capital and there we see some of the largest and finest stores, dealing in fine silver and glass. Oslo is also the largest city in Norway. There we are shown at the Open Air Museum a collection of Viking ships dug out of a burial mound a few years ago. They date back to about A. D. 850, and are almost intact.

We leave Norway and enter Sweden, but not yet Stockholm, its capital. We have docked at Visby — the city of "Roses and Ruins." One is really intrigued with Visby. Different from every other city, it seems to hold out both arms to you and to say: Here is rest and contentment. It is on the Island of Gotland. It is one of the most ancient cities visited on our cruise. It was an important trading center during the Middle Ages and the first of the Hanseatic League cities to assume commercial and political leadership in the Baltic regions. Its mighty walls are overgrown with roses. The gallows, where they hanged the pirates and thus broke up the strongly entrenched piratical rule in that part of the world, still stands. It is somewhat rusty from long disuse, but may be useful as a reminder.

From Visby, which is a part of Sweden, we leave Sweden temporarily but will visit Stockholm before the cruise is ended. We next make a short visit to Tallin, the capital and largest city of Estonia. This is one of the small Baltic States invaded by Germany, but later won from Germany by Russia. It remains to be seen what disposition Russia will make of it. My guess is that she will retain some kind of control over it, as well as over Lithuania and Latvia, other Baltic States.

And now Russia – the Union of Soviet Socialistic Republics. Russia is the great question mark. It is the country that revolted against the most extreme dictatorial totalitarianism to become, ostensibly, the most democratic government of the proletariat which history has known.

The Soviet when organized was called a government by the proletariat. That is a government by the laboring class or wage earners. That may have been the plan or conception of Lenin and others of its earliest leaders; but it has become, as well as can be determined by the lights afforded us, a dictatorship of the few—an oligarchy.

Russia is large in area and in population. All on the cruise are curious to know how the Russian people look, and how we will be received, and whether we shall be permitted to see inside the Kremlin. Some even wished to taste Russian vodka – with one taste, that curiosity ended. In fact, one curiosity ended before we reached Russia; it was officially announced that the Kremlin was closed for repairs and that there would be no admittance. Arriving at the docks in Leningrad, we saw that the few Russians in sight went about their business with scarcely a glance at the big Swedish-American liner. Transferred to automobiles and set off upon a sight-seeing tour, we observed the same solemn demeanor of the Russian people. There was sign neither of dislike nor welcome. It was like the weather they could do nothing about. The number of working men strolling the streets seemed large, but it was explained they were on a 5-day shift, one-fifth being idle every day. They all wore caps, jackets, and apparently cloth shoes. One peculiar thing was that women were working on the street car tracks, turning switches. No tourist could ride on a street car because only Russian money was acceptable for fare, and no tourist was allowed to have any Russian money.

The same difficulty was encountered as to stores. There were special stores for tourists where money of any country was accepted, but no Russian money. Russians could not trade in these tourist stores, called "Torgsin." More than that, in 1935, different stores were provided for different classes of Russians. The army, public officers, the private citizens, with the real proletariat at the bottom of the list, traded at different stores which offered varying grades of goods. The army was at the top, the proletariat at the bottom. Of course, we learned these facts from different sources, since we could trade only in Torgsin. We depended upon our guides to do all bargaining, since we spoke no Russian.

The most beautiful building in Leningrad is the Cathedral of St. Isaacs, begun in 1819, completed in 1858, costing some twenty million dollars. In 1935 it was used as an anti-religious museum. The Soviet changed the name of the city from St. Petersburg to Leningrad. and they changed the capital of Russia from this city to Moscow. They seemed to have abandoned Leningrad to decay. The streets were full of holes in 1935; the buildings needed paint and many windowpanes were missing from buildings on prominent streets. Both Leningrad and Moscow are very large cities, two million people being claimed by the former at the time we were there, with Moscow claiming three and a half millions. Both probably had even larger populations prior to the revolution of 1917. Many points of interest are in both — palaces, art galleries, cathedrals. For small fees tourists were guided through the Palace of Peter the Great, the Marble Palace, and, just outside Leningrad, the former Tsorskoye Selo, where the royal family resided up to the time of their arrest and from whence they were said to have been taken to Siberia, or the Urals, after which they were never heard of. Apparently nothing had been changed in the Royal Palace. The pictures (one of Rasputin in the Czarina's chamber), the draperies, beds, the Czar's writing room, and even a letter the Czar was writing when the blow fell — all were unchanged. The guide pointed to a bullet hole in the glass window near the Czar's desk — the bullet obviously having miscarried. The most unexpected exhibition was the Crown Jewels in the Hermitage Palace. I could hardly believe my eyes, for I had supposed that the chaos following the revolution had scattered all such things, royal or private. On the contrary, perfect order and control over these marvelous gems were maintained, all property being preserved for the new government. Peterhoff, to my mind, was the most beautiful of all the palaces in Russia, and considered with its setting it is likely the most beautiful in the world. The fountains are considered more beautiful than those at Versailles. They extend down the sides of flights of stairs leading from terrace to terrace as far as the eye can see. The figures in the fountain are gilded and in sunlight shine like gold through the myriad sprays of water.

Having left Leningrad at 10:00 p. m., we arrived in Moscow at 11 o'clock the next morning. The Russians call the city Moskva, for the river that runs through it. Moscow is the great city of Russia. Again quoting Stoddard: "Moscow is farther east than Jerusalem. Like Constantinople, it is situated where the two great divisions of our globe, the Orient and the Occident, forever gaze into each other's eyes." This must be kept in mind when we endeavor to understand the Russians, and especially when we think of Josef Stalin, the present ruler. He is a native of that Georgia which is a part of Russia in its Transcaucasian region. It borders on Turkey and Armenia. Russia is so large that it contains Orientals and Occidentals. It has many tribes speaking so many dialects that many do not understand the language of others. There are cultured people, even great artists, among the Russian people, but they also have illiterates, semi-barbarians, half-civilized races. Russia reaches from Poland to China. It soon may extend its borders to the region of East Prussia, thus taking off a slice of the German Fatherland. Moscow, unlike Leningrad (I like the old name, St. Petersburg), has not been neglected. Although already a beautiful city, it is being constantly more beautified by the widening of streets and erection of modern buildings. The government owns all the real estate and thus may tear down or put up buildings at its own pleasure. I was told by a high Russian official that the entire city would be made new, especially as to all streets, and that the population would be limited to five millions. The

Kremlin is the pride of Moscow, and the object of curiosity to all visitors. Few succeed in gratifying their curiosity. It was originally inclosed by walls of wood. The towers on the river side reach 100 feet above it. The Kremlin has been called the "Acropolis of Moscow."

The most magnificent church in Moscow is "The Church of the Savior," which was begun in 1813. It stands out above all other structures and may be seen from all parts of the city. Its splendor rivals that of any church in the world. The cost is not known but must have been enormous. "Red Square" has been heard of all over the world since the revolution that inaugurated the present government. To most people the name denotes bloodshed and horror. When there we were told by our guide that the square, very old, had always been known by that name which, in Russian, means "beautiful." I do not vouch for the accuracy of that statement. But this is true: there is nothing about this square to justify the word beautiful. It is large and suitable as a drill or parade ground for troops. Across one side is a wall of the Kremlin and next to the wall are tiers of seats used by spectators on gala occasions when troops are reviewed. About middle way of this side, just in front of the seats, is the tomb of Lenin. It was constantly under guard and was regarded as sacred.

It was my pleasure and honor to be included in a small party invited to the American Embassy for lunch with Ambassador Bullitt. I was informed by our chauffeur that, from my hotel, The Metropole, to the Embassy we traversed the same boulevard used by Napoleon when he led his army into Moscow and to disaster. The Ambassador was a delightful host, an interesting conversationist, and not an "all out" believer in Soviet or Bolshevist governments. I also had the honor of attending a dinner given by four Soviet officials in a private dining room of the National Hotel. The invitation was arranged for by our friend Hugh Richardson who, with Mrs. Richardson, their daughter Louise, and friend Miss Anne Alston, all of Atlanta, had preceded me to Moscow. The dinner was modern, served in a fashionable way; the food was excellent. Four fish courses were served, beginning with caviar (which I do not like) and ending with salmon (which I do not like) and including two other fish courses prepared in different ways. There were five other courses, quite familiar. Several wines were served also.

After returning to Leningrad, we proceeded across the Gulf of Finland, landing at Helsingfors, called Helsinki by the Finns. It is the capital and largest city of Finland. It was formerly a Grand Duchy of Russia. At the fall of Czar Nicholas, it formed an independent republic in 1917. As a small, independent government, it soon won the sympathy of the world and something more than sympathy in America by continuing the payment of the interest on its "World War I" debt to the United States. The country's population prior to the war was about three and a half millions. They are a hardened, industrious, patriotic people. They earn their living under most adverse conditions. In part the country is a watery wilderness, the northern part being habitable only to those of stamina and indomitable courage. They, despite all adversities, are an educated, clean, upright people and deserve the best of treatment at the Peace Table.

Stockholm! The Swedes call it the loveliest city in Europe. What they really mean, and are fully justified in saying, is that Stockholm is the loveliest city in the world. Everyone exaggerates when speaking of his home city, but in the case of Stockholm only slight exaggeration is required. Any stranger becomes eloquent in its praise.

Sweden has other cities, such as Gothenburg, but Stockholm, the capital, is the center of learning and culture, both as to the old and as to the new or progressive age. They claim that their Town Hall is the finest piece of architecture in the world of the modern type. It cost ten million dollars. Its interior is "a stunning room in a gold mosaic." You approach Stockholm through a blue channel studded with green islands. It is built partly on thirteen islands, and partly on the mainland, all connected by attractive bridges, reminding one of Amsterdam and Venice. In fact, it is called "the Venice of the North." It has a population of more than half a million and is a friendly city, with good hotels and excellent shops that show fair dealing. No beggars were observed, no slums were seen; they have very little crime.

While there I visited a court, witnessing the trial of a criminal case. On the day before, at a luncheon attended by a large party, a gentleman approached me, inquiring if there was any special thing I wished to see. I replied I wished to see a Swedish court in action. He at once handed me his engraved card, showing that he was a retired Naval officer, and said that if I would call at his office the next day he would introduce a Swedish lawyer who would be delighted to escort me to a court. Promptly at 10 o'clock the next morning I was there, and met an attractive lawyer, a graduate of Columbia University, New York. He afforded me a pleasant morning and a chance to observe a Swedish court. No juries are employed in Swedish trials. I asked the lawyer if he were familiar with the jury system in New York. He replied in the affirmative but stated that he preferred the Swedish system and that the Swedish Bar had no desire to institute the jury system.

In American cities the section along rivers usually is

given over to the "tough" or criminal element, and "dives" are to be expected there. Not so in Stockholm. Its most attractive section is around the bend of the watercourse. The finest hotels, stores, even the Royal Palace, front the water, reminding one of some fashionable resort. The terrain rises from the waterfront to high points on overhanging mountains. On well-paved roads one may drive up on the mountain to the loveliest points of recreation and entertainment.

Gothenburg, the second city, with a population of a quarter-million, is attractive and picturesque. There is a valley around the bend of the shore, and then the terrain takes an upturn, much like Honolulu. It is the eastern terminus of the Swedish-American Line and the home of many of its officers. At an outdoor luncheon, elaborate and well-served, we heard an excellent orchestra play "Dixie." A group of us took a beautiful drive through the country to the home of the president of the Swedish-American Line, where we were entertained at a most elaborate outdoor tea. It gave us a fine impression of the well-kept country homes.

And now Denmark, with its reminder of the great play *Hamlet* and Kronborg Castle at Elsinore. At Helsinki we had received a wire from Mr. North Winship of Macon, Georgia, Counsel for the American Embassy, inviting us to tea. It was a delightful hour with him and his charming wife. Earlier, Mrs. Ruth Bryan Owen, Minister to Denmark from the United States, had invited us for the same afternoon; so we also had an hour with that beautiful and charming woman, daughter of William Jennings Bryan and today Mrs. Borge Rohde.

The highlight of the trip was the visit to Elsinore, a short distance outside Copenhagen. Here Shakespeare laid the scene of his play *Hamlet*. The castle is still there, well preserved and used as a garrison for soldiers. There is a moat surrounding the castle, the beautiful, clear waters flowing freely, and there is a drawbridge and portcullis. The courtyard within the four walls of the castle is large enough for drill by a company of soldiers. Opening onto the courtyard is a small chapel. Townspeople can show you where Hamlet walked on a terrace when delivering his famous soliloquy. Outside the grounds are souvenir shops. May that castle remain to the end of time!

The streets of Copenhagen are busy with many bicycle riders. Denmark is mainly agricultural, exporting bacon, eggs, and butter all over the world. Like all Scandinavian countries, it is a constitutional monarchy with a homogeneous population and hardly any foreign population. It seems a sacrilege for a strong, brutal country like Nazi Germany to have subjugated such a land as Denmark. But the God of Justice has redeemed these excellent people from such slavery. May He ever afterward paralyze the arm that strikes them!

All these Scandinavian people command the respect and admiration of every tourist. Their respect for the law makes it almost unnecessary for one to watch his personal property anywhere in the Scandinavian countries.

We took on board the *Kingsholm*, as it bade farewell to Copenhagen, a good supply of Coca-Cola to last the party until its return to New York, out next port of entry. When we reached that port, our friends welcomed us back to Manhattan Island and beyond to the hinterlands of America—where we found the best of all the countries of the globe. We also, I must add, found the customs officers in full force. There, also, "Honesty is the Best Policy!"

I shall continue to detail my travels in Europe, through lands which since were overrun by Hitler. In some of them the Germans overran extensive lands, then outran the Allies getting out — out of Russia, out of Tunis, out of Normandy, Paris, Marseilles, through Belgium, out of Aachen. But I refer to the war only because it has covered lands I visited; I would not undertake here to deal with the war *per se*. Bad as was the subjugation of Czechoslovakia and Poland, the outstanding shock came with the fall of France in 1940. Proud and brave as France had been through the ages, it seemed a shame beyond conception for this country to go down before Hitler's hordes as readily as she did. Many of us felt indignant toward France as well as toward Germany. It appears now that the future historians must record that the land had considerably decayed internally. It had been infested with political heresies that divided the land into numerous groups and parties, dissipating its national strength. Its fall was a mere "push-over" for Germany. We are reminded of conditions that led to the French Revolution. The French Revolution was a drunken debauch from an overdose of democracy, led by barbarians.

My visits to Paris left lasting impressions though they were certainly of the surface variety. Outward evidences disclosed, with respect to the people there, an excitable nature even as to matters of small moment and about matters with which they were little connected. For instance, on one of our visits to Paris, the New York *Herald*, published there, had printed for several days news of Sacco and Vanzetti, the two anarchists whose murder trials had dragged along for seven years and whose execution had been postponed several times. Finally, one morning the paper came out with the news that the two had been put to death in Massachusetts. Immediately a riot started in Paris streets, and by nightfall pedestrians were scurrying for cover, while firing was heard in several streets. Our hotel room opened upon the boulevard; we could see the crowds and hear the noise. The next day small stores and fruit and news stands refused to sell to people from *Amerique*. Soon a long line of artillery was seen moving on a street parallel to the Seine. It had come in from an army barracks to quiet the rioters. A million dollars' worth of French property had been destroyed on streets and boulevards, and all because, at the end of a long and costly trial which had been reviewed by the Supreme Court of Massachusetts, two anarchists had been convicted of cold-blooded murder of a fellow being in the U. S. A., not in France! It is highly doubtful if on that day a French redcap could have been induced to touch a single piece of American baggage at any price.

Paris has many beauty spots of great historic interest. Its food is famous; and shops, large and small, delight the women. It has wonderful public buildings and gardens. The outlying country is in harmony. Its cathedrals, *Notre Dame* and the *Madeleine* in Paris, those of Chartres and Rheims, the ancient palaces, such as Fontainebleau and Versailles — all speak to us of a glorious past. We are all tremendously gratified that France is free again to establish her own government and take up her career where it was so suddenly and brutally cut off by the enemy. What her people have suffered in the interval cannot now be known, nor shall I attempt to describe it.

We in the United States of America are a peace-loving people; our foremost wish is to so live in the family of nations that we may do business on a basis of merit with all of them.

During a tour of the South, just following the close of the Spanish-American War, the late President William McKinley said in a public address: "It is the triumphs of peace that the American people are striving for today.

We are not a pirate power; we are a peace power. We love peace better than war and our swords should never be drawn except in a righteous cause and then never until every effort at peace and arbitration has been exhausted." We ardently hope to visit other countries as neighbors, enjoy their arts and objects of interest, and to meet and deal with them on terms of cordiality. We look for no return of our huge loans to other lands made after World War I, for only little Finland has acknowledged the indebtedness even so much as to pay any interest. We do not begrudge this money, since we ourselves became involved in war. In World War II we are repeating this philanthropy, notwithstanding our experience in the last war. We do not overlook our own interest in this, but we do not forget that from the first act of war by Germany we aided France and Britain promptly. After the first World War, those with whom we had fought made complaint against us, and even today complaints against us are coming out of various sections of Europe, particularly Italy and France. The DeGaulle regime especially complained, notwithstanding the fact that our men waded through water and faced German bullets in order to land in Normandy and elsewhere in France to free the country.

Dunkirk! Following the French debacle came Dunkirk and loss of the British and Belgian armies fighting with the French, save the comparatively few who escaped back to Britain. It is said the British succeeded in evacuating 300,000 men, despite their losses. That evacuation was the most amazing achievement in the world's war history. The British have known obstacles only to overcome them. The full story of this amazing enterprise must await a later day for the telling; but all the world recognizes it as a great achievement. Editorially, the New

York *Times* declared on June 1, 1940: "So long as the English tongue survives, the word Dunkirk will be spoken with reverence. For in that harbor, in such a hell as never blazed on earth before at the end of a lost battle, the rags and blemishes that have hidden the soul of democracy fall away. There, beaten, but unconquered, in shining splendor, she faced the enemy. . . . It was the common man of the free countries rising in all his glory out of mill, office, factory, mine, farm, and ship, applying to war the lessons learned when he went down the shaft to bring up trapped comrades, when he hurled the lifeboat through the surf, when he endured poverty and hard work for his children's sake. This shining thing in the souls of free men, Hitler cannot command, or attain, or conquer. He has crushed it where he could from German hearts."

Germany, at the zenith of her power, failed to invade Britain. But England worked on, improving each shining hour, getting ready to strike back at the enemy. Many Americans trace their families back to England. My Gilbert ancestors came from Devonshire, called the Garden of England. I have driven over it time after time to enjoy its unsurpassed scenery. As you traverse its well-paved highways and hedge-bordered lanes and see its verdant slopes and note the limpid streams, you greatly admire the lovely villages and rural homes. These scenes are such as to fill one with peace and contentment. But Devon is not all of England that comes close to the heart and will not depart. There are Salisbury, Winchester, and Stratford-on-Avon with its everlasting memories of Shakespeare. Then there are Sulgrave Manor, home of George Washington's ancestors, Oxford, Cambridge, and Canterbury. There are large cities like Bristol, where Wesley preached and built his first church, near which today stands his equestrian statue, commemorating his circuit-rider days. Then there is the great city, London, of imperishable history. There things are right "because they have always been that way." In London, on being shown our hotel room the first day, we called the maid's attention to a rather obvious sink in one of the mattresses. She promptly replied: "It's always been that way, sir." You wonder at the magnitude of the parks, the traffic never out of control of policemen who carry no weapons. Do you ask why? The answer: "This is England; the policeman is the law; the law is obeyed. When the policeman lifts his hand, that's the hand of the law."

You look about for historic points. Where did Dickens, Ben Jonson, and other immortals work and live; where were their favorite coffee houses? You are shown, and you may have your roast or your stew and the cup that cheers where these immortals gathered; and then you may see upon the walls the pictures of their times which have hung there these many years. You rise and take a stroll, walking across London Bridge, to the Houses of Parliament and Westminster Abbey, wandering into the ancient halls of the latter to see the names on the tombs centuries old, where lie those who made history. If you are a lawyer, as was I, you visit "Old Bailey," the Inns of Court, and famous places adjacent to them. No wonder the world could not stand by and see England invaded and subjugated. The United States, after Pearl Harbor, and the British Empire, after Dunkirk, lost no time; no effort was spared to defend both homelands. Since "the best defense is offense," the latter was chosen. The utmost efforts of both countries, happily reinforced by the almost limitless manpower of Russia, have paid large dividends. England was saved; France, Belgium, Holland, Greece, and many smaller countries have been freed from the iron heel of Germany.

CHAPTER XV

Georgia History and Men Who Made It

THE deeds leading to the American Declaration of Independence are too well set forth in that immortal document to require recounting here. A number of little known events transpired in Georgia, besides her well-known participation in the war. Colonial Governor Wright of Georgia was loyal to Britain, but the state had a patriot Council of Safety. On January 17, 1776, several British war vessels appeared at the mouth of the Savannah River; and in order to prevent Governor Wright from communicating with them, the Council of Safety ordered his arrest. The next day, with a party selected by himself, Major Joseph Habersham volunteered to secure the Governor, and, passing the sentinel at the door of the Governor's council chamber, he placed the Governor under arrest. However, on February 11, Governor Wright, who had been allowed to remain in his mansion on his solemn promise not to communicate with the British ships, broke his word and escaped to Bonaventure, the home of his friend, John Mulryne, near Savannah. He boarded a British ship in the river and took with him the Seal of the Province of Georgia. On August 10, 1776, news reached Georgia that her delegates in Congress, Button Gwinnett, Lyman Hall, and George Walton, had signed the Declaration of Independence on July 4th. In October, 1776, the first Constitutional Convention in Georgia met at Savannah. On February 5, 1777, the first regular Constitution of the State of Georgia was promulgated. The power of government was vested in a Legislature of a single house, which was to elect annually a Governor and an Advisory Council. All members of the Council were required to be landowners and Protestants. Courts of law were provided. The Constitution embraced a Bill of Rights. A new Seal for the State was adopted (another being adopted in 1799, the present one, whose date was changed to 1776, by legislative act in 1914); parishes were abolished and counties established in their stead. Thus Georgia's first General Assembly was unicameral — an assembly of only one house.

When the Constitution of the United States was formed and submitted to the states, Georgia was fourth to ratify it, and was one of the three which alone ratified unanimously. The Constitution was submitted in 1787; Georgia was the first to ratify in 1788, the year of most of the ratifications.

Soon after Georgia became a state, she lost a vast stretch of territory from the Mississippi River eastward to the Tombigbee River, because of that stupendous swindle known as the "Yazoo Fraud" (so called from the Yazoo River in Mississippi). The lost lands comprised nine-tenths of the present State of Mississippi, one-half or more of the present State of Alabama, and a fraction of the present State of Tennessee. To settle the numerous land claims growing out of this episode, the United States purchased from Georgia all of the lands between the Chattahoochee and Mississippi Rivers.

Next came the War Between the States and the defeat of the Southern Armies, leaving Georgia prostrate. Sufferings from hunger, destruction of every form of property, and subjugation faced our people, ruled over by a Federal Army controlled by a Congress which was bitterly vindictive toward the South. The Supreme Court

Georgia History and Men Who Made It 243

declared void all secession ordinances, yet Congress refused to permit Senators and Representatives from the South to resume their seats as members, save upon compliance with humiliating oaths of allegiance and objectionable amendments to the Constitution. Under such heart-breaking conditions Georgians — men, women, and children — labored without assistance or encouragement from without, and built a new civilization, the equal of any in the world. This is said only as a matter of pride — not of rancor. When finally our members were seated in Congress, Georgia's great orator and statesman, Benjamin H. Hill, delivered in the Senate words that will never die: "The South is here, and here she intends to remain . . . We are here, we are in the house of our fathers, our brothers are our companions, and we are at home to stay, thank God."

Many are the names which stud the bright diadem of Georgia's renown. There are some of true greatness who are remembered so little. I feel impelled to do what I may here toward perpetuating the name of one of them. Mirabeau Buonaparte Lamar was born at Louisville, Georgia, on August 16, 1798, of French Huguenot lineage. He was private secretary to Governor George M. Troup of Georgia, in 1823, and aided in working out the plans for the removal westward of the Indians of this state. In 1826 he married Tabitha Jordan of Perry, Alabama, then moved to Columbus, Georgia, where he founded one of the state's oldest newspapers, the Columbus *Enquirer*. It was a State's Rights paper. Having been defeated for Congress and his wife having died, Lamar moved to Texas in 1835. He joined General Sam Houston in the War for Texan Independence, the results of which were so successful. In the Republic of Texas he became Attorney General and Secretary of War. He was the Republic's first Vice President (General Houston being its first President). In 1836 he was elected to succeed General Houston as President and in 1838 was re-elected for a 3-year term. Lamar founded the city of Austin. In 1841 Houston was elected to succeed Lamar as President. After annexation of Texas to the American Union, Lamar declined the post of Minister to Argentina, but in 1858 went as Minister to Nicaragua and Costa Rica. He died at his home in Richmond, Texas, on December 19, 1859.

Today his nephew is better remembered than he, though likely did not influence history as much. That nephew was L. Q. C. Lamar, native of Georgia, graduate of Emory College at old Oxford, Georgia, who later represented the State of Mississippi in the United States Senate; who became Secretary of the Interior; and who ended his versatile career as a Justice of the Supreme Court of the United States.

Georgia is outstanding not only for her men who have won renown but for a number of notable events and achievements, only a few of which may be designated here.

Georgia was the first of the American colonies to ban slavery — this being in January, 1735. The colony also banned lawyers and spiritous liquors, but not wine. The bans were not long lived. When the colony was taken over by the Crown from the Trustees, the ban on slaves was lifted, as well as other bans. However, Georgia was the first state in the Union to forbid the importation of Negro slaves constitutionally. Such importation had been prohibited by *statute* law in Virginia and Massachusetts earlier, but the first State Constitution of any in the land forbidding importation of slaves was the Georgia Constitution of 1798. This constitution did not forbid domestic slavery, the holding of slaves with respect to Negroes born in this country, but did forbid the importation from Africa or any other foreign land of Negroes for any purpose, prohibiting also the importation or immigration into Georgia of free Negroes and providing that if free Negroes did get in they were to be made slaves. The state thus early registered its disapproval of any increase in Negro population of any status whatever.

Bethesda Orphanage, the oldest organized charity in America, was established near Savannah in March, 1740, by George Whitefield, the foremost pulpit orator known to the English-speaking world.

Georgia was the first state in the Union to abrogate the law of entails and primogeniture — in 1777. This did away with the practice (contrary to good public policy) of leaving property by will or otherwise to a specified class of persons, excluding all others. It forbade *entailing* (enchaining, as it were) property upon the first-born, leaving all other children with nothing; and thus liberalized wealth, enlarging its benefits to more persons.

An Act of 1783 of the Georgia Legislature established an academy at Augusta, Richmond County, known for generations as Richmond Academy. It is the oldest legally established academy in the land.

On January 27, 1785, a charter granting the right to set up a state-supported educational institution was voted by Georgia to Abraham Baldwin and others. This was the beginning of the University of Georgia, the first State University to be chartered in America.

In 1790 William Longstreet of Augusta attached a steam engine to a boat and forced the craft up the Savannah River at a rate of five miles an hour. However, it was not until 1808, a year after Robert Fulton had made a successful run up the Hudson River with his steamboat, *Clermont*, that Longstreet convinced a doubting public that steam would run a ship.

Eli Whitney, by common credit, invented the first cotton gin at Mulberry Grove Plantation near Savannah in 1793. It has been respectably claimed, however, that cotton gins were in use in South Carolina earlier; and also that Whitney took his idea from a Georgian.

On May 22, 1819, the *Savannah*, the first steamship ever to cross the Atlantic Ocean, sailed from Savannah, Georgia, bound for Liverpool, England. The voyage was completed in 29 days, 11 hours.

Georgia was the first state to require the registration of births — 1823.

Sequoyah, the Cherokee half-breed who invented the alphabet of the Cherokee Nation of Indians in 1825, was certainly one of the most remarkable men ever to live on Georgia soil. It has been said that he "leaped over centuries of progress to a phonetic system." He removed West, and the giant redwood trees of California were ultimately to bear his name.

By Act of December 23, 1836, the Legislature of Georgia chartered or incorporated "Georgia Female College" at Macon. This institution, renamed Wesleyan Female College (for John Wesley) and today known simply as Wesleyan College, still at Macon, was the first educational institution in the world ever to award a degree to a woman by authority of law. In other words, Wesleyan College was the first *chartered* institution to ever grant a degree to women. Of course, there is no way of knowing whether prior to 1836 any private institution ever did so.

Dr. Crawford W. Long was born in Georgia in 1815 and was graduated at the University of Georgia in 1835 and in medicine at the University of Pennsylvania in 1839. He discovered anaesthesia, and performed the first surgical operation without pain on March 30, 1842. This event took place in Georgia. The discovery has been one of mankind's greatest boons.

Georgia's Constitution of 1861 was the first to provide not only that laws in conflict with it were void but also that the courts *must* so declare.

Georgia was the first state in the Union to promulgate a Code embracing all the law of force within the state. This was on January 1, 1863. By express statute Georgia thus adopted all the common law of England, applicable to our institutions, into the state's system of jurisprudence.

Georgia was among the very first states to free the property of women from arbitrary control of husbands by making the property of women unavailable as security for the debts of husbands. This was in 1866.

In Columbus, Georgia, the first machine for making ice was manufactured and sold commercially. It was based on a process patented by Andrew Muhl. In 1872 the Columbus Ice Manufacturing Company was incorporated and began the business of making and selling ice.

The philanthropic institution, Berry School, now Berry College, is the greatest of its kind in the world. It was founded, directed, and made famous by the late Miss Martha Berry. The campus of the college comprises 25,000 acres.

Tallulah Falls School for Georgia mountain children, owned and operated by the Georgia Federation of Women's Clubs, is the only school so owned and operated. It is aptly called the "Light in the Mountains."

Mrs. Rebecca Latimer Felton of Georgia was the first woman United States Senator. She served only two days, November 21 and 22, 1922, by Executive appointment.

In 1932 Dr. Charles H. Herty's research on wood-pulp production from slash pine won for him the medal of the American Institute of Chemists. In November, 1933, newsprint paper made from such wood-pulp was used by Atlanta newspapers for the first time.

Georgia's Great Seal, adopted in 1799, expresses the noblest sentiments of her people. The device on one side shows three pillars, supporting an arch on which is the word, "Constitution." On the first pillar appears the word, "Wisdom;" on the second, "Justice;" and on the third, "Moderation." The three represent the ideal conception of the three departments of government — the Legislative, the Judicial, and the Executive. The key meaning to the device is that each and all of these three are absolutely necessary for the support of a Constitution.

Georgia's former Governor, John M. Slaton, has wisely declared that "Georgia stands first in many things, but is at the glorious bottom in the matter of bonded debt."

CHAPTER XVI

Higher Education in Georgia

TWO natives of the State of Connecticut, both graduates of Yale College, a great university, are entitled to be remembered as the fathers of our State University. They are Lyman Hall, signer of the Declaration of Independence for Georgia and later Governor of Georgia; and Abraham Baldwin, signer for Georgia of the United States Constitution, afterwards Governor of Georgia, Representative in Congress, then U. S. Senator from Georgia, and first president of the State University of Georgia. Governor Lyman Hall, in 1783, in a message to the Legislature, stressed the importance of education and seminaries of learning. In 1784 an act was passed recognizing this need. It seems certain that Hall and Baldwin collaborated on the subject of education; for in 1785 Baldwin, who had drawn a charter for the University of Georgia, obtained its passage by the General Assembly of Georgia, and it became a legal entity, lacking only an organization and the acceptance of the charter. It is most notable to observe here that this charter was couched in language providing by implication for ultimate inclusion of women in the student body – and that as far back as 1785! Because of the chaotic conditions resulting from the Revolution and because of the limited resources of the state which had become sovereign only nine years before, organization of a university was delayed.

The Act of 1784 was the first in America looking to the establishment of a college, statewide in its influence and benefits. These acts prove our fathers were in favor of educational facilities within this state — common schools and colleges. The Act of 1785 made the University a reality and proclaimed the exalted plane upon which it was established. It has had a long and distinguished career under able presidents and professors. It has educated a large portion of our leading statesmen, lawyers, judges, teachers, business men, and men in every calling. The temptation is great to name a long list of them but space forbids. It is easy to call to mind Governor Nat E. Harris, Henry W. Grady, Robert Toombs, and many others eminent in state and country.

The University of Georgia at Athens is the oldest institution of higher learning in the state. Today the University is presided over by the able Harmon W. Caldwell, a leader in educational circles. Other able men have preceded him, and still others of ability will follow.

The Georgia State College for Women, the largest senior women's college, was established by act of the General Assembly in 1889 when I was a member from Muscogee County. I supported this measure with all my energy. It has surpassed the most extravagant dreams of its most optimistic champions in the Legislature. It is located at Milledgeville, Georgia, and has a large and beautiful campus, with many dormitories, auditoriums, and lecture rooms. It is continuing to grow under its able and resourceful president, Guy H. Wells. The president lives in the old Governor's Mansion, still owned by the state and set aside for such residence.

Milledgeville was named for a former Governor and was for many years the capital of the state. The old Executive Mansion is the show place of Milledgeville, being in a better state of preservation than any other old building of the city. It was built in 1838, thus being today more than a hundred years old. Its ceilings on the

OLD GOVERNORS' MANSION AT MILLEDGEVILLE

first floor are eighteen feet high; its doors are thick and unwarped. In 1944 I was a guest there and slept in a room which had been occupied in past days by eight successive Governors of Georgia. I did not discern a single architectural fault in the building.

Milledgeville was selected as the capital before there was any settlement there. When the town was laid off, the streets were named for distinguished Georgians and other Americans. It was at Milledgeville, while it was the capital, that Georgia's Ordinance of Secession was adopted over the strenuous objection of Herschel V. Johnson, Benjamin H. Hill, Alexander H. Stephens, and a good number of other Georgians, some eminent, some unknown. The vote was close, and it has always since been a mooted question what the vote would have been had not former Governor Johnson been prevented from concluding his speech against secession. It was in the midst of this seemingly successful and very masterly argument that a request of him was made to suspend until after dinner. He agreed, but after dinner when he resumed, it was apparent that something tragic had occurred. Whether it was by accident or design will never be known. The important fact was that he was unable to go forward with the eloquence and logic characterizing the beginning of his deliverance. The contest was lost; the Ordinance was adopted.

The Georgia Constitutional Convention of 1865 and that of 1868 were beld in Milledgeville. The latter was attended largely by carpetbaggers, scalawags, and Negroes, though there were some able and respected members. Governor Joseph E. Brown was a member and was considered to be a man of excellent judgment. The convention did provide, in the constitution it adopted, for free education. This was by no means the first Georgia adoption of such a provision. Georgia's first constitution, in fact, that of 1777, adopted such a provision. As stated above, the General Assembly in 1866 provided that the wife's property should not be subject to the husband's debts. This principle was adopted in the 1868 constitution. This constitution also provided for the levy of a poll tax as qualification for voting; and it provided for the removal of the capital of the state to the city of Atlanta. Macon, probably, would have afforded equal facilities, but Atlanta's enterprise won. Duelling was made a penal offense and its participants disfranchised.

The Georgia School of Technology vies with the University proper in attendance and prowess. It is the foremost technological institution in the Southeast, and it is not a wild guess to predict that it will soon be the equal of any in America. Dr. Marion Luther Brittain, its president for twenty years, by his unceasing loyalty and brilliant mind brought this school to its present status. At his insistence, the Board of Regents of the University System retired him on July 1, 1944, electing him President Emeritus. At the same time good fortune smiled on the Board by affording an opportunity to select in Dr. Brittain's place Colonel Blake R. Van Leer, a distinguished engineer and former professor in many prominent technological schools. Georgia School of Technology is located in Atlanta and was created by act of the General Assembly in 1885 (the centenary of the act creating the State University), pursuant to a bill introduced by Senator Nat E. Harris of Macon, Bibb County. He was made the first chairman of the Board of Trustees, in which office he continued until his death. He probably always will be called the "father of Georgia Tech." Though Governor of Georgia later (1915-1917), he always insisted he would rather be chairman of the Georgia Tech Board

CHAPEL, UNIVERSITY OF GEORGIA

Library, Georgia School of Technology

than be Governor. Such is the nature of "fathers." He at least was a father worthy of the name and the affectionate remembrance of every lover of great schools. My only living child, Price Gilbert, Jr., is a graduate of Georgia Tech.

The outstanding achievement of the administration of Governor Richard B. Russell, Jr., now United States Senator, was the creation by law of the Board of Regents of the University System of Georgia. He signed the act on August 28, 1931, and it became effective on January 1, 1932. That act vested in the Board of Regents the responsibility for twenty-six institutions of higher learning and the agricultural experimentation. Prior to this date each of the institutions had its own governing board and executive officers. The only influence coordinating them at the time was the Governor and General Assembly. After a competent survey, the Regents reduced the number of institutions to seventeen, and then set up in Atlanta the University System Evening Center, looking to its ultimate absorption by the University of Georgia.

The Board of Regents consists of fifteen members, five from the state at large and one from each of the ten Congressional Districts. Formerly the Board was of statutory creation, the Governor being an ex-officio member. The present Board was created by constitutional amendment under which the Governor was omitted, this step being taken at the suggestion of Governor Ellis Arnall. The power was put in the Governor to appoint the Board members, under the amendment, just as the statute had formerly done; but it was notable with respect to the present Board that it was selected by the Governor without an application or an endorsement. The Governor has greatly impressed the Board members by his refusal to dictate its policies or interfere in its administration of educational affairs. Three of the present Board have formerly served as chairmen, and their experience is thus greatly beneficial. I was one of the appointees of Governor Arnall and now serve a term ending in 1950.

The Chancellor of the University System of Georgia is the executive officer of the Board of Regents. The work thus requires a man of untiring energy and business ability, being itself a "big business." Executive ability is required in administering the affairs of large educational institutions — as much so as with respect to large corporations. It might at first seem beyond the capability of one man to keep in mind the needs of so many units as those comprising this System. But the eminent and efficient Chancellor S. V. Sanford, recently deceased, during days of peace and the more strenuous days of war, fully measured up to the requirements of his office.

In his Report for 1941 to the Board of Regents, Chancellor Sanford said: "As the University System is something unique in the United States and as it has made such progress in the past decade, it has attracted national attention. No person knows better than I that bricks and mortar do not make a great university system. Buildings, laboratories, equipment, gifts are only the visible evidences of progress within an educational system. The real work is found in the work and activities of the teaching staff, in the stimulation given students, and in the encouragement which the University System gives to productive intellectual effort."

Because I, too, believe in the great purpose and the future of education in Georgia, I am making my final service to my state by serving as a member of the Board of Regents. I am happy to serve in the cause of helping others "to follow truth wherever it may lead," a cause to which Thomas Jefferson dedicated the University of

Higher Education in Georgia

Virginia. My feelings are so completely expressed in some remarks that I made on the occasion of presenting the Gilbert Memorial Infirmary to the University of Georgia on June 4, 1943, that I insert them here to close my pleasant task of writing about the people I admire and the state I love.

I am now entering the University of Georgia — somewhat delayed. It should have taken place more than sixty years ago. Instead, I entered another great university (not situated in this state) receiving my degree in 1883. In the fall of 1883, I entered another great university (not situated in this state), for the study of law, receiving my LL.B. in 1885. My choices were wrong, and I mean no disrespect to nor disparagement of these institutions. They have done and are doing wonderful work, but I have chosen another Alma Mater.

Being Georgia-born of Georgia-born parents, it was a gross mistake to lose the golden opportunity of drinking deeply from the Pierian Spring at the beloved university of my own state. Our splendid School of Technology had not then been established. A merciful Providence has granted me a long life, in which sorrows and happiness, hardships and good luck, defeats and triumphs, sickness and good health, have all been frequent companions along the road that I have travelled — but that road has all been in Georgia, and I have travelled with and among my beloved Georgians. Above the roar of conflicting sounds, and clashing interests, if I listened closely, there were heard voices of friendship, of cheer, of encouragement, of affection and confidence. These were the voices of my Georgia neighbors, and my loved ones at my own fireside — To them I owe all.

No wonder then, that I am abidingly grateful to Georgia and Georgians and wish above all things to evidence that gratitude. Most of my contemporaries are gone — but their children and grandchildren, our future citizens and future leaders, are here. On their preparation depends what kind of citizens they shall be and how they shall lead.

Education is the light of the world! Ignorance is the darkness. War is the child of ignorance, and just now it spreads its black shadow over the bleeding world. Education, broad education that reaches every need, is the life-line by which God may lead us to green pastures and beside the still waters of peace.

All Georgians should feel a thrill of pride in what has already been accomplished by our educational system. We must determine to make it more and more adequate.

Diseased bodies and unenlightened minds offer the most fruitful fields for the activities for evil, selfish, and designing influences. Poverty, embittered minds, and corrupt government follow as the night follows the day. Sound minds in sound bodies love the light and cast off darkness — "*Wisdom — Justice — Moderation*" find lodgment and make happy lives.

I am happy today to formally present to the University the Gilbert Memorial Infirmary, with the ardent hope that it may accomplish something helpful to the young men and women who seek instruction here amid these classic shades.

The Infirmary is a memorial to my father, Jasper Newton Gilbert, M.D., Augusta Medical College, 1855, and to my deceased son, Francis Howard Gilbert, who received his degree at the University of Georgia, 1927. My father's life was a priceless benefaction to me. My son was the fulfillment of all that his parents' hearts could wish.

GILBERT MEMORIAL INFIRMARY

In conclusion, please permit me to read some lines written by Miss Will Allen Dromgoole of Tennessee — They will furnish a key to the sentiment pervading this whole happy experience.

> An old man, going a lone highway,
> Came at the evening, cold and gray,
> To a chasm vast and wide and steep,
> With waters rolling cold and deep;
> The old man crossed in the twilight dim,
> For that sullen stream had no fear for him;
> But he turned when safe on the other side
> And built a bridge to span the tide.
>
> "Old man," said a fellow pilgrim near,
> "You are wasting your strength with building here;
> Your journey will end with the ending day,
> And you ne'er again will pass this way;
> You've crossed the chasm deep and wide;
> Why build you the bridge at eventide?"
>
> The builder lifted his old gray head,
> "Good friend, in the path I have come," he said,
> "There followeth after me today,
> A youth whose feet must pass this way.
> This chasm that has been as naught to me,
> To that fair-haired youth may a pitfall be;
> He, too, must cross in the twilight dim,—
> Good friend, I am building this bridge for him!"

In Memoriam
STEADMAN VINCENT SANFORD
1871—1945
CHANCELLOR, UNIVERSITY SYSTEM OF
GEORGIA, 1935-1945

www.ingramcontent.com/pod-product-compliance
Lightning Source LLC
Chambersburg PA
CBHW030131240426
43672CB00005B/100